GEMSTONES

GEMSTONES

A Jewelry Maker's Guide to Identifying and Using Beautiful Rocks

JUDITH CROWE

Interweave

Published in North America
by Interweave,
an imprint of F+W Media, Inc.
10151 Carver Road, Suite 300,
Blue Ash, Ohio 45242
www.interweave.com
All rights reserved.

Conceived, edited and designed by
Quarto Publishing plc
an imprint of The Quarto Group
The Old Brewery
6 Blundell Street
London N7 9BH
www.quartoknows.com

QUAR 305055

ISBN: 978-1-63250-682-5

SRN: 19JM01

Senior editor: Kate Burkett
Designer: Gemma Wilson
Photographer: Phil Wilkins
Art director: Jess Hibbert
Publisher: Samantha Warrington

Printed in China

10 9 8 7 6 5 4 3 2 1

Contents

About this Book

This comprehensive guide to identifying, buying, using, and caring for a dazzling array of jewels and gems is a complete reference for goldsmiths, jewelers, and jewelry makers. Charts, timelines, illustrations, and photography help you to identify different gemstones and demonstrate how they can be used in different designs and settings.

The front section of the book is your starting point. It covers the basic steps of identification, providing practical advice that is intended to prompt you into considering the various gemmological properties that make a gem identifiable. Further articles cover gem-related topics such as the mining, selection, and usage of rough material, the designing and cutting of gemstones, and pricing.

Synthetics and Imitations

For centuries, synthetic and imitation stones have been used in jewelry to make them more affordable, given the high value of natural gemstones. Often worn alongside the real gems, imitations could supplement the few pieces of gem-set jewelry owned by an individual. Inexpensive imitations also offered a choice of "gemstone look"—from diamonds to sapphires and opals—allowing buyers to purchase the colors and cuts they liked.

34

SYNTHETIC GEMSTONES
Synthetic gemstones are laboratory-grown gemstones that have the same chemistry and structure as the natural stone. The refractive index, hardness, and density/specific gravity will be the same, but it only takes a matter of months to grow a synthetic boule crystal. The basic method has been used since the early 1900s: powdered ingredients are melted under extreme heat to form the boule slowly and are then cut in the same way as the natural gemstone. There are synthetics of the most important gems, including Linde star sapphires and rubies that display asterism, and synthetic color-change gems. These have slightly different color zoning and growth lines to the natural stone. Synthetic emeralds are formed in a slightly different "flux-melt" process in which the powdered ingredients are mixed in a solvent at a high temperature for many months and then cooled very slowly. A synthetic emerald contains inclusions, which can fool many people, but they are different to those that occur in a natural emerald.

IMITATION GEMSTONES
Imitation gemstones are primarily made from cheaper materials such as lead glass, and have been used since Ancient Roman times. Glass stones have various names, such as paste, Strasse, rhinestones, diamanté, and crystal. From the 1700s they were manufactured in France and Eastern Europe, with factories along the Rhine: hence the name, rhinestones. They were often set in closed-back collets so that the foil could be placed behind them for extra brilliance. Well-known makers of imitation glass stones are Gilson, Swarovski, and Gripoix, poured glass. They can imitate a variety of gemstones such as emeralds, opals, and coral, but do not have the same properties as the natural gemstones. Identification is fairly easy; glass has little brilliance and it is a soft stone, so the facets become worn, chipped, and scratched. The imitations also contain bubbles and can discolor over time. A real diamond will retain sharp facet edges and exhibit brilliance and fire due to the hardness.

COMPOSITES
Composites are part natural stone and part glass or synthetic. A solid opal can be expensive, so doublets and triplets reduce the price. Emerald doublets are similar in make-up. These stones can be identified from a side view.

Synthetic stones
Synthetic stones have been available since early 1900s.

Paste lizard brooch
Made between 1890 and 1910, this brooch was fabricated using silver.

35

SYNTHETICS AND IMITATIONS

Faux pearls
Faux "glass" pearls can be identified by the grainy surface quality. These Marvella pearls have a great luster and value.

Glass jewelry
Vauxhall Glass and high-quality glass jewelry molded into shapes.

DIAMOND SIMULANTS
There are simulants of most gemstones. Diamonds, however, have lots of simulants because they are such expensive stones. Modern manufactured gems have replaced traditional paste as diamond simulants. They are more hard-wearing and have more "sparkle." The most popular simulants are:

CUBIC ZIRCONIA (CZ) is very cheap. It has the look of diamond and imitates other gemstones like tanzanite and emerald. It has more fire than diamond and is nearly as brilliant. Cubic zirconia can be identified because it is nearly 75 percent heavier than diamond and may be scratched with a fine carbide scriber.

YAG (YTTRIUM ALUMINUM GARNET), AKA DIAMONIQUE is used in fashion jewelry as a diamond simulant because it is hard (8.5 Mohs) and durable. However, it has low dispersion and so has little fire.

MOISSANITE is a good simulant as it has greater brilliance and dispersion than both diamond and cubic zirconia. It is also hard and durable. But it is not as cheap as cubic zirconia, costing between 10 and 20 percent of the price of an equivalent diamond.

LABORATORY-GROWN SYNTHETIC DIAMONDS are available, but these are expensive to produce and so are unviable. They are not identical to a diamond and can be identified by a laboratory. They are marketed as being eco-friendly as they do not have the same impact as mining on the environment and are not used to finance civil wars.

NOTE When purchasing any gemstone or piece of gem-set jewelry of high value, ask for a laboratory certificate or gemstone report as a guarantee of what you're buying. A certificate will state what the gemstone is, its characteristics, the treatments it has undergone, and sometimes the origin.

Cubic zirconia (left) and moissanite (right)
Two modern diamond simulants, CZs have been available since 1970 and moissanite since 1998. Both have high dispersion and good brilliance.

Species

Gemstones are organized into species, which helps to identify them. Some gemstones do not belong to a species (indicated by a white triangle).

Header

Refers to the name of the individual gemstone.

Gemmological information panel

Comparable information on the gemstone's properties, including hardness, density, and luster.

Imagery

The visuals illustrate the gem in its raw state, as a polished stone, and set in exquisite pieces of jewelry. Close-ups of the gemstones give you a closer look at their form, how they've been cut, any optical properties—such as inclusions and color zoning—or treatments.

GEMSTONE DIRECTORY

The directory is ordered according to hardness, from 10 Mohs (diamond) to 3.5 Mohs (amber).

Each entry in the directory covers the many practical considerations around using a particular stone: its visual and physical properties, color treatments, availability, and how to handle it, and wonderful imagery shows you the gem in its raw state, as a polished stone, and set in exquisite pieces of jewelry.

Gemstone Identification

This book aims to help gem enthusiasts identify the gemstones they come across, whether at a trade show, antiques fair, yard sale, local auction, or on the Internet. You might be a professional in the trade, a self-employed buyer or seller, a hobbyist, or just someone who has an interest in jewelry and gems. The same identification process can be used for most situations.

You cannot always rely on a seller or trader knowing what they have or to have checked and tested the gemstones themselves. In busy environments such as antiques fairs and yard sales, there often isn't the time or space to talk to traders in detail and discuss each piece with them. There won't be access to a laboratory or any technical equipment, so you'll be faced with a stone or piece of jewelry and limited information. Here is the basic checklist that I go through mentally when I'm at an event, auction, or fair.

Indicolite (tourmaline)

The gemstone is blue and bi-colored, so it's from a parti-colored crystal. It weighs 51 carats and is long and narrow. The stone has two different color directions, making it pleochroic.

CHECKLIST

1 COLOR
What color is the gem and which gemstones are this color? For example, consider which stones are always green and which stones can occur in green. Does the gemstone have color banding or is it bi- or tri-colored?
See Color, pages 14–17.

2 LUSTER AND HARDNESS
What luster and hardness is this gem? Is it a dense/heavy gemstone? If it is rough material, what is the crystal system and habit?
See Gemmological Information, pages 18–19.

3 OPTICAL PROPERTIES
Does the stone have any unusual or specific optical or color properties that help identify it? Does it exhibit pleochroism, color change, fluorescence, asterism, chatoyance, color-play, aventurescence, opalescence, or iridescence? Which gemstones have these properties?
See Optical Properties, pages 22–25.

4 DISPERSION
Does the stone have high dispersion, showing "fire," and is it a brilliant, lively stone? Certain gemstones with high dispersion show colors or "fire" when they sparkle—this is white light splitting into spectral colors.
See Optical Properties, pages 22–25.

5 INCLUSIONS
What inclusions can you see in the stone and do they help identify it? Look for rutile needles, lily pads, color zoning, small crystals, or metallic platelets.
See Inclusions, page 26.

Tanzanian natural rubies
Red with a hint of blue, these stones are small at 1.05ct each. Possible stones include garnet, ruby, or rubellite, but garnet and rubellite are not quite this color and are larger.

Iolite cushion cabochon
This gemstone is a blue-purple when viewed from above and clear or gray when seen from the side—an optical effect called pleochroism. This stone is trichroic.

6 AGE AND SOURCE
What do I know about the age and source of the gemstone? Is it an old stone and where might it have come from?
See Sources, pages 27–29.

7 TREATMENTS
Has the stone undergone any treatments, such as heating, dyeing, or fracture filling? Does this help date the piece?
See Gemstone Treatments, pages 30–33.

8 IMITATIONS
Is the stone an imitation (glass), synthetic, or composite?
See Synthetics and Imitations, pages 34–35.
See Sources, pages 27–29.

9 SIZE
What is the size of the stone? Is it large and clean or small? What is the shape and cut of the stone? Is it a narrow step cut, a round brilliant cut, or an old cut?
See Cutting, pages 36–39.

10 SPECIES
Could the gem come from one of the species of stones—Corundum, Beryl, Tourmaline, Garnet, Quartz, or Feldspar? Or is it a single or idiochromatic gem?

11 FURTHER INFORMATION
Do I need to go through any further technical procedures to help confirm the gem's identity? Or does the gem need to go to a laboratory?
See Technical Methods of Identification, pages 12–13.

Gemstone Appraisal

The identification of a gemstone (see pages 8–9) is nearly always combined with an appraisal of the gem; the two processes go together. As I check the identity, I'm also running through a mental checklist that assesses the quality of the stone.

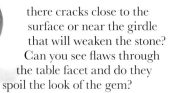

1 QUALITY OF COLOR is the most important aspect of a colored stone—it can be worth up to 50 percent of the total value of the stone. A good color is usually a sign of good quality. If the color is poor, then clarity and cut become more important. Ideally, look for a pure hue without any brown or gray tones. Check for color zoning and stability of color.

2 TREATMENTS are used on various gemstones, so it's important that you get to know the type of gem you are inspecting. Always ask the trader you are buying from, as they have a duty to disclose such information, but also check for treatments yourself. Are they permanent and how do they affect the value? Be on the lookout for composite stones and simulants/synthetics.

3 CLARITY is worth 20 to 30 percent of the total value of the gemstone. Ideally, a "clean" stone is preferred rather than one with visible or ugly inclusions. However, some inclusions are a good thing because they can provide information on origin, identity, and treatments. Some stones, such as emeralds, will always have inclusions. Look at the positioning of the flaws—are there cracks close to the surface or near the girdle that will weaken the stone? Can you see flaws through the table facet and do they spoil the look of the gem?

4 DURABILITY of a gemstone affects its wearability. Check whether the gemstone is fragile and suitable for the intended wear and tear. Does the gem have perfect cleavage (a plane of weak atomic bonding) where it can break if knocked, as is the case for topaz and kunzite?

5 CUT AND SYMMETRY account for 10 to 20 percent of the total value of a gemstone. It is less critical than other criteria, as it can be changed. Poor cutting can affect durability and brilliance, thus devaluing the gem. Avoid shallow and very deep stones, as they will be glassy or dull and lifeless. Stones are often cut for weight and there is the option of re-cutting them to better proportions. Individual custom-cut stones are normally better quality than those cut in quantity.

6 POLISH accounts for about 10 percent of the value. Look for surface abrasions such as scratches and chipping. If the stone has a value, then you are justified in asking the dealer to re-polish the stone as a condition of sale.

Cut and symmetry: Natural blue topaz (above)

This is a large topaz showing perfect proportions; there are no big windows, no dullness, or lack of brilliance.

Color: Rose quartz (top left)

Quality of color is worth up to 50% of the total value. This rose quartz has a strong peachy-pink that's enhanced by the stone's translucency.

Clarity: Emerald-cut diamond (bottom left)

For an emerald-cut diamond, good clarity is essential as the step-cut facets on the pavilion will show any inclusions.

ALWAYS TAKE A "GEM KIT" WITH YOU FOR EVALUATION PURPOSES

×10 LOUPE (1) This is essential when buying at trade fairs and events. Purchase a good-quality, x10 magnification loupe. The magnification doesn't need to be any higher, and I prefer not to have an LED light attached to the loupe. To use, hold the loupe close to your eye and bring the item up until it's in focus.

TWEEZERS (2) I have a pair of locking tweezers with fine tips that are excellent for diamonds. The locking mechanism keeps the stone secure as you look at it.

LINT-FREE CLOTH (3) Grease can affect the look of the stone, so it's worth cleaning the stone prior to louping.

PEN FLASHLIGHT (4) I use a non-LED, pen-type flashlight to check cabochons for inclusions, view rough material, check color, and study cat's-eye and star stones. I also have a dual-action flashlight with both fluorescent and daylight bulbs. They are handy for color-change stones and checking for fluorescence.

×2.5 MAGNIFICATION READING GLASSES (5) These are very useful for checking stones and jewelry when you're on the move.

DIAMOND TESTER (6) I take a tester that checks for diamonds and moissanite. It's worth the financial investment for the speed of testing it provides and to avoid making expensive mistakes.

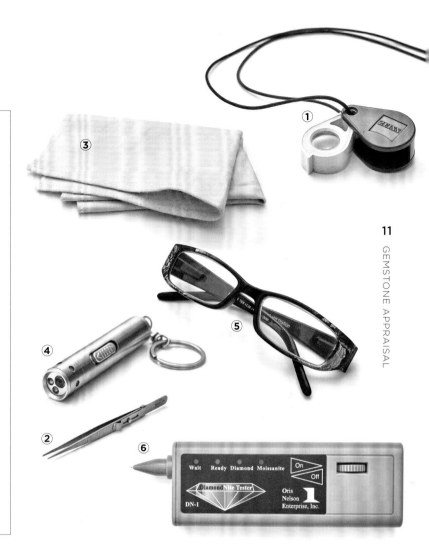

7 **SIZE AND SHAPE** of the gem depend on the rough material; some gemstones, such as Brazilian paraiba tourmalines, only occur in small sizes. The crystal habit usually dictates the shape of the gemstone, so a fancy cut often produces more wastage and will be more expensive.

8 **OPTICAL EFFECTS** such as asterism, color change, and chatoyance need to be as good as the color and clarity. Use a flashlight to check. In the case of asterims, does the "star" sit centrally on the stone and is it clearly visible? Is the color change clear and attractive?

9 **CERTIFICATES** will add to the price of the gemstone, but they do give reassurance. They are important if the gemstone is rare or priced according to a certain grading.

10 **RARITY** affects the value of a gemstone. The gemstone might be rare for a number of reasons, including the color, size, origin, and type of stone, so receipts need to state the origin, color, etc. Get to know the carat prices of the gems you're looking at and bear in mind that prices increase at certain weights such as 1 carat, 3 carats, and above.

Optical effects: Chatoyance (far left)

The quartz cat's eye has a very sharp eye that sits centrally on the stone. The cabochon is fairly clean, although you can see some fibers lying perpendicular to the eye, which have been orientated to produce the chatoyance.

Rarity: Paraiba (below)

The turquoise-blue suggests paraiba tourmaline. Rarity equates to high value, so ask for a laboratory certificate.

Technical Methods of Identification

There are times when a more formal verification is required, especially if the stone is valuable or priced on the basis of a specific property, such as its color or origin. Formal identification in the form of a laboratory report is sometimes requested by the buyer as a condition of sale and, occasionally, a dealer needs a verbal identification on a stone they are considering buying.

A laboratory provides the following services:

A FORMAL IDENTIFICATION if there is any uncertainty—for instance, is a row of beads jadeite or dyed quartzite? It prevents misrepresentation and gives a quick verbal identification that's 100 percent accurate.

A TEST FOR GEM TREATMENTS or to test if a stone is natural, which will affect the value.

IDENTIFICATION OF SOURCE indicates, for example, whether a stone is a Burmese ruby or a Sri Lankan sapphire.

IDENTIFICATION OF NATURAL PEARLS using X-ray.

A GEMSTONE APPRAISAL that sets out the individual characteristics of a gemstone, giving color assessment, clarity grading, weight, measurements, and optical properties.

REASSURANCE for insurance companies.

A VERBAL IDENTIFICATION followed by a report or certificate if the stone checks out.

AN OPINION ON CLARITY ENHANCEMENTS, including glass- or fracture-filling of Corundum or Colombian emeralds.

Laboratories can vary in quality, so check out the reputable firms. The top laboratories, such as the Gemmological Institute of America (GIA), HRD Antwerp Institute of Gemmology, Diamant PrufLabor GMBH (DPL), GemResearch Swisslab AG (GRS), Swiss Gemmological Institute (SSEF), and Gubelin, in Switzerland, will be more expensive and can take up to six weeks to test the stone, so these are best used for valuable diamonds and colored stones.

Laboratories use the following devices and techniques to assess a stone:

TO TEST THE DENSITY OF A GEMSTONE, laboratories use a carat scale that weighs to $1/100th$ of a carat and can be switched to grams.

TO TEST FOR THE REFRACTIVE INDEX, a refractometer is used. These are essential for formal identification and are a heavily used piece of equipment. They can be bought at a range of prices, but it can be difficult to get a reading from the cheaper ones. It's useful to have RI liquid that allows you to read off higher RIs, but this too can be expensive.

TO IDENTIFY CHROMIUM-RICH STONES laboratories use a Chelsea filter, which is a very simple tool. It is a loupe-type filter that distinguishes chromium-colored emeralds from other green gemstones such as sapphire and peridot, which do not contain chromium. It also helps identify other chromium-rich stones such as jadeite and chrome tourmaline.

TO CHECK THE ABSORPTION SPECTRUM OF A STONE a spectroscope is used.

TO MEASURE STONES AND PEARLS, a leveridge gauge measures to $1/10th$ of a millimeter and is very useful when buying small calibrated diamonds and colored stones. It also gives accurate readings on larger stones. It is possible to use a caliper gauge, but a leveridge gauge is easier and has a very handy booklet that allows you to calculate weights from measurements of different-shaped diamonds.

TO IDENTIFY PLEOCHROIC ROUGH MATERIAL AND DISTINGUISH IT FROM OTHER NON-PLEOCHROIC GEMS, a dichroscope is used to show the true colors along each color axis and help a cutter orientate the material before cutting, so the best color is shown through the table.

Tools for a manual assessment

Most dealers will perform a preliminary assessment of the stone using tweezers and a loupe to cover clarity, inclusions, symmetry, proportions, cut, and polish.

THE GEM & PEARL LABORATORY

The Gem Lab

09277

PEARL REPORT

21 January

Description:	LOOSE UNDRILLED 'PEARL'
Shape:	IRREGULAR SHAPED
Colour:	IRIDESCENT GREY/BLACK
Weight:	12.23 ct
Measurements:	13.4 – 15.4 x 8.5 mm
Result:	NATURAL PEARL (SALTWATER)
Comments:	No evidence of treatment was observed

The Gem & Pearl Laboratory Limited follows the guidelines of the World Jewellery Confederation (CIBJO).

This report is issued subject to the conditions printed on the report cover.

Only the original report with signature, security foil, ultra violet fluorescent watermark, and embossed stamp is a valid identification document.

John Smith

For and on the behalf of
The Gem Lab
123 Back Street
London

Laboratory certificate

A certificate for a natural saltwater pearl, which has been X-rayed, weighed, and measured.

Laboratory

A technician inspects a parcel of gemstones under the microscope. She will be looking at the internal characteristics of the stones to identify them and ascertain any treatments.

Color

The most important factor when buying a colored gemstone is the quality of the color. This aspect is worth approximately half the total value of the gem.

Purity of hue and saturation or intensity of color will increase the value of a gemstone considerably. In addition, the finer the color, the less impact clarity, weight, and cutting will have on the value, but a very pale or overly dark stone will need good clarity and cutting in order to sell. It is useful to know the various colors of gems in order to assess them, but it is essential for purposes of identification.

COLOR PROPERTIES or the way a colored gem displays color depends on the way it absorbs light. White light enters the stone and splits into its spectral colors—the colors of the rainbow. Some of those colors will be absorbed by the stone, while others will be reflected back, giving the gem its color. For example, if a stone absorbs all the colors except blue, the stone will appear blue. Gemstones can be identified by their absorption spectrum—a unique color identifier. This can be viewed using a spectroscope.

ALLOCHROMATIC GEMSTONES are white or colorless in their pure form, but can also occur in different colors as a result of the trace elements, metal oxides, and impurities that were around the crystal as it formed. For instance, a ruby is colored by varying amounts of chromium and iron. These stones are commonly treated with heat or irradiation to enhance or change their color. Treatments for color add a premium to the price of a natural (untreated) stone.

IDIOCHROMATIC GEMSTONES are always one color, because the chemical that causes the color is a part of its chemical composition. For instance, malachite is always green because copper is part of its composition.

Some gemstones are parti-colored and the crystal will have two, three, or more colors and produce a bi- or tri-colored gem. Ametrine consists of purple amethyst and yellow citrine, while watermelon tourmaline crystals have a green "rind" and a pink core. Sapphire can also be bi-colored, as can Beryl, kunzite, fluorite, and topaz. This is a distinguishing factor in identification.

COLOR ZONING is an important factor when assessing gems. There are a number of gems that have an irregular distribution of color; it is common with colored Diamonds, Corundum, Quartz, and Tourmaline. Zoning often corresponds to growth layers or lines in the crystal. To check for this, simply turn the stone upside down and lay it on white paper because, usually, the cutter will "hide" or disguise the zoning, making the cut stone appear evenly colored. Zoning is also disguised by the brilliance of a gem, as a result of good faceting. Sometimes there will only be a tiny bit of color in the bottom of the culet, which can be seen when viewing the stone side on. However, careful and clever cutting will make the stone appear a uniform color when viewed from the top.

PLEOCHROISM is another property of color that helps to distinguish a stone. Pleochroic stones display different colors when viewed from different angles. Iolite, for example, shows purple, gray, and/or colorless when viewed from the top and sides. This property depends on the crystal system. Cubic and amorphous gems have one color only. Trigonal, hexagonal, and tetragonal gems show two color directions, so are dichroic. Monoclinic, triclinic, and orthorhombic systems can show three color directions, so are trichroic. *(For more on pleochroism, see page 22.)*

COLOR-CHANGE GEMSTONES are rare and this property only occurs in a few gems, such as alexandrite, garnet, sapphire, spinel, and diaspore. In daylight they exhibit one color and then in incandescent light they display another. Alexandrite is well known for having this property; it shows green-blue in daylight and red-brown in incandescent light.

Idiochromatic gems

These peridot cabochons will always be green because they are idiochromatic. Iron impurities are not only the coloring agent of the gem but also an important part of peridot's chemical composition.

Parti-colored stone

A watermelon tourmaline pear-shaped pendeloque. Certain minerals, such as watermelon tourmaline, ametrine, and sapphire, occur as parti-colored crystals.

Color zoning in quartz and amethyst

Quartz (above, left) frequently has color zoning based on crystal growth lines. To see it clearly, place the gem upside down as per the amethyst (left).

Allochromatic stones

Tourmaline faceted beads showing the wide range of colors that the gemstone can be found in. Tourmaline is colorless in its pure form, but trace elements and chemicals will give the gem a variety of colors.

Color-change gems

Certain gems such as alexandrite, sapphire, and garnet have a rare color-change property according to the light source. This garnet changes from brownish-red in incandescent light to green in daylight.

COLOR KEY

Gemstones are found in a range of beautiful colors, with many occurring in more than one color. This key is intended to help you begin identifying a stone based on its color, as well as to source stones in colors you like.

 COLORLESS	WHITE	 YELLOW	ORANGE	RED	PINK
Apatite	Agate	Amber	Amber	Alexandrite	Alexandrite
Crystal opal	**Amber**	Apatite	Andesine	Almandine garnet	**Bi-color**
Dendritic quartz	Chalcedony	Boulder opal	Carnelian	Amber	**tourmaline**
Diamond	**Coral**	Cat's-eye quartz	Citrine	**Andalusite**	Boulder opal
Fluorite	Dendritic agate	Chrysoberyl	Coral	Andesine	**Chalcedony**
Goshenite	**Fossilized coral**	**Citrine**	**Fire opal**	**Bixbite**	Color-change
Madagascan	Freshwater pearls	Diamond	Freshwater pearls	Boulder opal	garnet
moonstone	**Jadeite**	**Fire opal**	**Grossular**	**Carnelian**	**Coral**
Moonstone, blue	Moonstone	Fluorite	**hessonite**	Color-change	Diamond
Orthoclase	**Natural pearls**	**Fossilized coral**	Jadeite	garnet	**Fluorite**
Quartz with	Nephrite	Fossilized wood	**Moonstone**	**Coral**	Grossular garnet
inclusions	**Precious white**	**Freshwater pearls**	Padparadscha	Diamond	**Freshwater pearls**
Quartz/Rock	**opal**	Heliodor	sapphire	**Fire opal**	Kunzite
crystal	Saltwater pearls	**Jadeite**	**Rhodochrosite**	Fossilized coral	**Morganite**
Sapphire	**Sardonyx**	Moonstone	Sapphire	**Grossular**	Rhodochrosite
Scapolite		**Orthoclase**	**Sardonyx**	**hessonite**	**Rhodolite garnet**
Spinel		Prehnite	Spessartite garnet	**Hematite**	Rose quartz
Topaz		**Rutile quartz**	**Sphene**	**Jasper**	**Rubellite**
Tourmaline		Saltwater pearls	Sunstone	Moonstone	**Ruby**
Zircon		**Sapphire**	**Topaz**	**Pyrope and**	**Saltwater pearls**
		Scapolite	Zircon	**Almandine**	Sapphire
		Sphene		**garnet**	**Scapolite**
		Tektites moldavite		Rubellite	Spinel
		Topaz		**Ruby**	**Sugilite**
		Verdelite		Rutile quartz	Topaz
		Zircon		**Sapphire**	
				Scapolite	
				Spessartite	
				garnet	
				Spinel	
				Sunstone	
				Zircon	

PURPLE

Almandine garnet
Amethyst
Apatite
Black opal
Blue chalcedony
Boulder opal
Chalcedony
Fluorite
Freshwater pearls
Iolite
Kunzite
Lavender jadeite
Natural pearls
**Paraiba
  tourmaline**
Sapphire
Scapolite
Spinel
Sugilite
Tanzanite

BLUE

Alexandrite
Amazonite
Amber
Andean opal
Apatite
Aquamarine
Bi-color
  tourmaline
Blue chalcedony
Boulder opal
Chalcedony
Chrysocolla
**Color-change
  garnet**
Diamond
Fluorite
Indicolite
Iolite
Kyanite
Lapis lazuli
Madagascan
  moonstone
Moonstone, blue
Paraiba tourmaline
Saltwater pearls
Sapphire
Scapolite
Sugilite
Tanzanite
Topaz
Turquoise
Zircon

GREEN

Alexandrite
Amazonite
Amber
Andalusite
Andean opal
Apatite
Aquamarine
Aventurine quartz
Bi-color
  tourmaline
Boulder opal
Cat's-eye quartz
Chrome diopside
Chrome
  tourmaline
Chrysoberyl
Chrysocolla
Chrysoprase
Color-change
  garnet
Demantoid garnet
Diamond
Diopside
Emerald
Fluorite
Fossilized wood
Green beryl
Hiddenite
Indicolite
Jadeite
Malachite
Moonstone
Moss agate
Nephrite
**Paraiba
  tourmaline**
Peridot
Prasiolite
Prehnite
Sapphire
Sphene
**Tektites
  moldavite**
Topaz
Tsavorite garnet
Turquoise
Verdelite
Watermelon
  tourmaline
Zircon

BROWN

Agates
Amber
Andalusite
Aventurine quartz
Boulder opal
Cat's-eye quartz
Chrysoberyl
Citrine
Color-change
  garnet
Dendritic agate
Diamond
Dravite
Fire agate
Fossilized coral
Fossilized wood
**Grossular
  hessonite**
Jadeite
Jasper
Moonstone
Moss agate
Sardonyx
Smoky quartz
Spessartite garnet
Topaz
Zircon

GREY

Agates
Black opal
Cat's-eye quartz
Hematite
Jadeite
Labradorite
Moonstone
Natural pearls
Obsidian natural
  glass
Saltwater pearls
Scapolite
Spectrolite

BLACK

Black opal
Boulder opal
Coral
Dendritic agate
Diamond
Hematite
Jadeite
Kyanite
Moonstone
Natural pearls
Nephrite
**Obsidian natural
  glass**
Quartz with
  inclusions
Sardonyx
Schorl
Spinel
Star diopside
Tektite

Gemmological Information

Each of the gemstones in the Gemstone Directory *has a list of the important gemmological information for that stone. This will help you identify a stone, enable you to compare different stones, and, if you're a jeweler or cutter, assist you when working with the gem.*

CRYSTAL SYSTEM AND CRYSTAL HABIT are both key in identifying gemstones. The crystal system is the internal atomic structure of the crystal; a gemstone will have one of seven systems according to its symmetry. The crystal habit is the external shape or form of the crystal. There can be more than one habit; for instance, diamond has the cubic/isometric system, which has the highest symmetry, but has cubic, macle, pentagonal, dodecahedral, and octahedral habits. *(For more on crystal systems and habits, see page 20.)*

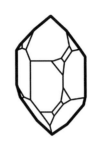

Crystal system and habit

The line drawing shows the Quartz trigonal crystal system and common habit, which is trigonal prismatic with pyramidal ends.

HARDNESS of gemstones is measured according to a scale of hardness known as the Mohs scale. The scale starts at 1 (the softest) and goes up to 10 (the hardest). Diamond is 10 Mohs and talc is 1 Mohs. Usually, gemstones for jewelry are 5 Mohs and above. A few gems are softer, and need particular care.

REFRACTIVE INDEX (RI) of a gemstone is used as a means of identification. The RI measures the amount that white light bends as it

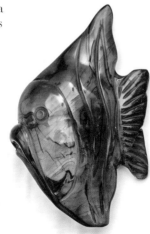

Specific Gravity: Carved amber fish

Amber is an organic gem with low density, so it feels very light in weight. Density can help identify certain gems.

enters the stone. The stone has a different optical density to air and so the light slows and bends—it is refracted. It is calculated using a refractometer, which is a prism that produces a numbered grading. Some stones have birefringence or double refraction (DR). This means the light rays are split in two, giving two readings on the refractometer. The difference between the two readings gives the stone its birefringence. The cubic crystal system is always singly refractive, while zircon, which has the tetragonal system, is doubly refractive. So when the gemstone is viewed from the top, looking through the table, you can see a doubling of the back facets of the pavilion.

SPECIFIC GRAVITY (SG) indicates the gemstone's density. The greater the SG, the heavier a stone will feel and weigh. Some gems are denser than others. For example, opal and turquoise (2.10 and 2.80 SG) are low density, but sapphire (4.0 SG) and hematite (5.2 SG) are higher density. They will feel heavier in the hand and weigh more. This can be helpful in identifying a gemstone. For instance, if you have two colorless faceted gems and don't know which stone is a diamond and which is a simulant such as cubic zirconia, just weigh them. A cubic zirconia (CZ) is 75 percent denser than a diamond and you will feel the difference in density.

LUSTER is the overall look of a stone, and refers to the way in which light is reflected off the surface. The harder the gemstone, such as a diamond (10 Mohs), the greater the luster, and it is described as having "adamantine" luster. The lusters of some rough stones can be earthy or dull, and some massive material, such as jadeite, can be greasy. Most faceted gemstones have a hardness of 5 Mohs or above because softer stones are not suitable for faceting. These are described as having a "vitreous" luster. There are a number of descriptions, including waxy, resinous, pearly, and metallic.

CHEMICAL COMPOSITION of a crystal mineral is the result of a combination of chemicals under intense heat and pressure. Some gemstones derive their color from

—

Luster

Luster is how the light is reflected off the surface of a stone. It can range from vitreous and adamantine on hard stones to greasy and dull on softer stones. These nephrite jade beads have a greasy luster.

impurities and metal oxides around the crystal, while other gems get their color from the chemicals in their composition (these are called idiochromatic gems).

TREATMENTS are applied to gemstones to enhance their appearance. They are used to change the color and improve clarity and luster. Some treatments are very common and accepted, while others are used to deceive buyers. *(See Gemstone Treatments, pages 30–33.)*

OPTICAL PROPERTIES of gemstones include asterism and chatoyance, color change, dispersion, brilliance, pleochroism, and aventurescence. Some of these properties, such as color change or asterism, are quite rare, and only a handful of gems exhibit them. However, this can be used to help identify a gemstone. *(See Optical Properties, pages 22–25.)*

CUTTING AND CUTS must take account of the cleavage and fracture of a gemstone. The cleavage and fracture refer to the ways in which a gemstone can break. Cleavage relates to the crystal's atomic structure; there are planes of weak atomic bonding which can be separated with a blow or knock. Before the development of cutting technology, diamonds would be cleaved so they could be used in jewelry. The lapidary knew that if the diamond crystal was hit/cleaved at a certain point, then a clean, smooth break could be made. Fracture, however, relates to breakage that is unrelated to a mineral's internal atomic structure. The remaining surfaces after breakage are described in a variety of ways, including conchoidal (shell-like), splintery, and uneven fractures. Due to factors such as hardness and dispersion, there are gemstone cuts that are traditionally

used for certain gems. For instance, emerald is brittle and contains many cracks and flaws. As a result, the emerald step cut was developed so that corners wouldn't break off during setting. *(See Cutting, pages 36–39.)*

IMITATIONS include paste and glass stones, like diamanté, plus man-made/manufactured simulants such as cubic zirconia, Yttrium Aluminum Garnet (YAG), and moissanite. Synthetics are lab-grown gemstones such as ruby and sapphire which contain the same chemicals as those found in the natural gems. The ingredients are put under heat and pressure so boules (crystals) form over a few months. There are also composite stones such as doublets and triplets. *(See Synthetics and Imitations, pages 34–35.)*

Cutting and Cuts: Golden-yellow topaz faceted pears

Some gemstones have planes of weak atomic bonding (cleavage). Topaz has cleavage such as this, so if it is used in a ring it requires a protective setting.

Properties of Gemstone Material

An understanding of the optical and physical properties of the original material is a prerequisite to knowing the best ways of working with gemstones and making the most of their inherent qualities.

CRYSTAL FORM

Most minerals are crystalline; they grow atom by atom, layer by layer, into a regular 3-D atomic structure. In most rocks, the crystals are too small to be seen without the use of a microscope (microcrystalline or cryptocrystalline), or the crystals are too small or irregular to be used as gemstones. A few minerals are amorphous, which means that they have a weak crystal structure or lack one altogether. Crystalline material may form with an irregular shape (massive), but there will be an internal regular 3-D atomic structure, even though no crystal faces are visible. The physical properties of crystals (i.e. their hardness, durability, and the way they break or fracture) and their optical properties (the way light is reflected off surfaces or travels through them) are all related to the atomic structure.

CRYSTAL HABITS

The orientation of the flat faces of a crystal and their rate of growth control the final appearance of the crystal—that is, its crystal habit. Most gemstones have a typical crystal habit, such as the acicular (needle-like) crystals of rutile found as inclusions within quartz, amethyst prisms, spinel octahedra, and fluorite cubes. Others have a number of habits. *(For more on crystal habits, see page 18.)*

CRYSTAL HABIT

OCTAHEDRON
Diamond crystal habit

PLANE OF SYMMETRY

HEXAGONAL PRISM
Beryl crystal habit

TRIGONAL PRISM
Quartz crystal habit

Colourless Beryl (goshenite) crystal (right)

The crystal system of Beryl is hexagonal. The typical crystal habit is long columnar crystals that are hexagonal prismatic with flat ends and bevel edges.

Chalcedony (carnelian) (far right)

This specimen shows chalcedony's botryoidal microcrystalline habit, which is a compact mass of tiny trigonal Quartz crystals.

Rutilated quartz crystals
Colorless quartz containing needle-like crystals of rutile. The Quartz crystal system is trigonal with a crystal habit that's usually hexagonal prismatic with pyramidal ends. It has striations perpendicular to the length.

CRYSTAL SYSTEMS

Geologists, mineralogists, and gemologists use symmetry to divide crystals into different systems. Diamond, for example, forms as a structure of carbon atoms, bonded in such a way that cubes, octahedra (bipyramids), and other cubic crystal habits are created. Diamond, like spinel and garnet, therefore belongs to the cubic system. There are seven main crystal systems, which are defined by their minimum symmetry. *(For more on crystal systems, see page 18.)*

CRYSTAL SYSTEMS

CUBIC
Three four-fold axes

TETRAGONAL
One vertical four-fold axis

HEXAGONAL
One vertical six-fold axis

TRIGONAL
One vertical three-fold axis

ORTHORHOMBIC
Either one two-fold axis at the intersection of two mutually perpendicular planes or three mutually perpendicular two-fold axes.

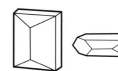

MONOCLINIC
One two-fold axis.

TRICLINIC
Either a center of symmetry or no symmetry

Optical Properties

A good way to identify gemstones is to look at the optical properties and effects exhibited by certain gems, which makes them special. For instance, only a small number of gems display asterism (stars) and chatoyance (cat's eyes), and this makes them easy to identify. So, when you're on the hunt for something special, or are trying to figure out the identity of a gem, keep your flashlight handy as this simple piece of equipment will "bring out" any special optical properties.

This section provides a list of the most common, and also rare, optical features that you might come across, as well as the correct gemmological terminology. It tells you which stones exhibit these properties and explains what is happening inside the stone and what you need to look for. It also guides you to the entries for individual gemstones in the *Gemstone Directory*.

BRILLIANCE is produced by light refracting in a transparent faceted gemstone with a high refractive index and a hardness value above 7 Mohs. The white light reflects off the polished facets within the pavilion and then comes back out through the table facet, creating high brilliance and sparkle. The brilliant cut was developed to produce maximum "life" and brilliance in a diamond. Measurements and proportions for the brilliant cut were calculated and established as the "ideal cut." If you see a very brilliant stone, it will have a high Mohs/hardness and RI.

Sunstone ring by Kent Raible

An impressive 18kt gold ring set with an Oregon sunstone cabochon (5.47ct), cognac diamonds, and red/orange sapphires. The ring contains many optical effects: the sunstone's aventurescence plus the fire and brilliance of the diamonds and sapphires.

DISPERSION occurs when white light enters the gemstone and splits into spectral colors, producing colorful fire.

PLEOCHROISM describes a gemstone that has two or three color directions when viewed from different angles. Tetragonal, trigonal, and hexagonal stones show two colors (dichroic). Monoclinic, orthorhombic, and triclinic stones can show three colors (trichroic). Cubic and amorphous stones do not have this property. *(For more on pleochroism, see page 14.)*

ASTERISM refers to the four-ray or six-ray star that hovers over the surface of the stone. It is produced when light hits two or three sets of fibers, rutile needles, or cavities within the stone. The lapidary has to ensure that the fibers lie parallel to the base of the cabochon.

CHATOYANCE (cat's eye) is a white silvery line that sits across the middle of the stone. It occurs when light enters the cabochon and reflects off internal inclusions such as cavities, rutile needles, or fibers. The lapidary has to orientate the material so that the inclusions lie parallel to the base of the stone.

FLUORESCENCE occurs when ultraviolet (UV) daylight enters certain gemstones, such as diamonds or fluorite. They will fluoresce either yellow or blue, and can make a diamond appear whiter or have a yellowish tint in daylight.

SILK is the silky/translucent appearance of a stone as a result of light reflecting off fine rutile needles. It is commonly seen in Corundum.

COLOR-CHANGE gemstones exhibit a change of color when moved from daylight to incandescent light. Alexandrite, for example, is green in daylight and reddish-brown in incandescent light.

HIGH BRILLIANCE
Diamond • Zircon • Chrysoberyl • Spinel • Spessartite garnet

DISPERSION
Diamond • **Sphene** • Demantoid garnet

PLEOCHROISM
Morganite • Aquamarine • Dravite • Indicolite • Rubellite • Verdelite • Tanzanite • **Iolite** • Apatite • Andalusite • Kunzite • Sphene

ASTERISM

SIX-RAY
Sapphire • **Ruby** • Spinel • Rose quartz • Smoky quartz

FOUR-RAY
Almandine garnet • Star diopside • Spinel

CHATOYANCE
Chrysoberyl • Alexandrite Aquamarine • Heliodor Tourmaline • Cat's-eye quartz Nephrite • Obsidian Prehnite • Scapolite Apatite • Yellow orthoclase (Feldspar) • **Fire opal**

FLUORESCENCE
Ruby • **Diamond** • Fluorite

SILK
Ruby • **Sapphire** • Prehnite

COLOR CHANGE
Alexandrite • **Sapphire** • Garnet • Tanzanite • Fluorite

Names in **bold** identify gem shown.

INTERFERENCE
Labradorite • Moonstone •
Hematite • **Opal**

OPALESCENCE /
ADULARESCENCE
Colorless orthoclase (Feldspar) •
Moonstone

COLOR-PLAY
Opals

SCHILLER
Moonstone • **Labradorite**

IRIDESCENCE
Obsidian • Opal • Fire agate •
Hematite • Obsidian •
Pearls (organic) • **Labradorite**

ORIENT
Pearls (organic)

AVENTURESCENCE
Aventurine quartz • **Sunstone** •
Labradorite • Obsidian

BIREFRINGENCE
Zircon • Peridot •
Sphene • Tourmaline

*Burmese ruby and
diamond ring*
The ruby's optical properties
include fluorescence, while
the fine old-cut diamonds
exhibit brilliance and fire as
a result of the high refractive
index and dispersion.

INTERFERENCE is the reflection of light off structures, such as layers, inside a gemstone or, in the case of opal, tiny silica spheres. The interference can produce spectral colors in the form of color-play.

OPALESCENCE / ADULARESCENCE is a white or blue shimmering effect over the surface of a stone, which is produced when light hits the internal layers.

COLOR-PLAY describes the colorful iridescent patches and pinpoints produced when white light hits the lattice of tiny silica spheres that form an opal. The colors should move as the opal is rotated through 360 degrees.

SCHILLER is a shimmering effect or sheen produced when light hits the internal layers in a gemstone. It sits just below the surface of the stone.

IRIDESCENCE is a colorful rainbow effect that is produced when white light hits internal structures within a gemstone.

ORIENT is the iridescent luster that's created when light hits the overlapping concentric layers of pearly nacre (aragonite platelets) produced by a pearl.

AVENTURESCENCE is a glittering, metallic effect caused by light reflecting off internal platelet inclusions of minerals such as fuchsite, mica, pyrite, or goethite.

BIREFRINGENCE OR DOUBLE REFRACTION (DR) occurs when white light splits into two on entering the stone. The DR reading is the measured difference between the two rays. When viewed through the table facet, the back facets of the pavilion will look as if they are doubled.

Inclusions

Inclusions are the internal structures and features found inside a crystal or gemstone; they can be solids (such as small crystals of another mineral), liquids (such as silica droplets), or gases, or they can be semi-filled fractures or cleavage breaks. They occur during the formation of the crystal, which can envelope the inclusion as it forms or, in the case of fractures, occur at the same time as the host material is forming. Some inclusions are unique to particular gemstones, such as insects in amber, or they are common to a variety of minerals, such as rutile needles. Many jewelers and buyers consider them to be flaws, and they are removed or "hidden" during the cutting of the stone to produce a clean gem. However, inclusions can be advantageous, as well as fascinating, and they do have their uses.

Inclusions, such as peridot "lily pads," sunstone platelets, hexagonal zoning in Corundum, and "horsetail" (asbestos fiber) inclusions in demantoid garnets, can be used to establish the identity of a gemstone. They prove that a stone is natural and has not been heated; small crystals and rutile needles in ruby and sapphire alter during heat treatment.

Inclusions can prove that a stone is not a synthetic or imitation. For example, the inclusions of a natural emerald are different to those in a synthetic emerald.

And, lastly, inclusions can indicate a source, which can be a huge bonus in selling a gemstone. For example, Burmese rubies typically contain rutile needles, while Brazilian Paraiba tourmalines can have copper inclusions, which are not found in other tourmalines. Colombian emeralds can have pyrite crystals and a rare trapiche formation; Sri Lankan spinel contains zircon crystals; and peridot from Pakistan can be identified by black Ludwig needles.

Amber cabochon with insect inclusion (top)

Amber was the sticky resin of pine trees, so inclusions of plants and insects can frequently be found. This cabochon has a fully intact fly-insect inclusion, which gives it added interest and value.

Faceted emerald (middle)

This Colombian emerald has small, jagged three-phase inclusions consisting of liquid, gas bubble with crystal element (commonly pyrite).

Dendritic agate (bottom)

A great example of dendritic agate showing the black dendrite crystal formations in the milky agate, which look like trapped plant-life but are small crystals. It is completely natural—no treatments have been used.

Sources

Many dealers prefer to buy old gemstone stock because the material is often of better quality than more modern stones. Large and fine imperial, pink, and golden topaz and indicolite (tourmaline) from Brazil is getting harder to find as the mines are not producing the quality crystals that they used to. Russian demantoid garnet is rarely seen in the market place and is viewed as the "Holy Grail" of demantoid because it is of a finer quality than newer sources. Large rubellite with a good color is in short supply; Mozambique once supplied lovely material in large sizes, but this supply has tailed off over the years.

As mines are "mined out," the size of the uncut gem material often gets smaller. Therefore, high-quality natural gemstones above 3 carats in weight become rarer, and so have a higher value and keep that value over time. In addition, a great deal of "old" gem material is untreated, while nowadays new material undergoes a host of treatments, such as glass filling and epoxy filling, often at source, and diamonds that have undergone high pressure, high temperature (HPHT) treatment and lattice diffusion-treated sapphires are widely available. So, old gems and jewelry are a good source of unusual, untreated, and sought-after stones.

Source has a major impact on price, especially for the more important stones, in terms of the color, size, or simply the rarity of deposits, for example. Russian alexandrite has never really been matched due to its fine color and the size of the gemstones. Other countries, such as Brazil and Madagascar, also produce alexandrite, but stones originating there have a lower value because they are of inferior quality and size. Dealers speculate on Burmese ruby and sapphire, and wonder how much longer the famous Mogok mines (which yield very fine ruby and have been heavily exploited for years) can keep producing. Demand for Myanmar stock is huge and uncertainty over supply adds a premium to the price of Burmese goods. When this source is mined-out, the prices will rocket. Fortunately, Mozambique has come on-line with some very nice ruby rough that's not dissimilar to Burmese ruby. It's a beautiful color and the prices can be good, giving buyers an attractive alternative to Myanmar.

Sapphire mine, Madagascar

Madagascar is rich in colored gemstones with deposits of labradorite, alexandrite, and sapphire. Using low-tech, small-scale methods of extraction, these miners are washing the paydirt to separate host rock from sapphire crystals.

MINING MAP
This map shows the most important and valuable sources of gemstones worldwide.

SARDINIA, ITALY Red coral

CANADA Diamond

USA Turquoise; sapphire; morganite; tourmaline; natural freshwater pearls

MEXICO Fire opal

CARIBBEAN Conch pearls and natural pearls

COLOMBIA Emerald

BRAZIL Paraiba, rubellite, and indicolite tourmaline; chrysoberyl; diamond; aquamarine (Santa Maria); pink, imperial, and golden topaz; amethyst and citrine (Rio Grande); emerald; fine agates

NIGERIA Tourmaline; aquamarine

NAMIBIA Diamond; mandarin garnet; tourmaline

SOUTH AFRICA, ZAIRE, AND BOTSWANA Diamond (de Beers)

ZAMBIA Emerald

ZIMBABWE Sandawana emerald

IRAN Turquoise

AFGHANISTAN Aquamarine; ruby; lapis lazuli

PAKISTAN Emerald

RUSSIA (SIBERIA) Demantoid garnet; alexandrite (chrysoberyl); diamond; Siberian amethyst; nephrite jade (white and green); aquamarine

JAPAN Cultured saltwater Akoya pearls and saltwater keshi (natural) pearls; coral

CHINA Freshwater pearls

MYANMAR Ruby; sapphire; jadeite; spinel; peridot; blue moonstone

THAILAND Ruby; sapphire

INDIA Kashmir blue sapphire; Golconda diamond; chrysoberyl

SRI LANKA Sapphire and padparadscha sapphires; chrysoberyl; blue moonstone; topaz

MADAGASCAR Tourmaline; aquamarine

TANZANIA Tanzanite; ruby

MOZAMBIQUE Ruby; aquamarine; rubellite and Paraiba-type tourmaline (Brazilian is more valuable); garnet

PERSIAN GULF Natural saltwater pearls

EGYPT Peridot

ETHIOPIA Opal

KENYA Tsavorite (garnet)

AUSTRALIA Black and precious opal; saltwater, South Sea, and Tahitian pearls; diamond

TAHITI AND INDONESIA South Sea and Tahitian pearls

Gemstone Treatments

Records show that gemstones have been treated for many centuries. In fact, some gemstones can be dated by studying the treatments they have undergone, which also helps to identify them. The timeline on pages 32–33 gives the dates that various treatments arrived on the market, so you can work out which stones are natural or untreated. Without treatments, some gems would be so rare that they would become prohibitively expensive or too fragile to use. Certain treatments are commonplace, so always assume that your stone has been treated. Treatments do affect the price and should always be declared by the trader. A laboratory will be able to identify most treatments, but some can be identified just by using a loupe.

1 HEAT TREATMENT is often performed on gemstones in the Corundum, Beryl, and Quartz species as an accepted practice. Up to 95 percent of rubies, sapphires, and aquamarines are heated, so assume that the stone has been heated unless told otherwise. The heating process develops and intensifies the gem's natural color and also changes the internal structures. There are different types and levels of heating, ranging from very slight to extreme, and the prices of the resulting gemstones vary.

🔍 *Heat treatment can be seen in rubies and sapphires using a loupe.*

2 HIGH PRESSURE, HIGH TEMPERATURE (HPHT) treatments on diamonds can change their color. Unpopular brownish stones can become vibrant pinks, blues, greens, black, or colorless.

3 LATTICE DIFFUSION occurs with rubies, sapphires, and some feldspars. It is a form of extreme heat treatment in the presence of chemicals such as beryllium or titanium. It makes the colors more vivid and can improve asterism. It's generally performed on poor material; the treatment changes brownish rubies to bright reds, for example. It often stays in the outer layer of the gemstone and is not always permanent. Diffused-treated sapphires are much cheaper than normal heated ones. Lattice diffusion should be declared.

4 GLASS FILLING is performed on many rubies and sapphires, and some diamonds. The material is heated with flux and the glass/filler is pushed under vacuum into the cracks and feathers of the stone to make it look cleaner and improve the color. The treatment is not stable, so heat and chemicals must be avoided. This treatment should be declared, because it dramatically reduces the price. The treated stones are called composite sapphires and rubies. It's possible to see glass bubbles and the blue-orange flashes of the lead glass in a stone.

🔍 *Glass filling can be seen in rubies and sapphires using a loupe.*

5 OILING is part of the lapidary process for emeralds and is used to fill surface-reaching cracks and to improve clarity. Ninety-five percent of emeralds are enhanced by oiling. The oil can dry out over time, so it is not completely permanent. Colored oils are not acceptable.

6 EPOXY FILLING is a step further than simply oiling. Fillers such as epoxy resin are forced under mild heat into the open pores of the emerald. It is done under vacuum so that the filler is absorbed into the cracks and feathers, making it look cleaner by hiding the whiteish inclusions. The treatment should be declared.

🔍 *Fracture filling can be seen in emeralds using a loupe.*

7 LASER DRILLING involves lasering a tiny bore hole in a diamond to reach a black carbon inclusion. Sulfuric acid is then pushed through

the bore hole to dissolve or remove the black inclusion. The bore hole can be seen with a loupe and the process should be declared.

🔍 *Laser drilling can be seen in diamonds using a loupe.*

8   **IRRADIATION** involves exposing a gemstone to gamma radiation with chemicals to change the color of the stone. It's regularly used on diamonds, topaz, quartz, and pearls, and is sometimes backed up with heating. It can be inconsistent and fade. Irradiation treatment can normally be spotted, as the colors are not natural.

9   **STABILIZING** is performed on crumbly, soft gem material such as turquoise, hematite, and opal. An adhesive bonding agent such as plastic is introduced into porous microcrystalline material. It improves hardness, reduces porosity, and increases density. Sometimes color is introduced as well.

10   **IMPREGNATION** is the infusion of a foreign material such as a wax, polymer, or resin into a porous gemstone to improve stability and durability, and is often performed at source. Keep such gems away from heat, because the waxes may melt.

11   **BLEACHING** is performed on gems prior to dyeing; it removes the color entirely or partially. The stone is then often impregnated with a polymer to improve its durability, as the bleaching can make the item more porous and brittle. Bleaching is performed on pearls that have spots or marks in the nacre or conchiolin, to even out the color.

12   **DYEING AND STAINING** are performed on stones such as chalcedony, agates, coral, and jadeite that are porous with fine cracks. Pearls are commonly dyed to "fashion" colors or produce colors that are more "expensive." These treatments can be checked for using acetone and are long-lasting if done well.

🔍 *Dyeing and staining can be seen using a loupe.*

13   **RECONSTITUTION AND PRESSING** involve mixing powdered gem with a resin or PVA-type material. The resulting substance is then compressed and cut into stones; sometimes a dye is also added. Turquoise and amber have both been reconstituted for years and the treatment should be declared by the trader.

14   **COATING** is a process that applies a layer of color to the back of a low-grade gem to improve how it looks. It's performed on diamonds and pearls, and will break down and peel off over time.

🔍 *Coating can usually be seen using a loupe.*

15   **BUFFING** with a wax or chemical polish is performed on pearls such as saltwater Akoya pearls to improve their luster and surface quality.

KEY 🔍 = treatments you can see using a loupe.

TIMELINE

Some gemstones can be dated by analyzing the treatments they've undergone, which is useful in the case of antique jewelry as it helps identify the gemstone. Below is a timeline giving the dates that the various treatments arrived on the market—it means you can work out which stones are natural or untreated. The dates of the introduction of imitation and synthetic stones have also been included.

Georgian paste earrings
Paste jewelry was very popular in France from the 1700s.

Akoya cultured pearls
Mikimoto developed the process of culturing saltwater Akoya pearls in the early 1900s. Prior to that, pearls were all natural.

AD 1048 Records show that heat treatment of rubies was occurring

1720 Paste stones were being made by Georges Strasse in France

1877 Synthetic emeralds developed

1800s Paste imported from Czechoslovakia

1823 Dyeing of agates recorded

1905-1910 Synthetic ruby and sapphire on the market

1915 Heating performed

1920 Cultured pearls from Mikimoto

1949 Synthetic Linde star sapphires

1960 Hydrothermal synthetic emeralds appeared on the market

EARLY 1960s Irradiation of pearls

Reconstituted amber
Art Deco earrings (Ambroid/reconstituted amber has been made for several hundred years, so will be found in jewelry from 1700s).

Art Deco paste jewelry
This pendant was made in the 1920s and is set with a synthetic sapphire and paste stones.

Irradiated lemon citrine

Quartz was irradiated to change its color from 1970.

Glass-filled rubies

Glass-filled rubies are misrepresented on the market as heated rubies.

1970 India started irradiation processes

1950 Diffusion treatments

1990s Chromium-diffused rubies

1960s Laser drilling of diamonds for clarity enhancement

1970s Cubic zirconia manufactured

1970s Slocum opals marketed

1990–2000 Glass-filled rubies

1998 Moissanite marketed

1999 HPHT diamonds by General Electric

EARLY 2000 Synthetic diamonds

2000 Beryllium treatments of Corundum

Synthetic opals

1970s Gilson and Slocum opals.

Mystic topaz

First seen in 1998, this topaz was coated and heated to achieve this appearance.

Synthetics and Imitations

For centuries, synthetic and imitation stones have been used in jewelry to make them more affordable, given the high value of natural gemstones. Often worn alongside the real gems, imitations would supplement the few pieces of gem-set jewelry owned by an individual. Inexpensive imitations also offered a choice of "gemstone look"—from diamonds to sapphires and opals—allowing buyers to purchase the colors and cuts they liked.

SYNTHETIC GEMSTONES

Synthetic gemstones are laboratory-grown gemstones that have the same chemistry and structure as the natural stone. The refractive index, hardness, and density/specific gravity will be the same, but it only takes a matter of months to grow a synthetic boule (crystal). The basic method has been used since the early 1900s: powdered ingredients are melted under extreme heat to form the boule slowly and are then cut in the same way as the natural gemstone. There are synthetics of the most important gems, including Linde star sapphires and rubies that display asterism, and synthetic color-change gems. These have slightly different color zoning and growth lines to the natural stone. Synthetic emeralds are formed in a slightly different "flux-melt" process in which the powdered ingredients are mixed in a solvent at a high temperature for many months and then cooled very slowly. A synthetic emerald contains inclusions, which can fool many people, but they are different to those that occur in a natural emerald.

IMITATION GEMSTONES

Imitation gemstones are primarily made from cheaper materials such as lead glass, and have been used since Ancient Roman times. Glass stones have various names, such as paste, Strasse, rhinestones, diamanté, and crystal. From the 1700s they were manufactured in France and Eastern Europe, with factories along the Rhine (hence the name, rhinestones). They were often set in closed-back collets so that the foil could be placed behind them for extra brilliance. Well-known makers of imitation glass stones are Gilson, Swarovski, and Gripoix (poured glass). They can imitate a variety of gemstones such as emeralds, opals, and coral, but do not have the same properties as the natural gemstones. Identification is fairly easy; glass has little brilliance and it is a soft stone, so the facets become worn, chipped, and scratched. The imitations also contain bubbles and can discolor over time. A real diamond will retain sharp facet edges and exhibit brilliance and fire due to the hardness.

COMPOSITES

Composites are part natural stone and part glass or synthetic. A solid opal can be expensive, so doublets and triplets reduce the price Emerald doublets are similar in make-up. These stones can be identified from a side view.

Synthetic stones
Synthetic stones have been available since early 1900s.

Paste lizard brooch
Made between 1890 and 1910, this brooch was fabricated using silver.

Faux pearls

Faux "glass" pearls can be identified by the grainy surface quality. These Marvella pearls have a great luster and value.

Glass jewelry

Vauxhall Glass sold high-quality glass jewelry molded into shapes.

DIAMOND SIMULANTS

There are simulants of most gemstones. Diamonds, however, have lots of simulants because they're such expensive stones. Modern manufactured gems have replaced traditional paste as diamond simulants. They are more hard-wearing and have more "sparkle." The most popular simulants are:

CUBIC ZIRCONIA (CZ) is very cheap; it has the look of diamond and imitates other gemstones like tanzanite and emerald. It has more fire than diamond and is nearly as brilliant. Cubic zirconia can be identified because it is nearly 75 percent heavier than diamond and may be scratched with a fine carbide scriber.

YAG (YTTRIUM ALUMINUM GARNET), AKA DIAMONIQUE is used in fashion jewelry as a diamond simulant because it is hard (8.5 Mohs) and durable. However, it has low dispersion and so has little fire.

MOISSANITE is a good simulant as it has greater brilliance and dispersion than both diamond and cubic zirconia. It is also hard and durable. But it is not as cheap as cubic zirconia, costing between 10 and 20 percent of the price of an equivalent diamond.

LABORATORY-GROWN SYNTHETIC DIAMONDS are available, but these are expensive to produce and so are unviable. They are not identical to a diamond and can be identified by a laboratory. They are marketed as being eco-friendly as they do not have the same impact as mining on the environment and are not used to finance civil wars.

NOTE When purchasing any gemstone or piece of gem-set jewelry of high value, ask for a laboratory certificate or gemstone report as a guarantee of what you're buying. A certificate will state what the gemstone is, its characteristics, the treatments it has undergone, and sometimes the origin.

Cubic zirconia (left) and moissanite (right)

Two modern diamond simulants, CZs have been available since 1970 and moissanite since 1998. Both have high dispersion and good brilliance.

Cutting

The selection of rough material and the cutting of a faceted gemstone are skilled jobs, with numerous factors to consider. Cutting requires an understanding of the way light refracts in a gemstone, the characteristics of specific gems, and how certain gemstones "behave." In addition, rough material is often valuable and so the lapidary is expected to make every carat count.

A faceted gemstone requires a good-sized crystal with reasonable clarity and an even spread of color. However, on average, only about 10 percent of what's mined is of the required quality for faceting; the remaining gem material is then used for cabochons, carvings, beads, and industrial purposes instead. Many gems cut at source have what's called "native cutting," which means that the stone is cut to maximize the weight in order to achieve the best price. In the West, buyers prefer stones that have good symmetry and correct proportions, so stones are often re-cut to look their best.

WHY ARE GEMSTONES CUT THE WAY THEY ARE?

Crystal shape and size dictate the cut, as the yield needs to be maximized. The crystal shape affects the type of cut used. For instance, tourmaline has long, columnar crystals, so rectangular baguettes and emerald cuts are common. Octahedral diamond crystals are perfect for cutting rounds and princess cuts, but baguette cuts create more wastage and so often cost more.

A pale or colorless gemstone needs to be cut to produce brilliance and fire, while colored stones are often cut as step cuts, which display the color best.

PARTS OF A FACETED GEMSTONE

These are the terms for the different parts of a round brilliant-cut gemstone. Their varying proportions will affect the brilliance, beauty and colour of the stone.

GIRDLE The outer edge of the perimeter of a gemstone, where the crown meets the pavilion

CROWN The top portion of a stone, above the girdle

PAVILION The lower part of a stone, from the girdle to the culet

TABLE The flat surface on top of a stone, the largest facet or face

CULET The lowest part of the stone, which appears as a point or ridge

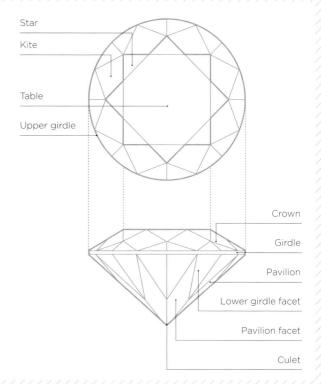

Star
Kite
Table
Upper girdle

Crown
Girdle
Pavilion
Lower girdle facet
Pavilion facet
Culet

Rectangular baguettes
The buff-top indicolite baguette is rectangular.

Cleavage planes
This faceted kunzite octagon shows great cleavage planes.

Perfect cleavage
This fluorite displays perfect cleavage.

Inclusions
This chatoyant quartz cabochon has rutile inclusions.

Some gems are pleochroic—they have two or three color directions. The lapidary has to orientate the rough material correctly to achieve the best color on the table facet.

Optical effects, such as asterism and schiller, need to be maximized, so the crystal has to be orientated correctly to display the effect. For example, with asterism, the rutile needles should be parallel to the base of the stone.

Cutting a gemstone is never a "done deal"; there can be hidden or invisible flaws, or there can be tension within the crystal so that it breaks or cracks as the cutter is working.

Some gemstones have perfect cleavage, which is a plane of weak atomic bonding that usually lies perpendicular to the long axis of the crystal. The cutter has to orientate the rough so that he/she is not cutting on a cleavage plane.

Best value or return means that the finished stone has to reach a certain price. Rough material is expensive. It's important to get a good yield, as wastage can reduce profit. Weight and price bands have to be considered.

Many gems contain inclusions, so the lapidary has to map out the crystal and place the inclusions in an area that isn't too visible. An obvious inclusion will spoil the look of the stone and an internal crack can cause fragility if it is too close to the girdle. There is computer technology available that offers cutting options for valuable material.

Machine cutting is used for smaller calibrated gemstones, but larger and more valuable stones are generally custom cut by a lapidary. The quality of the finished gem will be better in a "custom cut."

CABOCHONS

Usually, faceted gems are prized over unfaceted cabochons. However, over the years, cabochons have become more valued, largely thanks to the cutters in Idar Oberstein, Germany, where there is a tradition of cutting high-grade cabochons using quality gem material. The prices of cabochons are always lower than those of faceted gems, enabling jewelry designers to create accessible and affordable jewelry.

CUTTING HISTORY

The development of cutting was led by diamonds because of their high value. Other gemstones, including paste, were either cut in the same way or used as small polished pebbles.

Until the 1400s, uncut octahedral diamond crystals were used with the rough edges smoothed and flat surfaces polished using another diamond. From the early 1400s, the point cut was used to enhance the diamond's octahedral shape and show off its transparency.

In the late 1500s, an understanding of gemmology and cleavage allowed cutters to shape diamonds into a hogback cut, which is similar to the roof of a building. The crystal was cleaved to make flat, regular surfaces parallel to the crystal's triangular faces. Between 1500 and 1700, the table cut was used; a diamond crystal had the top point and lower point of the octahedral crystal cleaved to create a table facet and culet. To set them, high-karat gold was simply burnished around the stone.

Between 1600 and early 1700, basic cutting technology led to the rose cut, which used flat diamond rough. The rose cut could have just three triangular facets or more, in multiples of six. Foil was placed behind them to bring light into the stone. Briolettes were based on the rose cut.

In early 1700, the old cut—also known as the old mine cut—was developed. It was the precursor of the modern brilliant cut and

Table cut

This is a very old diamond that's a development of the early table cut. Based on an octahedron, the top and bottom points were cleaved, leaving a very high crown and deep pavilion.

Rose cut

The rose cut arrived in the 1600s. It has a flat base and a faceted upper surface. It could be adapted to different shapes and have more or fewer facets.

Georgian garnet brooch and pendant

An important early piece set with shallow antique-cut almandine garnets.

was based around the shape of an octahedral diamond crystal. The old cut was used up until the early 1900s.

In 1919, Marcel Tolkowsky developed the modern brilliant cut. It had calculated angles, measurements, and proportions to promote the natural brilliance of a diamond. It coincided with the advent of high-grade diamond rough coming out of South Africa. This cut gave us calibration, where a certain size equates to a certain weight—for example, a 6.5mm-diameter, round, brilliant-cut diamond should weigh 1 carat.

The 1920s brought electricity and precision cutting, so more cuts were developed. Up until the 1920s, the only square cuts were baguette step cuts; they were designed to show off color, but didn't produce much brilliance. So the Asscher cut was developed, which had an Art Deco appearance and produced more "life" than the step cut.

During the 20th century, the square radiant cut and the princess or quadrillion cut were developed. They were based on the modern brilliant cut, displaying much more brilliance than a step cut. Also the trilliant arrived, which was effectively a triangular brilliant cut that was shallow in depth and ideal for use as shoulder stones.

Princess cut

The princess cut is basically a square brilliant cut, originally with 58 facets.

DIFFERENT TYPES OF CUT

HOW TO SPOT AN OLD CUT

- 58 facets

- Deep pavilion and crown, which retains weight and produces fire

- Cushiony-round outline that follows the shape of the crystal

- Large open culet

- Small table

   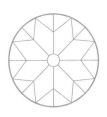

side view   top view   bottom view

HOW TO SPOT A BRILLIANT CUT

- 58 facets

- Less deep than the old cut. The crown is approximately one-third of the depth of the pavilion

- Round outline

- More brilliance than an old cut, but not as much fire

- No culet facet

   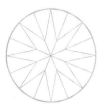

side view   top view   bottom view

HOW TO SPOT AN ASSCHER CUT

- Square shape

- Angular corners

- Small table

- High crown

- Open square culet

  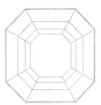 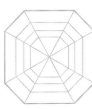

side view   top view   bottom view

Pricing and Grading

Cut or faceted gemstones cost what they do due to a number of factors: the rarity of material, the size and quality of mining deposits, and the production and mining costs involved, including the difficulty of extraction and the cost of finding more deposits and gem material.

RARITY

Some gemstones, such as quartzes and agates, are plentiful and occur worldwide, so there's no shortage and they are inexpensive. However, certain gemstones are rare and the yield of fine faceting material from a mine is very low, which means that every carat has to count in terms of financial return. Rare geology also affects the pricing of some gems; basically, the geology required for certain gems to form just doesn't occur very often, so there are very few deposits worldwide. A finite supply will always raise the price.

SIZE AND QUALITY OF DEPOSITS

The price of faceted gems also comes down to the quality of deposits and the grade of crystals. Sometimes there will only be small pockets of good material suitable for faceting, while the remaining material is mediocre. Mines can get quickly mined-out of the best rough and, as time goes by, the supply of material tails off. The limited supply of fine-grade crystals can make certain colored gemstones more valuable than diamonds. A clean, 4-carat, unheated Burmese ruby in "Pigeon's Blood" red is rarer than a diamond, as is a

Sri Lankan mine

A low-tech, low-impact mine in Sri Lanka involving a simple shaft shored up with wooden beams.

De Beers mine

Redundant open-pit diamond mine in South Africa that would have yielded approximately 14 million carats of diamonds.

*"Pigeon's Blood" ruby
and diamond ring by Graff*

This is a very fine and
expensive ruby; it appears
to be very clean, which is
unusual, and it has a perfect
ruby color. Treatments and
source unknown.

fine, untreated Colombian emerald with good clarity
and color.

PRODUCTION COSTS

Colored stones are typically collected using cheaper,
low-tech mining methods, while diamonds are mined
on a huge scale with high-impact extraction techniques.
The ruby and sapphire mines in Mogok, Myanmar, still
use traditional wicker baskets and "people power"
instead of heavy and expensive equipment. Smaller
artisanal mining is beneficial to both the local ecology
and the end buyer, as long as it doesn't risk the health
and safety of the miners.

Difficulty of extraction is another factor in pricing;
some gem deposits are more difficult and expensive to
access. Mines in Siberia, Russia, are affected by freezing
temperatures and permafrost, and extraction can only
take place for about six months of the year. In Brazil, the
famously rich gem deposits of Minas Gerais are not only
difficult to extract, but there are also significant physical
dangers and risks from armed bandits in the region.

PRESSURE OF DEMAND

Some gem deposits, such as Burmese jadeite and Baltic
amber, will continue to yield material for centuries to
come, while others dwindle and new sources have to be
found. Such is the size of the market and the constant
demand for diamonds that, even with the millions of
carats coming out of Africa, Australia, Russia, and
more recently, Canada, new deposits need to be found.
Expensive viability studies using high-tech geological
mapping are performed to ensure that the yield will be
financially worthwhile.

COLORED STONES

Unlike diamonds, colored stones have no set prices and
there is no pricing index. The value of colored stones
depends on all the above factors, and buyers will have a
choice of prices depending on the source, grade, and
how many hands the gem has passed through. If the
material is from a mine or local cutter, then the price
will be lower than from a major trading center where
dealers are trying to get the best price. Blue sapphires
vary widely in price, depending on their origin, size,
color, clarity, and treatments, so buyers need to decide
on a budget and/or grade of stone before looking. A
cheap sapphire will be pale in color and included, a
mid-range, heated stone will have better color and
clarity, and a natural, unheated, cornflower-blue
sapphire will be the most expensive. Bear in mind that,
as the weight increases, so does the price; it will go up at
1 carat, 2 carats, and 3 carats-plus, and a certified stone
costs more. Because of the range of factors involved in
the pricing of colored stones and the sheer range of
available gemstones, a set price list would be both
cumbersome and confusing.

Sri Lankan blue sapphire

An unheated royal blue
Sri Lankan sapphire with
minor inclusions. It has a
good depth of color and the
cutting is generally good.

GEMSTONE
DIRECTORY

*The following 140 pages form the Gemstone Directory,
which gives the gemmological properties and characteristics
of the individual gemstones.*

DIAMOND

The exceptional brilliance and luster that arise from the crystal structure and hardness of diamond cannot be matched by any other natural mineral. Diamonds are incredibly durable and difficult to damage, so can survive many centuries of wear in jewelry.

Diamond in its pure form is colorless but, depending on the presence of trace elements, "Natural Fancy" yellow, brown, pink, blue, green, gray, black, and even red diamonds can occur. In general, bright white stones are the most desirable and graded by certifying bodies such as the GIA. This grades D as the best blue-white diamond and then moves down the alphabet, with yellow or brown tints being seen from I onward. The price and value decrease with the grade. The best way to see the color of a white diamond is to place it upside down and look through the side of the stone. If you look through the table, the brilliance will confuse and hide the color. A certificate will state the color grading of a stone—dependable certifying bodies include the GIA, as well as HRD, DPL, and IGI.

The rare and valuable "Fancy Colors" are priced separately to white diamonds. They often have color zoning in layers and bands, and will carry more inclusions than white diamonds. Fancy colors need good saturation and purity of color, with a uniformity or even spread of color. It's essential that you obtain a certificate for any natural-colored diamond.

White diamonds are not particularly rare and are mined on a large scale. Deposits form deep in the Earth's crust from 110 to 250 miles (177–402km) down. The crystals are brought to the surface by rising magma in naturally occuring Kimberlite pipes, and require open-pit mining to excavate the diamond-bearing rock. Sometimes, secondary

—
Group of uncut rough diamonds
Approximately 15% of what's mined are gem grade. The cubic crystal system gives the highest symmetry and enables them to be cut with minimum waste.

GEMMOLOGICAL INFORMATION

CRYSTAL SYSTEM Isometric/cubic. Crystal shapes are octahedrons, cubes, macles, rhombic dodecahedrons, and plates.

MOHS HARDNESS 10 (diamond is the hardest known mineral)

REFRACTIVE INDEX 2.417–2.419

SPECIFIC GRAVITY/DENSITY 3.50–3.53

LUSTER Adamantine

CHEMICAL COMPOSITION Crystallized carbon

COMMON TREATMENTS High Pressure High Temperature (HPHT) treatments, irradiation, coating, fracture filling, and clarity enhancement.

OPTICAL PROPERTIES High RI and high dispersion produce brilliance and fire. Fluorescence under UV light in certain types of diamond—namely, blue, yellow, and green.

CUTTING AND STONE CUTS Perfect cleavage allows diamonds to be cut or cleaved along a cleavage plane. The presence of different grains in the crystal enables cutting with another diamond. Diamonds have led the way in cutting technology for all other gemstones. The recent use of lasers has made cutting diamonds much easier. Octahedron crystals can produce two round brilliant cuts or two square princess cuts with the minimum of wastage.

IMITATIONS/SYNTHETICS From the 1600s, a paste (called Strasse) was used to simulate diamonds. From the 20th century, cubic zirconia, YAG/diamonique, strontium titanite/fabulite, and moissanite were popular imitations. From 1970 onward, gem-grade diamond synthetics have been produced.

NOT TO BE CONFUSED WITH... White sapphire, topaz, quartz, zircon, goshenite beryl.

Asscher cut (left)

The Asscher cut has a geometric Art Deco feel. which makes it a popular choice for jewelry. As a square cut, the Asscher has more life and brilliance than a standard step-cut emerald cut.

deposits such as alluvial diamonds are found in river gravels and seabeds. The famous diamond-producing kingdom of Golconda in 16th-century India mined alluvial deposits, while the fine white South African diamonds found in the late 1800s were in Kimberlite pipes. In the late 20th century, Eastern Siberia produced diamonds on a huge scale, with Canada coming "online" at the beginning of the 21st century.

Approximately 15 percent of what's mined are gem-grade crystals; the remainder are either near-gem grade, with 50 percent being used for industrial purposes. Gem-grade diamonds are transparent, uniformly shaped crystals—50 percent of them are octahedrons, which have the highest yield. Diamond has a cubic crystal habit and an orderly atomic structure, with the atoms arranged in neat, repetitive patterns; as a result, the crystals have well-formed shapes. The crystal structure affects the hardness and density, as well as the way light travels through the crystal. This is why diamond has high dispersion and fire, and also an adamantine luster resulting from hardness.

Graff necklace

An impressive diamond necklace from Graff, which features a huge 53.94ct Fancy Intense yellow emerald-cut diamond pendant surrounded by flawless white diamonds. Traditionally, the emerald cut was designed to display color in a stone with its large table facet, while the parallel step cuts brought light into the rear of the stone.

From left to right: Round brilliant cut, princess cut, and emerald cut

The emerald cut has the best D color and is internally flawless. The round brilliant cut may have a J color grade, but there is little visible tint and it has a VS clarity (see page 46). The princess cut is a typical commercial-grade diamond.

Early old-cut diamonds

These diamonds were in a pair of antique earrings and weigh 1.97ct and 1.63ct. They have been cut according to the shape of an octahedral crystal.

Common inclusions are cleavage feathers; these are white or transparent internal breaks that can weaken the structure and extend over time, resulting in separation. There are small crystal inclusions such as garnet and spinel, plus tiny diamonds. White or black pinpoints can also occur. These pinpoints are tiny solid deposits that are often miniature rough diamonds. Clouds are groups of white pinpoints that give a hazy effect. Finally, stress inclusions caused by internal structural changes may occur and can cause breakage during cutting. These are common in colored diamonds. A good certificate will map the number and type of any inclusions in your stone. In general, the cutter will tuck inclusions away along the girdle of the stone under the crown facets, leaving the large table facet clear. The GIA clarity grading system starts with IF (internally flawless) and then grades from VVS (very very small inclusions) to VS (very small inclusions) to SI (small inclusions) and then I (inclusions).

The aim of cutting is to achieve a stone with good clarity, good proportions, and good weight. Correct proportions produce brilliance and fire, while a good weight brings the best price. Lasers and computer technology have made a huge difference in how diamonds are cut. Traditionally, a crystal would be polished on one side so the cutter could look into the stone and map any inclusions. Nowadays, computers are used to "map" the rough material and give simulations of the cutting options. Lasers also provide greater cutting options as they can cut away from cleavage planes—the cleavage is used to indictate where the crystal could be cut. Common diamond cuts are the brilliant cuts, which have 52 facets and were developed for diamonds in 1920s, the princess cut, and trillions.

Rose-cut diamond rings by Louise O'Neill

These articulated rings are an original way of using rose-cut diamonds. Three pear-shaped roses of different colors have been bezel-set in brushed white, rose, and yellow gold.

Three antique rings

Top: 1930s Art Deco ring in 18kt white gold set with three round brilliant-cut diamonds. Center: Early Art Deco diamond ring set with old cuts in an 18kt gold band and silver mount. Bottom: Edwardian "shell" ring in 18kt gold and platinum set with old-cut diamonds.

The Eternal Twins

Earrings by Graff using a pair of D flawless
emerald-cut diamonds that are suspended from a
shower of emerald- and round-cut diamonds.

Numerous treatments exist for diamonds, including HPHT. The HPHT process was developed by General Electric and can turn brown diamonds into colorless whites and, if irradiated and HPHT heated, yellowish diamonds can be turned into fancy vivid colors. This is a controversial process and the GIA will only grade the diamonds as "HPHT annealed" or "Artificially Irradiated," and the stones must also be laser-inscribed as "HPHT processed" or "Irradiated." Black diamonds are produced in this way—they are fairly cheap, but the process seems to make them softer than natural white diamonds. They are often pitted and can chip during setting, which isn't the case with natural diamonds.

Other treatments are fracture filling with lead glass in order to improve clarity, but bear in mind that ultrasonic jewelry cleaners can remove any fillers in the stone. Other clarity enhancements exist, such as drilling a small bore hole with a laser to black carbon inclusions and then removing them with sulfuric acid. The bore hole can be seen with a x10 magnification loupe.

Cut diamond ring (1968) by Charlotte De Syllas

A niello ring using 18kt yellow and white gold set
with a diamond that has been cut simply with only
three facets at the top and bottom.

The diamond-producing countries want to maintain the high prices of diamonds to ensure that they remain an attractive investment, so they hold back diamond rough to keep the prices high! The Diamond Producer's Association (DPA) consists of the top seven producers, the most important of these being De Beers (Africa), Alrosa (Russia), Rio Tinto (Australia), Canada, and India. Jewelry sales are increasing year on year. The USA is the fastest-growing market, with 42 percent of total sales (approximately $32 billion). China buys 16 percent, with India and the Persian Gulf at 8 percent each. The DPA estimates that demand will outstrip production by 2020, so there is pressure to find new sources of quality diamonds. This is why De Beers is using marine mining on the seabed and investing around $3 billion in its mines in Africa and Canada.

Diamonds are durable stones, but they are not unbreakable. They are attracted to grease, so need to be cleaned regularly to keep them looking their best. A dirty diamond can lose up to two grades of whiteness! They can be cleaned quite simply using hot soapy water and a toothbrush.

Cubic zirconia

Available since the 1970s, cublic zirconias (CZs) are best known as a diamond simulant. They have higher dispersion and fire than a diamond, but can be scratched and are much heavier.

Spun ring with natural fancy brown diamond by Emma Farquharson

The band of this ring is made of spun silver and has a yellow gold rub-over collet, which offsets the rich, deep brown color of the brilliant-cut diamond. At this size, natural browns are good value and come in a range of tones.

Natural fancy yellow and dark orange brown diamonds

Both of these natural colored diamonds are certified by reputable laboratories. Because of the cost of colored diamonds and the use of treatments to change color, it is advisable to buy stones that are certified as natural.

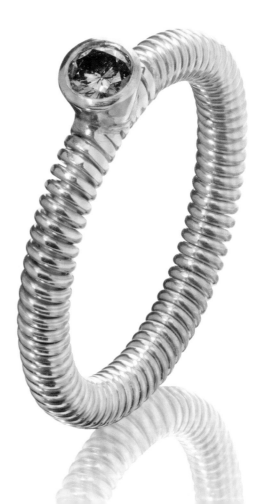

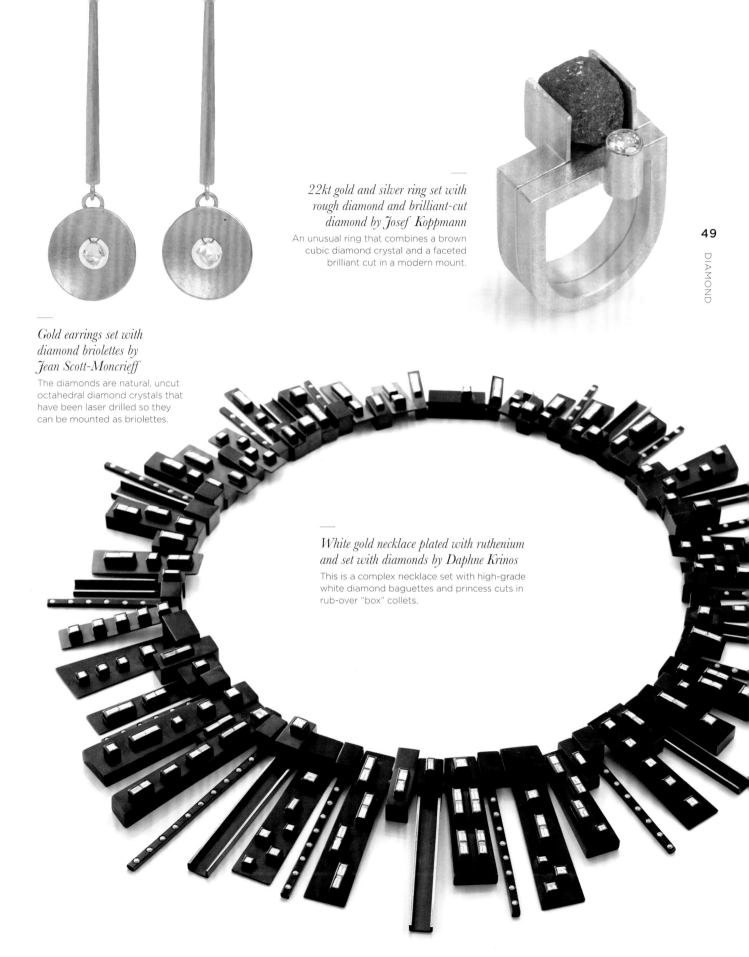

22kt gold and silver ring set with rough diamond and brilliant-cut diamond by Josef Koppmann

An unusual ring that combines a brown cubic diamond crystal and a faceted brilliant cut in a modern mount.

Gold earrings set with diamond briolettes by Jean Scott-Moncrieff

The diamonds are natural, uncut octahedral diamond crystals that have been laser drilled so they can be mounted as briolettes.

White gold necklace plated with ruthenium and set with diamonds by Daphne Krinos

This is a complex necklace set with high-grade white diamond baguettes and princess cuts in rub-over "box" collets.

RUBY

Ruby has a rich pinkish to purplish-red color that often becomes more saturated and "hotter" under UV and incandescent light as it fluoresces. If the stone is translucent or opaque, you'll frequently see stepped, hexagonal growth lines in the material.

Ruby belongs to the Corundum species, which is an allochromatic gemstone that's colorless in its pure form. Ruby is colored by chromium and iron impurities. It should have a medium to dark tone; if lighter in color, it is described as pink sapphire, which is also part of the Corundum species. As the crystal grows it forms new layers, resulting in color variations called zoning within the ruby. The color often relates to the geographical origin—for example, Myanmar produces pinkish-red stones and Thai rubies are brownish-red/garnet in color. The perfect color of ruby is pure red with a hint of blue; this is called Pigeon's Blood red.

Typical inclusions are small crystals, growth structures and zoning, and fluid-filled cavities and canals. Rutile inclusions in the form of small needles are common in Burmese rubies—they can give the stone a silky appearance as light reflects off them. There are several inclusions to help identify rubies as natural and untreated, including "fingerprints," which are healed fractures or fluid inclusions. It's not really possible to detect origin and heat treatment in a flawless, clean stone.

The main sources of ruby are Myanmar, Thailand, Pakistan, Vietnam, and, more recently, Mozambique, Tanzania, and Madagascar. Russia, Australia, and the USA are other sources.

GEMMOLOGICAL INFORMATION

CRYSTAL SYSTEM Trigonal habit. Barrel-shaped hexagonal crystals with double-pointed pyramidal ends.

MOHS HARDNESS 9

REFRACTIVE INDEX 1.762–1.778

SPECIFIC GRAVITY/DENSITY 3.97–4.05 (weighs heavy compared with diamond)

LUSTER Dull and greasy when rough, but vitreous to adamantine when faceted and polished.

CHEMICAL COMPOSITION Aluminum oxide

COMMON TREATMENTS Heat treatment, beryllium heat-treated, diffusion-treated, dyed with red ruby oil, and glass-filled.

OPTICAL PROPERTIES Strong pleochroism—a dichroscope will show yellow/orange-red in one direction and deep carmine/purplish-red in another. Color zoning according to layers of growth, which lie parallel to the prismatic crystal faces. Fluorescence under long- and short-wave UV light—some stones will fluoresce in sunlight and halogen light. Fluoresence doesn't usually occur in Thai and some African rubies, as they have a higher iron content. Asterism (six-ray star). Trapiches (six prismatic crystals co-joined).

CUTTING AND STONE CUTS No cleavage, but slightly brittle. Faceted into cushions, ovals, and octagons (mixed cuts, step cuts, and brilliant cuts), and cabochons.

IMITATIONS/SYNTHETICS Glass and verneuil flame-fusion synthetics were available from 1902; they have curved growth lines. In the 1980s, flux-melt and hydrothermal synthetics were developed—these carry inclusions, making them difficult to detect. Linde star rubies were produced from 1950 and are still sold today.

NOT TO BE CONFUSED WITH... Garnet, rubellite tourmaline, spinel; glass and dyed quartz; garnet and glass doublets.

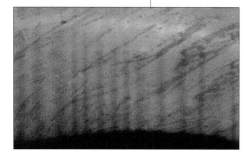

Burmese rubies

Left: The close-up of this 5.55ct unheated Burmese ruby cabochon shows rutile needles. Above right: The faceted round-cut Burmese ruby typically contains inclusions, such as small crystals.

Ruby rough is tightly controlled by the producing country, so it's very hard to get hold of nice cutting material. "Native" cutting can be an issue with rubies, as they're usually cut to maximize the weight in the country in which they are mined. It's common to get deep stones with off-center culets, "windows," and poor proportions, making the gem glassy or dull. So a re-cut can be worth considering to increase the value of the stone, despite losing weight. Low-grade ruby material is used for cabochons, beads, and carvings, as well as for grinding and polishing.

Approximately 95 percent of rubies are heated and treated to improve their clarity and color. The Mong Hsu mines in Myanmar produce large amounts of ruby, but all the material requires heating to make it an acceptable ruby color. As a precaution, avoid heating rubies when working on jewelry because this can cause a color change in the stone.

Diffusion treatments increase the rutile needle content in the ruby, which produces a better "star." Beryllium heat treatment, which began in the early 2000s, obtains pleasing ruby colors from brownish-dark Corundum that did not respond to standard heating.

Rubies can be more expensive than diamonds due to their rarity. The origin affects pricing, with Burmese rubies being the most valuable. Prices vary depending on the type of treatments—basic heating does not lower the value significantly, but beryllium heating,

Ruby and diamond eternity band by Graff

This is a high-grade ring; the emerald-cut rubies are all matched for color, clarity, and cut.

Rough ruby with faceted stone

A ruby crystal in prismatic habit attached to matrix. The crystal is included and the color is a brownish pinky-red, not the bright red of the oval-cut stone that sits next to it. It is a low-grade crystal.

2.84ct Thai ruby faceted cushion

This is a natural, unheated Thai ruby from an old collection. It has good "spread" for its weight due to its relatively shallow depth. It's very clean, barring some small crystal inclusions.

surface diffusion, and dyeing will have a big impact on price. The market has been swamped with glass-filled rubies in the last 15 years and these are now commonplace, with some dealers describing them erroneously as just "heated"—they are not.

"Naturals" carry a premium, so will require a certificate. A 2-carat-plus natural ruby with good color saturation, purity, and strong fluorescence is very desirable. The price increases exponentially with the weight. Rubies of 1 to 1.5 carats are easy to source, so have a moderate price, but a 2 to 2.5-carat stone becomes more difficult to find, with 3 carats-plus being rarer and much more expensive.

Variations of rubies
Lattice diffusion or beryllium-treated (left) and flame-fusion synthetic (right) rubies.

Ruby and diamond halo bombé cluster ring by Graff
A contemporary ring comprising a floral cluster of fine, brilliant-cut diamonds, which sits in the center of this ring as a focal point.

*Ruby and diamond
necklace by Graff*

Sensational ruby and diamond
necklace with three rows of perfectly
matched oval rubies and an important
oval faceted ruby in the central drop
section. The ruby is surrounded by
fine pear-shaped diamonds.

*Late Victorian ruby
and diamond ring*

The marquise shape was
popular at the turn of the
19th century and it featured
regularly in Victorian jewelry.
The ruby is small but a very
nice color; the diamonds have
good brilliance and clarity.

SAPPHIRE

Sapphires can be difficult to identify because of the sheer range of colors; however, a "Cornflower Blue" sapphire isn't matched by any other stone. Its identity can be confirmed by the angular hexagonal growth lines and color zoning common to sapphire.

Sapphire comes in every color except red, which is ruby. It is colorless in its pure form, with coloring agents producing the different colors. The presence of titanium and iron produces a blue sapphire, while chromium impurities give pink sapphires. Sapphire is more abundant than ruby, as the impurities required are more common. The most important blue sapphires come from Kashmir, but these are now rare as little is mined. Very fine stones are also found in Sri Lanka and Myanmar. Other sources are East Africa (Mozambique and Tanzania), Madagscar, the USA, and Australia.

The most valuable blue sapphire is medium- to dark-toned royal blue (also called Cornflower Blue) with a touch of violet. Padparadschas, which are a beautiful mix of pink and orange, are very rare and highly sought after—these sell for much higher prices. Green sapphires contain fine alternating bands of blue and yellow, and often have a khaki tone. In general, good color saturation is looked for, as long as the stone doesn't become too dark or lose brilliance. As the intense colors are more valuable, so pinks, yellows, oranges, and violet are treated to a more saturated hue. Color-change sapphires are a rare phenomenon; there is usually a blue to purple change as the stone is viewed in UV daylight and then incandescent light. More rarely, the change is red-brown to green.

5.96ct natural blue sapphire
A certified untreated Sri Lankan sapphire in an attractive royal blue. The stone has good clarity for a natural, which often contain inclusions.

GEMMOLOGICAL INFORMATION

CRYSTAL SYSTEM Trigonal habit. Barrel-shaped hexagonal crystals with double-pointed pyramidal ends.

MOHS HARDNESS 9

REFRACTIVE INDEX 1.762–1.788

SPECIFIC GRAVITY/DENSITY 3.95–4.03

LUSTER Vitreous

CHEMICAL COMPOSITION Aluminum oxide

COMMON TREATMENTS 95 percent of sapphires are heated. There are also lattice diffusion and beryllium/titanium treatments, plus glass-filling.

OPTICAL PROPERTIES Pleochroism. Sapphires are dichroic—green-blue in one direction and violet-blue in another. Color zoning and color-change stones (blue to purple and, rarely, red to green) also occur. Asterism is exhibited.

CUTTING AND STONE CUTS No cleavage. Sapphire is frequently cut deep due to the crystal shape and is often cut for weight. Cutters have to orientate the material so that the violet-blue direction is visible through the table facet. Color zoning means that cutters also have to orientate the color inside the stone so that the best color is viewed when set—for instance, color is often put in the culet.

IMITATIONS/SYNTHETICS Glass, synthetics dating from the 1900s, synthetic Linde star sapphires, and dyed sapphire.

NOT TO BE CONFUSED WITH... Tanzanite, iolite, kyanite, indicolite, spinel, zircon.

Sapphire variations
The natural blue pear-shaped cabochon (left) is a good size and has a lovely silky luster. Its color is often deeper than that of the Sri Lankan sapphire (right).

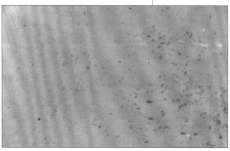

Close-up
This zoomed-in version of the pear-shaped cabochon shows color banding.

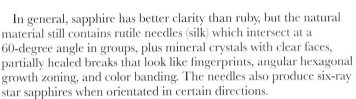

Triple pave butterfly cluster sapphire and diamond earrings by Graff

A beautiful pair of earrings with top-grade workmanship. The sapphires are a stunning cornflower blue and the quality of the pave setting is superb. Each butterfly has a bright white marquise-cut diamond as its body.

In general, sapphire has better clarity than ruby, but the natural material still contains rutile needles (silk) which intersect at a 60-degree angle in groups, plus mineral crystals with clear faces, partially healed breaks that look like fingerprints, angular hexagonal growth zoning, and color banding. The needles also produce six-ray star sapphires when orientated in certain directions.

Up to 70 percent of Sri Lankan sapphire (called geuda) has to be heated to a blue color—when mined, geuda is milky, pale gray, and semi-transparent, and has no value. Once heated, it becomes an attractive sapphire that looks natural and has value. Normal heat treatment also improves clarity by reducing and changing the inclusions—using a loupe you can see disk-like fractures that look like halos with mineral inclusions that have become rounded with a snowball-like appearance. The silk is semi-dissolved and broken, crystals are ruptured, and crystal faces around the girdle sintered.

Deep blue sapphire rough material

The matrix or host rock has been removed, leaving gem material ready for cutting. It might have been heated to improve color and clarity.

The color range of natural Corundum

A yellow cushion of 19.03ct, a pink octagon of 6.36ct, a green cushion of 7.98ct, a color-change sapphire (blue to purple) of 4.79ct, and a rare red to green color-change sapphire of 2.56ct illustrate the color range of natural Corundum.

Bentley and Skinner Victorian sapphire and diamond cluster necklace, c.*1870*

An impressive necklace with approximately 17 carats total of blue sapphire and approximately 9 carats of old-cut diamonds set in 32 clusters. The stones are perfectly matched for color and cut and are set in silver and yellow gold.

Panthère de Cartier ring

A famous design by Cartier, the Panther ring is made of platinum, blue sapphire, emerald, and white diamonds.

When the sapphire is treated with foreign material and extreme heat (lattice diffusion and beryllium/titanium treatments), the color becomes vivid. It also tends to run along the facet junctions and girdle, and becomes localized and blotchy, bleeding into pits and cracks. Sometimes the treatments can lighten the blue color and the stone ends up with a colorless zone on the outer edges. If the stone is glass-filled, it effectively becomes a composite mix of natural Corundum and lead glass, containing gas and glass bubble inclusions with blue/orange flashes when moved in the light. All these sapphires are without value, and the treatments should be declared. Imitations such as glass and cubic zirconia are common. Synthetic sapphires are produced by the flame-fusion process and have curved growth lines rather than straight. They often have irregular color distribution, with the color sitting in the outer edges of the boule. Synthetics have been used in jewelry from the early 1900s.

Multi-colored sapphire rings
by Louise O'Neill

Sapphires are so much more than a blue stone. These sapphire rings show the subtle mid-colors that can be found—the peachy-pinks, lilacs, greys, teals, and greens. The brushed finish of the gold enhances the delicate colors.

Grecian gold and blue sapphire
ring by Emma Chapman

A charming 18kt gold ring that uses design elements often seen in Ancient Greek jewelry. It is set with a faceted 7/5mm pear-shaped blue sapphire on a dainty 1mm gold band. The sapphire has a decorative bezel setting, which adds to the antique style of the ring.

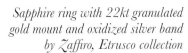

Sapphire ring with 22kt granulated
gold mount and oxidized silver band
by Zaffiro, Etrusco collection

The hexagonal color or growth zoning on the crystal slice tell us clearly that this is a sapphire.

EMERALD

The allure of a fine emerald is hard to ignore—it is pure emerald green in color, with just a hint of blue, and will typically have inclusions such as cracks and small crystals. Its price can be close to that of a diamond.

Emerald belongs to the Beryl species and is the most important gem of the group. It is also the most important green gemstone you can find. Historically, emerald has been highly prized, appearing in Mughal jewelry and also early European pieces.

Color is everything with emerald: the more intense the color, the more valuable the stone. The best color is a strong bluish-green that comes primarily from chromium and vanadium impurities with a tiny bit of iron. The color should be vivid and saturated, but not too dark, and there should be no zoning. Color is graded according to three categories: hue (the type of green, i.e. yellow- or bluish-green), tone (light, medium, or dark), and, most importantly, saturation (the intensity). With emeralds, the most attractive stones are those with vivid saturation and a medium tone. The hue is dependent on the source. Colombian emeralds are thought to have the best color; they are a more intense pure green, as they are colored primarily by chromium. They have secondary blue hues that give the stone a richer, warmer color. Brazilian and Zambian emeralds have vanadium as the primary coloring agent and have a higher blue tone.

Emerald crystals frequently have irregular color distribution and growth zoning. Complete transparency is rare. The Beryl group are hard stones, but also brittle due to stress and the violent geological

Emerald and diamond necklace by Graff

A magnificent piece of work that comprises more than 66 carats of emerald-cut emeralds haphazardly arranged among crisp white diamonds. The design has been carefully planned, however, with all the emeralds matched for color and clarity.

Colombian close-up

The close-up of the Colombian emerald (left) shows typical Colombian inclusions in the form of partially healed fissures.

Colombian and Zambian emerald

The Colombian emerald (left) came out of Colombia before fracture-filling treatments became the norm. It shows only minor clarity enhancement (oiling). The Zambian emerald (right) is a slightly cheaper alternative and, barring light oiling, they are not treated at source.

conditions under which they are formed. The GIA classes emeralds as Type III for clarity—they are nearly always included with cracks, feathers, rods, and long fibers of tremolite, liquid and gas bubbles, and other minerals. This is called the *jardin*, which is the French word for "garden," because the inclusions look like plant growth; they are accepted as normal. Eye-clean emerald is rare and expensive. Emerald is so included that sometimes 80–85 percent of the rough material must be cut away to produce a clean-looking stone, and this affects the price. Most people can't afford to buy a "clean" emerald, so there have to be inclusions in the stone.

Be aware that treatments can hide inclusions, with nearly all emeralds being oiled under vacuum to minimize feathers, cracks, and whitish inclusions. Cedar or synthetic oil, or polymers such as Opticon, are used very sparingly or in a heavy, "fracture-filling" way.

GEMMOLOGICAL INFORMATION

CRYSTAL SYSTEM Hexagonal prisms.

MOHS HARDNESS 7.5–8.0

REFRACTIVE INDEX 1.57–1.59 (birefringent)

SPECIFIC GRAVITY/DENSITY 2.69–2.80

LUSTER Vitreous

CHEMICAL COMPOSITION Beryllium aluminum silicate

COMMON TREATMENTS 99.5 percent of emeralds are oiled under vacuum for clarity. Colombian emeralds are fracture filled. Some undergo color enhancement.

OPTICAL PROPERTIES Vary according to source. Most emeralds have a jardin—crystals and cracks. Birefringence. Pleochroism. Trapiche.

CUTTING AND STONE CUTS Emerald has indistinct cleavage, but is brittle and sensitive to pressure, which is why stones are cut as emerald cuts without corners. Avoid heating.

IMITATIONS/SYNTHETICS Composite soude emeralds, plus glass and synthetic emeralds, have been produced since end of 19th century.

NOT TO BE CONFUSED WITH… Green sapphire, diopside, peridot, green tourmaline, demantoid garnet, and dioptase. "Oriental emeralds" are green sapphires.

Zambian crystal slice

An interesting polished crystal slice of Zambian emerald showing concentric color zoning and common emerald inclusions, such as two- and three-phase inclusions, black carbonaceous flakes, and actinolite (fine needles).

Cluster of Gilson synthetic emeralds

These are flux-melt synthetic emerald crystals grown in a laboratory. Powdered ingredients are mixed with a solvent to a high temperature and then slowly cooled over months, allowing crystals to form.

Soude emerald

Soude emeralds are composite stones; they are doublets that have a crown and pavilion of different materials, which are cemented together. Once set, they will look like an included emerald.

A laboratory will advise you of the clarity enhancements, but always ask the dealer about treatments. As clean emeralds are so rare and valuable, fracture filling is now performed on all stones coming out of Colombian mines—always assume that Colombian emeralds are treated unless certified otherwise. Since the early 2000s, GIA certificates classify levels of clarity treatment on an emerald from minor (slight oiling) to moderate to significant (fracture filling). Avoid ultrasonic cleaners, as these can strip out any polymer fillers and leave you with a pale included stone.

Colombia has always been viewed as the most important source of fine emerald—in the famous Muzo mine, emerald crystals were picked carefully by hand and produced beautiful, intensely green stones. However, on the whole, only one-third of Colombian emeralds are worth cutting. Good emeralds are also found in Brazil, namely in Bahia and Goiás, while from the 1980s good deposits were found in the Minas Gerais region. From the 1950s, Sandawana emeralds from Zimbabwe were mined. These have an intense color, but only come in small sizes. Zambia became a producer of good-quality emerald from the 1970s onward. Many people choose Zambian emeralds because they're not treated at source like

Art Deco emerald and diamond lizard pin, c.1920

Pave-set emeralds and a row of brilliant-cut diamonds create the perfect body for the lizard.

Diamond and emerald Panthère de Cartier ring in white gold

Two vivid emeralds have been set as the panther's eyes amid the geometric diamond-encrusted head.

Colombian emeralds. Other sources are Afghanistan, Australia, Ghana, India, Pakistan, Mozambique, and Nigeria.

An emerald needs to be cut to the correct proportions to prevent it from becoming a glassy shallow stone or a deep dull stone. The so-called emerald cut maximizes the weight of the rough crystal in terms of shape and has been designed to manage the brittle characteristics of the gemstone. The corners are "taken off" to avoid breakage as a claw is pushed over, and the depth will ensure good color saturation. Cabochons are a good alternative to faceted stones, as they are less fragile and can look stunning even with inclusions.

Emerald is dichroic, which means that it has two color directions: blue-green and yellow-green. The cutter has to orientate the table facet perpendicular to the crystal length to get a more bluish-green. Colombians may be difficult to cut as the crystals can have a greater intensity of color close to the surface, so if the cutter removes too much material from the upper part of the stone, the emerald will become paler.

Doublets (soude emeralds) are a composite of green glass or synthetic emerald cemented to a base of low-grade, included, pale beryl. Doublets can be identified by looking at the stone side on, but this can be difficult if they are mounted in an enclosed setting.

Antique emerald and diamond gold and silver ring, c.*1740*
The emerald in this stunning ring is undamaged and untreated. There are six rose-cut diamonds in closed-back bezel settings, which are typical of the period.

Raw stone
An aggregate of high-quality emerald crystals with a rich, saturated color.

Emeralds were first synthesized in 1877 using the flux-melt process. The inclusions are different—they have a veil and feather pattern instead of the usual crystals and internal cracks. The more recent laboratory-grown synthetics have fewer inclusions and flaws. They do, however, take time to "grow," which means there is a reasonable investment of time and so synthetics do have a value.

When evaluating an emerald, the criteria that need to be considered are color, durability, and inclusions. Emeralds are vulnerable to damage, so avoid significant fractures or fissures in the crystal. If there are cracks, these need to be checked when they are close to the surface. Also, the cut of the gemstone should be suitable—emerald cuts, ovals, and cushions are the safest. The color should be maximized, the proportions need to be correct, and the faceting should produce good brilliance. A stone can be re-cut to better proportions, but the inclusions and cracks in an emerald can make this difficult.

Emerald and gold ring by Emma Farquharson

A Zambian emerald has been bezel-set into a chunky 18kt gold band. The emerald has been cut into a curved freeform shape that contrasts well with the flat, angular facets of the band.

Emerald and diamond gold earrings by Judith Crowe

A fine pair of Zambian emerald pendeloques with diamond-set gold fittings. The emerald's color is deeper in tone than this image shows, with good saturation.

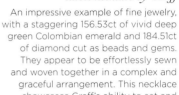

*Emerald and diamond beaded
tassel necklace by Graff*

An impressive example of fine jewelry,
with a staggering 156.53ct of vivid deep
green Colombian emerald and 184.51ct
of diamond cut as beads and gems.
They appear to be effortlessly sewn
and woven together in a complex and
graceful arrangement. This necklace
showcases Graff's ability to set and
display gemstones.

*Emerald and diamond
ring by Graff*

This unusual and beautiful 4.22ct
lozenge-shaped old-mine Colombian
emerald is a rare find; the color and
clarity are near perfect. The gem
has a rich emerald green hue that's
not too dark and the saturation
is excellent. The clarity gives the
emerald both depth and brilliance.

AQUAMARINE

Aquamarines are large gemstones that are generally free from inclusions, and are cut in a step cut. They can be blue with a hint of green or sky blue. Aquamarine belongs to the Beryl family. It is the sister stone to emerald, but doesn't have all the cracks and inclusions found in emerald. In general, its natural color is sea-green—hence the name, "sea water." Aquamarine is a lovely color, but the current fashion is for sky-blue stones, so most material is treated to change the color. It is possible to get a dark blue color, but this is rare and thus valuable. Santa Maria aquamarine from Caera, Brazil, produces a natural deep blue gem that is colored by the presence of iron.

There are sources that produce a natural sky-blue color—Mozambique, for example, is sometimes called Santa Maria Africana because of its intense color. Natural deep blue material also comes out of India, Nigeria, Mozambique, and Madagascar. Other sources of good aquamarine are Afghanistan and Zimbabwe. The finest color is deep blue without gray tones.

Aquamarine can be transparent and opaque, the latter type being used for cabochons and beads. If the crystals have inclusions, these tend to be long hollow, or liquid-filled, tubes. If the tubes are orientated correctly, the gem becomes chatoyant—in other words, it has a "cat's eye." In general, however, the crystals have good clarity and brilliance is good. Crystals can be very large, up to hundreds of carats. Aquamarine is pleochroistic and has two color directions—near colorless and strong blue. The blue color corresponds to the orientation that retains weight. The table facet is aligned parallel to the length of the crystal.

Unheated Mozambique faceted oval
The cutting of this beautiful sky-blue aquamarine from Mozambique—a source that is known for its depth of color—is excellent; the stone has good proportions and is not overly deep.

GEMMOLOGICAL INFORMATION

CRYSTAL SYSTEM Hexagonal prisms.

MOHS HARDNESS 7.5–8.0

REFRACTIVE INDEX 1.564–1.596

SPECIFIC GRAVITY/DENSITY 2.69–2.80

LUSTER Vitreous

CHEMICAL COMPOSITION Aluminum beryllium silicate

COMMON TREATMENTS Heating to 725–850°F (400–450°C). Neutron and gamma irradiation not permanent.

OPTICAL PROPERTIES Pleochroism, chatoyance, and, rarely, asterism.

CUTTING AND STONE CUTS Step cuts to show off color.

IMITATIONS/SYNTHETICS Synthetic spinel

NOT TO BE CONFUSED WITH... Blue topaz, tourmaline, zircon, kyanite.

Aquamarine and diamond brooch by Bentley and Skinner
A flower-head platinum brooch set with a central brilliant-cut diamond and four aquamarine heart-shaped petals measuring ³⁄₄in (18.5mm). The stalk is set with brilliant-cut diamonds. The aquamarine has a greenish tint to it, which usually indicates unheated material.

Two natural Brazilian "Santa Maria" aquamarines
The color of this old dark blue aquamarine (left) is so exceptional that many people assume it's topaz or synthetic spinel. The faceted cushion (right) also has an intense dark blue color.

Silver ring with 24kt gold set and faceted aquamarine by Josef Koppmann

The square-cut aquamarine may be heated, but this cannot be confirmed as there are generally no flaws in the stone to help indicate the use of heat.

Aquamarine crystal and gold clasp necklace by Daphne Krinos

This piece comprises of a row of natural aquamarine crystals that have been top drilled and strung with gold crystals.

There can be mishaps sometimes when cutting aquamarine; it has indistinct cleavage and can be slightly brittle. It is not always possible to see cleavage breaks in the material, so there can be occasional breakage during setting.

Aquamarine is commonly heated. Unless you are told otherwise, it is best to assume that the stone has gone through this process—laboratories can't really test for heating in a stone that carries no inclusions. Heating is a permanent treatment. Some aquamarines are irradiated to a dark blue color. This is not permanent, however, and the color fades over time. Irradiation can be identified by a laboratory, so it's worth getting expensive dark blue stones checked.

Aquamarine is a sturdy stone and can be used for all types of jewelry. It needs a regular clean, otherwise it looks gray and glassy.

Aquamarine rough material for cutting

It is a typically greenish-blue color, which is usually changed to sky blue by heating the material to 725–850°F (400–450°C). The material is transparent with some inclusions.

MORGANITE, HELIODOR, GOSHENITE, GREEN BERYL, AND BIXBITE

The Beryl species is a collection of colorful, clear gemstones with good brilliance in large sizes. Durability is fairly good, so facet edges stay clean and sharp over time.

MORGANITE is colored by manganese impurities and occurs in pink, peach, violet, and salmon-pink colors. It is found as short tabular prisms. Morganite is a dichroic gemstone—either colorless, plus one color, or two different colors. It often occurs in bi-color crystals with aquamarine and typically has liquid-filled inclusions. Morganite is usually pale in color and requires a faceted brilliant cut, princess cut, or trillion to produce maximum "life."

Morganite is found in Madagascar, Brazil (bi-color crystals), Elba, Mozambique, Namibia, and Pakistan.

HELIODOR is rarely treated and occurs in lemon-yellow to golden yellow colors. If heliodor is heated, it actually loses color. It's found alongside aquamarine in granite pegmatites. The typical inclusions are slender tubes, which are visible to the naked eye.

Heliodor is usually cut into step cuts to display its color, but brilliant cuts also work well. It's possible to find chatoyant cabochons.

Heliodor comes from the Russian Urals, Brazil (pale), Madagascar (fine color), Ukraine, Namibia, Sri Lanka, and the USA.

GEMMOLOGICAL INFORMATION

CRYSTAL SYSTEM Hexagonal prisms with bevel edges and flat ends.

MOHS HARDNESS 7.5–8.0

REFRACTIVE INDEX 1.562–1.602

SPECIFIC GRAVITY/DENSITY 2.66–2.87

LUSTER Vitreous

CHEMICAL COMPOSITION Beryllium aluminum silicate

COMMON TREATMENTS Heating to change color. Morganite can be irradiated and heated.

OPTICAL PROPERTIES Dichroism, bi-color crystals, chatoyance, and asterism.

CUTTING AND STONE CUTS Indistinct cleavage with brittle fracture. Sensitive to pressure. Often cut as step cuts for color.

IMITATIONS/SYNTHETICS Synthetic morganite

NOT TO BE CONFUSED WITH... Tourmaline, quartz, sapphire, yellow/pink topaz.

22kt gold morganite and blue diamond ring by Zaffiro

The faceted pear-shaped morganite has been set in 22kt gold, which has been granulated for decoration and then set with small blue diamonds.

Heliodor and morganite

Heliodor or yellow beryl (left) has a really vibrant color. To try to strengthen the soft peachy-pink color of the morganite (right), it has been cut slightly deep.

Green beryl cabochon

This large, translucent beryl cabochon is a beautiful blue-green, similar to Paraiba tourmaline or Andean blue opal. The cutter has made the most of the material, producing a high-dome square cushion, which could make a stunning ring. The inclusions enhance the color and give it depth.

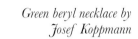

Blue-green beryl and goshenite

These beryl crystals show the prismatic crystal habit, with bevel edges and flat ends. They can be dichroic with two color directions and can be brittle.

*Green beryl necklace by
Josef Koppmann*

This necklace is fabricated from silver with 24kt gold on the bezel setting and bail. It is set with a prism-cut natural green beryl, which has few facets, displaying the color well.

GOSHENITE is pure colorless beryl. Historically, it was used to imitate diamond and emerald by placing colored metal foil behind the gemstone and placing it in a closed setting. At one time, goshenite was used for the lenses in glasses. It commonly has spiky inclusions and the crystals have an hexagonal outline with a tabular shape.

Goshenite originates in the USA (Goshen, Massachusetts), Canada, Brazil, Russia, China, and Mexico.

GREEN BERYL is not the same as emerald, because it's not a saturated, intense green. Usually green beryl is pale or yellowish-green and heated to 831–932°F (444–500°C) to turn it blue. It is rare to find green beryl with the color of the cabochon in the image above right.

Green beryl comes from Brazil (Cearà), India, Nigeria, Mozambique, Madagascar, Afghanistan, and Zimbabwe.

BIXBITE or **RED BERYL** is very rare. It has an intense red color as a result of manganese impurities and the crystals are prismatic. It's found in Utah, in the USA.

Very few treatments are performed on these stones. Morganite is the exception, with heating (to 752°F/400°C) and irradiation being used to remove yellow tints and intensify the pink color. Green beryl is commonly treated to a sky-blue color like aquamarine.

With the exception of bixbite, all the stones are good value. Morganite is the most expensive of the remaining four.

*22kt gold heliodor "Tatlin"
ring by Charlotte De Syllas*

A hand-carved ring using heliodor, which is suited to carving because the crystals are generally clean.

CHRYSOBERYL

The gemstone chrysoberyl actually refers to two stones—one is chatoyant cabochon (known as cat's eye) and the other a less well-known, brilliant, dichroic faceted gem.

Faceted chrysoberyl is both good-looking and inexpensive. It was called chrysolite in the 19th century, which is actually another name for peridot (also a green stone), and was very popular in Victorian and Edwardian England.

The color can be golden brown to yellowish-green to green, due to the presence of iron. It has low dispersion, which means that it has no fire, but is bright and lively because of its high RI. Faceted chrysoberyl can come in large sizes up to 30 carats.

When dealers discuss "cat's eyes," they are referring to chrysoberyl cat's eye. If the stone is not chrysoberyl, then the name of the gem material needs to be added—for instance, quartz cat's eye or cat's eye scapolite. The quality of the cat's eye is very important and will affect the price considerably. The body color ranges from dark yellow-brown to honey and green; sometimes it has a shimmering blue tone. The "eye" should be silver-white. The term "milk and honey" is occasionally used to describe the stone. It can have a high value. Cat's eyes have short needles and tubes that lie parallel to the long axis of the crystal—these produce the chatoyance.

Cat's eyes have been known in Asia for many centuries and were popular in 18th- and 19th-century England. They were also called *cymophane*—Greek for "waving light."

Sources of cat's eye are India, Sri Lanka, Brazil, Japan, Madagascar, and Tanzania. Faceted chrysoberyl is found in Sri Lanka, Brazil, Australia, Myanmar, and the USA.

Chrysoberyl is a hard stone but, when it comes to cutting, the lapidary needs to take care as it's sensitive to knocks and heat. Cutting is crucial with the cat's eye: the base needs to be level, with the fibers aligned so that the "eye" sits centrally.

Faceted chrysoberyl is not normally treated, but cat's eyes are sometimes dyed or oiled and can be irradiated for color. Flux-grown, faceted synthetic chrysoberyl has been produced since the early 20th century, while cat's-eye synthetics have been commercially available since the 1980s. There are also chrysoberyl cat's-eye doublets, which are composite stones.

Chrysoberyl cat's eye and diamond ring by Lang (right)
Two greenish-yellow chrysoberyl cat's-eye cabochons sit either side of a diagonal sweep of brilliant-cut diamonds in this unique ring design. The cabochons are easy to identify, nestling in their 18kt gold trumpet-like settings.

Raw stone
Chrysoberyl rough crystal in tabular habit from Analamanga Region, Madagascar. It shows the fibers that are required to produce chatoyancy (the cat's-eye effect).

Chrysoberyl faceted cushion and oval

Sadly, chrysoberyl is not a stone that people use very often, despite the hardness, brilliance, and attractive colors. The faceted chrysoberyls show brown and yellow pleochroism, which helps identify them.

GEMMOLOGICAL INFORMATION

CRYSTAL SYSTEM Orthorhombic. Tabular or prismatic crystals. Massive and alluvial pebbles. Thick-tabled, twins, and intergrown triplets.

MOHS HARDNESS 8.5

REFRACTIVE INDEX 1.746–1.763

SPECIFIC GRAVITY/DENSITY 3.70–3.78

LUSTER Vitreous

CHEMICAL COMPOSITION Beryllium aluminum oxide

COMMON TREATMENTS None on faceted chrysoberyl. Dye or oil, or irradiation, of cat's eye for color.

OPTICAL PROPERTIES Distinct pleochroism in yellow and brown for faceted chrysoberyl. Good brilliance and clarity of faceted stone. Chatoyance and, rarely, asterism.

CUTTING AND STONE CUTS Distinct cleavage in one direction in faceted gem. For the cat's eye, the alignment of the needles and base is essential.

IMITATIONS/SYNTHETICS Synthetic chrysoberyl and cat's eyes, plus doublets (composites), are available.

NOT TO BE CONFUSED WITH... Yellow sapphires, if the chrysoberyl is Australian with a very high RI, andalusite, golden beryl, hiddenite, peridot, scapolite, topaz, tourmaline, zircon.

Chrysoberyl cat's eyes

Two good cat's eyes. The stone on the left is lovely— very clean and the white eye sits centrally. The stone on the right has more inclusions; you can see parallel fibers running perpendicular to the eye that are producing the optical effect.

ALEXANDRITE

Alexandrite is a color-change gemstone; there are only four natural gems that have this property and this is the most important one. Always check gemstones in two lights—incandescent light and daylight—to fully identify a stone.

Alexandrite is a chromium-bearing stone, hence the color, while the other chrysoberyls are colored by iron. The usual color change is emerald-green to raspberry-red or bluish-green to pink. Occasionally, you'll find yellowish to pink, and Sri Lankan alexandrites tend to have a khaki-to-brown change. Alexandrite from Tanzania has lighter tones, but a good change. The color change is the result of strong absorption of light in the yellow and blue portions of the color spectrum.

Chatoyance can also occur from time to time, so it's possible to find cat's-eye cabochons in small sizes. Clarity is generally good, with Sri Lanka producing the cleanest stones with no visible inclusions.

Alexandrite was discovered in 1830 in the Russian Urals and named after Czar Alexander II. When alexandrite was first found, it was thought to be emerald as it was discovered in emerald mines in the Urals. Since Russia became mined out, the only large fine specimens are to be found in Minas Gerais, in Brazil. The color is well saturated and shows a blue-to-purplish change. Other sources are Sri Lanka, India, Madagascar, Namibia, Myanmar, Tanzania, and Zimbabwe.

Alexandrite is sensitive to heat and pressure, so care needs to be taken when cutting and setting. Large stones are very rare; the usual size is between 1 and 2.5 carats. It exhibits strong pleochroism, with emerald-green, red, orange, and yellow colors occurring when the stone is viewed from different angles or directions.

Alexandrite is not normally treated, but very occasionally dyeing and oiling occur. Imitations do exist because of alexandrite's high value, with synthetic alexandrite being available since the 1960s. Even synthetic stones are expensive, as it's a difficult production process and takes time. Often synthetic Corundum is used instead.

If the alexandrite is a high-grade stone, then it's one of the most expensive gems available. For quality stones you'll be paying fine emerald prices. Large pieces of alexandrite can only be found in antique Russian jewelry. English Victorian jewelry contains alexandrites, but these tend to be small. Ideally, it's desirable to have a stone with pure hues and a good, clear color change.

GEMMOLOGICAL INFORMATION

CRYSTAL SYSTEM Orthorhombic

MOHS HARDNESS 8.5

REFRACTIVE INDEX 1.746–1.763

SPECIFIC GRAVITY/DENSITY 3.70–3.78

LUSTER Vitreous

CHEMICAL COMPOSITION Beryllium aluminum oxide (cyclosilicate)

COMMON TREATMENTS None

OPTICAL PROPERTIES Color change, chatoyance, and pleochroism.

CUTTING AND STONE CUTS Small sizes in all cuts.

IMITATIONS/SYNTHETICS Synthetics are on the market, including other color-change gems.

NOT TO BE CONFUSED WITH... Synthetic Corundum or spinel; andalusite; color-change Corundum, spinel, and garnet.

Cat's-eye alexandrite

This cat's-eye alexandrite is an attractive teal-blue color, with a distinct white eye. It is similar to chrysoberyl cat's eye, with fibrous inclusions producing the chatoyance.

*Antique alexandrite and diamond ring,
Fellows private collection (above)*

The alexandrite has good clarity and is
surrounded by old-cut diamonds with
an estimated total weight of 1 carat. The
alexandrite has 11 claws keeping it safe.

Certified alexandrite faceted oval (below)

The color change is also very good, from an
attractive blue-green in daylight to a pink-purple
in incandescent light. The change in color is clean
and clear, which is desirable.

Raw stone (left)

Alexandrite rough material, displaying typical
crystal habits of rhombic prisms, pyramids, and
rhombic double pyramids. Generally, alexandrite
comes in small sizes and also has a fairly high
specific gravity, so it feels quite heavy.

SPINEL

It is difficult to miss a red spinel, as it is the only gemstone that has a true red color with such life and brilliance. Check for the tiny octahedral crystal inclusions, as they are a helpful indicator of its identity. Look out for spinel in antique jewelry.

The Spinel species comes in a range of colors because it's an allochromatic gemstone. The most well known is ruby spinel, also called balas ruby; this is slightly lighter in color than ruby, the red being closer to brick-red than the ruby's color. It is colored by chromium and iron.

Other colors are the flame spinel (also called rubicelle), which is a bright orange to orange-red color. Blue spinel, a dark blue or blue-green color, is colored by iron and, occasionally, cobalt (this is called cobalt spinel).

Another variety is blue gahnospinel or gahnite, which contains zinc. It has a higher density. Lilac to purple almandine spinel is truly beautiful, as is the color-change spinel found in Myanmar. This is gray-blue in daylight and lavender in incandescent light.

Picotite/chrome spinel, hercynite, and pleonaste/ceylonite are all dark green to black in color. Opaque black spinel has a good luster and polishes up really well. It's an affordable, durable, natural alternative to black diamond.

The most distinctive inclusions are angular "spangles"—rows and swirls of tiny, solid octahedral spinel crystals. Sometimes these occur as fingerprint inclusions with rows of tiny, octahedral-shaped negative crystals, which can be filled with calcite. At the edges of spinels it's possible to see iron-stained films and feathers, plus zircon

Red spinel faceted cushion

This orange-red spinel is also called flame spinel or rubicelle. The purity and saturation of color, together with great clarity, give it a high value.

GEMMOLOGICAL INFORMATION

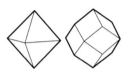

CRYSTAL SYSTEM Cubic with uniform octahedral, rhombic dodecahedron, and macle crystals.

MOHS HARDNESS 8

REFRACTIVE INDEX 1.712–1.762

SPECIFIC GRAVITY/DENSITY 3.54–3.63

LUSTER Vitreous

CHEMICAL COMPOSITION Magnesium aluminum oxide

COMMON TREATMENTS None

OPTICAL PROPERTIES High dispersion and brilliance. Strong red fluorescence in red stones under UV light. Color-change stones exist. Rarely asterism.

CUTTING AND STONE CUTS Indistinct cleavage. Not found in large sizes.

IMITATIONS/SYNTHETICS None. Flame-fusion synthetic spinel was developed in 1910, but is used to imitate aquamarine, Corundum, zircon, and tourmaline.

NOT TO BE CONFUSED WITH... Amethyst, pyrope garnet, sapphire, pink topaz, red/pink tourmaline, green and blue zircon.

Burmese pink spinel

This is a remarkable stone for its size; a transparent faceted spinel of 10 carats is very large. Usually the bright red spinels are the most popular, but the tone of this pink is very attractive. The gem can be identified by the tiny angular spangles inside the stone, which are solid octahedral spinel crystals.

Red oval cabochon and blue faceted oval

The term ruby spinel is often used to describe the red color (top left) that spinel is famous for. Few other gems exist in this pure red. Spinels can also be blue (bottom left), gray, and lilac and are often referred to as almandine spinel. These colors have a lower price than the reds.

haloes, which are inclusions of zircon that have a dark surround due to radioactivity. There can be feathers around the zircon inclusions due to stress and cracking.

Spinel often occurs naturally with Corundum (ruby), and in Myanmar spinel crystals can be found in the famous ruby mines of Mogok. Burmese spinel crystals typically have inclusions of calcite, apatite, dolomite, and olivine. In Sri Lankan deposits, common inclusions are of zircon (with brown haloes), sphene, apatite, and spinel. Star spinel is very rare, but it does occur with four- and six-ray stars.

Spinel has only been identified as a gem in its own right in the last 150 years. Before then, it was thought to be a variety of ruby, hence the names ruby spinel and rubicelle. Many important jewelry pieces have contained spinel rather than ruby. The Black Prince's Ruby in the Imperial State Crown of the United Kingdom is actually a spinel, as is the 361-carat Timur Ruby in the English Crown Jewels.

The most important sources of spinel are Myanmar, Sri Lanka, and Madagascar. Tanzania produces superb hot-pink spinel with a Padparadscha-look. Other deposits are to be found in Afghanistan, Pakistan, Brazil, Australia, Russia, the USA, Cambodia, and Nigeria.

Spinel has a high RI, which produces good brilliance when cut in correct proportions. It also possesses great dispersion and fire. You can find gemstones up to 4 to 4.5 carats in weight, but larger fine pieces are more difficult to source.

Spinel is a great natural alternative to ruby and sapphire, which nowadays undergo so many treatments and have numerous imitations. Fine ruby spinel is rarer than ruby of an equal color, but costs approximately 30 percent less. Unfortunately, the scarcity of spinel is due to a lack of demand because it's simply not marketed. The red colors are sought after and valuable, while the pinks and blues are reasonably priced.

Spinel and Herkimer ring by Milena Kovanovic

This is an unusual ring, as two crystals have been set side by side in a "molten" silver setting. The red spinel is in a typical triangular (macle) habit and the herkimer crystal is in a hexagonal quartz habit.

Raw spinel

Three red spinel crystals display a well-formed octahedral habit. The saturated color, hardness, vitreous luster, and high dispersion produce a gem with good brilliance and fire.

Gold and spinel necklace by Catherine Mannheim

A row of pink spinel beads is interspersed with decorative 18kt gold droplets. The rich colors work well and are reminiscent of Indian Moghul jewelry.

Spinel gold earrings by Jean Scott-Moncrieff

Elegant elongated drop earrings are terminated with small spinel beads wired together in a cluster. The color of spinel is so intense that only a small amount is needed and it creates a rich contrast to the 18kt and 22kt gold.

Spinel ring by Zaffiro

A cushion-shaped magenta spinel (1.03ct) is bezel set with small pink spinels either side in 22kt granulated gold. The color range of the spinel and granulated gold has a very rich appearance.

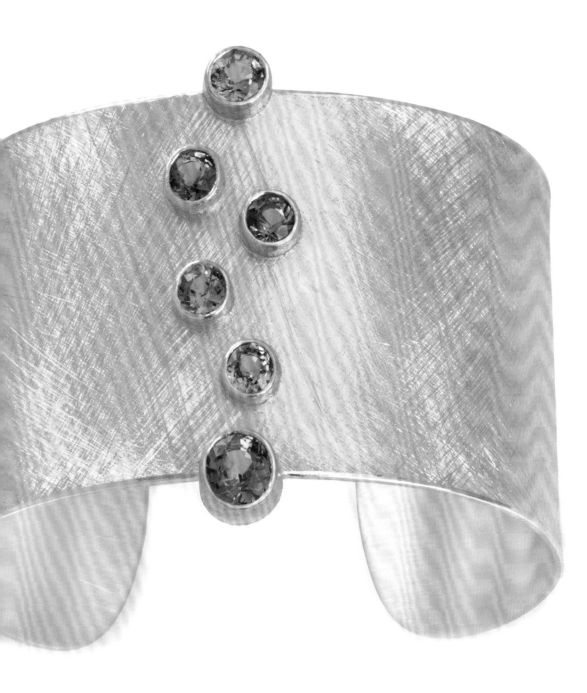

24kt gold and silver cuff set with
faceted spinels by Josef Koppmann

The chunky cuff shows off the lovely color range of
spinel with a mix of pink, blue, and lilac stones. The
gems are set off by the brushed 24kt gold finish.

TOPAZ

Topaz is a gemstone with two identities—the trio of treated blues (sky-blue, Swiss-blue, and London-blue) are easy to recognize. Look out for the rarer gentler colors of natural topaz in older jewelry.

The Topaz group of gemstones is allochromatic; the colors are derived from impurities and trace elements. Colorless topaz is common and usually treated to a blue. Yellow, brown, and natural blue are easy to find, but other colors are rare—only a couple of green crystals will be found in a large deposit. Precious pink, imperial (reddish-gold), and golden are the most important colors; they usually have a soft tone unless they've been heated. An intense natural color is very rare and expensive.

Blue and colorless topaz crystals can be very large, weighing up to 220 pounds (100kg). Topaz is a clean stone overall, but typical inclusions are cavities containing gas bubbles or liquids, liquid droplets, cracks, streaks, and veils. Very little precious topaz is available these days because deposits are dwindling. The best stones tend to be old/antique ones—their color is better, they're natural, and the gems are larger in size.

Natural golden topaz faceted octagon

An old stone with an antique cut, displaying a fine golden color. It's an exceptional stone for its size, purity of color and clarity, and the cutting is fabulous.

GEMMOLOGICAL INFORMATION

CRYSTAL SYSTEM
Orthorhombic. Prisms with faceted ends (wedge-shaped). Also eight-sided, lozenge-shaped cross-sections with striations parallel to the length.

MOHS HARDNESS 8

REFRACTIVE INDEX 1.609–1.643

SPECIFIC GRAVITY/DENSITY 3.49–3.57 (relatively dense, so weighs heavy)

LUSTER Vitreous

CHEMICAL COMPOSITION Fluor-containing aluminum silicate (aka aluminum fluoro-hydroxy-silicate)

COMMON TREATMENTS Heating, surface coating, and irradiation.

OPTICAL PROPERTIES Weak fluorescence. Pleochroism (yellow, blue, and red). Certain colors can fade in sunlight—for example, browns from Pakistan.

CUTTING AND STONE CUTS Perfect cleavage with conchoidal fracture.

IMITATIONS/SYNTHETICS None

NOT TO BE CONFUSED WITH... Blue (aquamarine, blue zircon); Pink (morganite, tourmaline, kunzite, sapphire); Sherry/golden (zircon, chrysoberyl, tourmaline); Yellow topaz (citrine—many Asian gem dealers call citrine yellow topaz, so beware).

Kai blue topaz and diamond ring

This stunning one-of-a-kind blue topaz ring has been handmade in our workshops by one of our top goldsmiths. The central blue topaz trillion-shaped gemstone is set in oxidized silver, overlaid with exquisite 18-karat gold flower and leaf motifs embedded with diamonds. This ring is a real beauty.

A trio of irradiated blue topaz

From right: A London blue oval, a Swiss blue octagon, and a sky blue square emerald cut. The sky blue is often mistaken for aquamarine.

The most important source of topaz has always been Minas Gerais in Brazil. Other sources are Afghanistan, Myanmar, China, Namibia, Nigeria, Pakistan, Russia, Sri Lanka, the USA, and Germany.

Topaz is a durable gemstone, as it's 8 Mohs, but cutting topaz can be difficult because it has perfect cleavage that is perpendicular to the length of the crystal. It's easy to chip or break the stone, so jewelers need to be careful when setting and mount it in a protective setting. Topaz stones are cut with step cuts or scissor cuts, as they are designed to display color, but if it's a pale stone, then a brilliant cut or princess cut will produce the best-looking gem.

Unfortunately, topaz is one of the most treated stones available. Most blue topaz is irradiated and requires certificates of origin in the USA. There were formerly concerns over the safety of irradiated blue topaz, so the American Nuclear Regulatory Commission (NRC) tested batches of this topaz and found there to be no health risk. The treatment process differs slightly from color to color: pale blue is either exposed to gamma rays in a cobalt irradiator or has electron bombardment in an accelerator (linac treatment). The most heavily treated are the dark blue colors; the material is exposed to fast neutrons in a nuclear reactor, resulting in residual radioactivity. The material must be held in a secure facility for up to three years to "cool" before cutting. Legislation requires the initial importer of irradiated gems to be licensed by the NRC.

Surface coating is a common treatment of topaz; colorless topaz is coated with metal oxides to create a variety of colors such as "mystic topaz." As the coating sits on the surface, rather than inside the stone, it can be scratched off along the facet edges.

Honey topaz pendant

This unique and exquisite pendant was hand made in our workshops. The central gemstone is a gorgeous honey topaz. The base is made from oxidized silver and covered with intricate 18-karat gold flower and silver leaf motifs. The gold flowers are embedded with diamonds. The pendant comes with a 22in (56cm) silk cord.

Natural blue topaz from Finland

There aren't huge deposits of quality natural blue topaz available, which is why so much irradiated blue topaz is produced. This image shows the inclusions commonly found in natural material.

Natural blue topaz faceted round cut and natural pink topaz

Topaz is not a very brilliant stone compared to gems such as sapphire or spinel, and it has low dispersion. As a result, it requires skilled cutting to show it at its best. The saturated color of the pink stones makes this untreated topaz rare and special. Very little natural pink topaz is available now.

Color zoning can occur in topaz, resulting in pink and yellow bi-colored crystals. When heated the yellow tone disappears, making the crystal pink overall, but this can also make the crystal more brittle and difficult to cut. Irradiated blue topaz is also heated to a specific tone. The treatments are permanent.

According to *Colored Stone* magazine, blue topaz is the second most popular gem in the world. Indeed, irradiated blue topaz, such as London blue, has risen in price significantly in recent years. Precious pink, imperial, and golden topaz have all increased in value due to the scarcity of material, especially large stones.

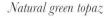

Natural green topaz

A large and rare faceted pear-shaped green topaz. The color is gentle and the clarity is good. It came from a Sri Lankan mine that had blue topaz deposits—this was the only green topaz to come out of the entire mine.

Georgian pink topaz necklace, c.*1820*

The cross pendant of this Georgian necklace has a cushion-shaped, pink topaz center and four rectangular, pink topaz arms. There is an oval pink topaz between each arm and an oval pink topaz pendant top with a detachable fitting. This is suspended from a necklace of alternating graduated rectangular and oval pink topazes to a concealed clasp, all cut-down set to a closed-back gold mount. The necklace measures approximately 16in (40cm) in length and has a gross weight of 42.44 grams.

Early Victorian cross brooch, c.*1840*

This early Victorian topaz-set brooch takes the form of a cross with nine round faceted topazes and a pear-shaped faceted topaz between each arm, estimated to weigh a total of 23.5 carats, all cut-down set to a gold mount with a brooch pin fitting. Gross weight of 12.8 grams.

*Imperial topaz gold necklace
by Jean Scott-Moncrieff*

This necklace is fabricated from 18kt and 22kt gold.
The warm pinkish-orange of the imperial topaz
baguette cuts complements the tones of the gold.

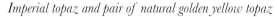

*Imperial topaz and gold necklace
by Louise O'Neill*

The faceted precious topaz buttons are a delicate
color, with some variation in the orange and pink
tones. The topaz is interspersed with bi-color gold
beads (white and yellow gold) that have a brushed
satin finish, which gives the necklace a lovely color
range.

Imperial topaz and pair of natural golden yellow topaz

Imperial topaz should have an orange tone and this stone
has just that. The clarity and size are good for imperial
material. The faceted pair is a good size. It's hard to find
matching pairs of fine topaz at this size, so they have value.

22kt gold topaz and diamond ring by Zaffiro

A soft brown topaz (sometimes called
champagne) is bezel set with pink sapphires
plus cognac and white diamonds. The
gemstones are all set in 22kt granulated gold.

INDICOLITE

Indicolite is a very attractive blue to blue-green gemstone. It has distinct dichroism, with the long axis of the crystal tending to be very dark. Consequently, indicolite is often cut in elongated step cuts in order to display the best color.

Gemstones in the Tourmaline group are some of the most popular on the market—they are offered in a wide range of colors and at different prices, and are available worldwide. The stones in the group have complex and different chemical compositions, with 14 known species. Tourmaline is colorless in its pure form (achroite), but iron, copper, and titanium give rise to light to dark blue and blue-green stones, and these are called indicolite. Crystals are often color zoned, with blue and green occurring together along the length of the crystal, and the color can get very dark, almost black, when viewed along the long axis. Pleochroism is very strong in indicolite and gives lapidaries a real challenge! In general, indicolite can be any shade as long as blue predominates; medium to light tones, without gray, are preferred.

Tourmaline crystals form in a rich liquid environment and some of the liquid is captured as inclusions. Thread-like cavities running parallel to the length of the crystal are common; under magnification, it's possible to see the cavities filled with liquid or gas bubbles. These irregular tubes can be capped with minute mineral crystals and produce a cat's-eye cabochon when aligned correctly. Indicolite has Type II clarity, making flawless stones rare.

Indicolite scissor-cut octagon

A lovely seafoam blue-green indicolite with excellent clarity and the color is pure and bright. The material is Brazilian and is untreated. Large, clean stones like this are becoming difficult to find now and the prices are high.

GEMMOLOGICAL INFORMATION

CRYSTAL SYSTEM Trigonal, often hexagonal, shape. Crystals are usually a long prismatic shape, heavily striated along the length, with flat ends.

MOHS HARDNESS 7.0–7.5

REFRACTIVE INDEX 1.603–1.820

SPECIFIC GRAVITY/DENSITY 3.05–3.11

LUSTER Vitreous

CHEMICAL COMPOSITION Complex borosilicate

COMMON TREATMENTS Heating, irradiation, acid treatment, and epoxy filling.

OPTICAL PROPERTIES Chatoyance, color change, and pleochroism.

CUTTING AND STONE CUTS No cleavage and slightly brittle. Indicolite is pyroelectric; it can have an electrical charge when heated.

IMITATIONS/SYNTHETICS No synthetic indicolite is produced, but synthetic spinel is used as an imitation.

NOT TO BE CONFUSED WITH... Sapphire, tanzanite, kyanite, zircon, topaz.

Bi-color indicolite faceted buff top

This large Brazilian bi-color indicolite with green and blue zoning is cut as an elongated buff-top baguette due to its columnar shape.

Pair of carved indicolite cabochons

An unusual pair of carved indicolite cabochons with a lovely blue-green color. The organic shell-like carvings were cut in the 1950s.

Indicolite tourmaline

These two crystals, from Minas Gerais in Brazil, a region famous for high-quality indicolite, show tourmaline's long prismatic habit, with heavy striations running the length of the crystal.

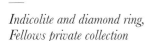

Indicolite and diamond ring,
Fellows private collection
A fine blue indicolite in a baguette cut that
displays its clarity. The color is enhanced by white
diamonds set on the shoulders and triple band.

The best cuts for larger, saturated indicolite are brilliant cuts
or checkerboard cuts, as these allow more light to enter the stone.
Indicolite will usually absorb more light down the length of the
crystal than across it, so often the best color is across the long axis.
From 5 carats onward, quality gemstone rough gets rarer, and
anything more than 10 carats that is eye-clean will be very expensive.

Many indicolites are heated to 1,202–1,292°F (650–700°C) to
remove or lighten green tones. Beware of indicolites with names such
as "Blue Ice" as these are normally treated colors. When you look at a
selection of blue tourmalines they should all differ slightly in color;
very rarely do natural stones all have the same hue and tone. Also,
there should be a slight color change between incandescent light and
daylight, and the dichroism will be present on natural stones. If the
tourmaline doesn't have any of these properties, then it's likely to
have been treated.

The current sources of indicolite are Brazil, Afghanistan, the
Russian Urals, Nigeria, Pakistan, Madagascar, the USA, and Namibia.

Faceted indicolite gold ring
and pendant by Zaffiro
The ring is set with an oval blue indicolite plus
blue-green indicolites and diamonds. Both pieces
use granulated 22kt gold and the band is twisted
18kt gold. The pendant is set with an oval blue-green
indicolite and diamonds. It is 3¼in (8.25cm) long.

RUBELLITE

Rubellite gives us saturated red to purplish hot-pink gemstones, frequently cut in step cuts. The red color is produced by manganese impurities, plus natural radiation.

Rubellite is one of the most popular and sought-after species of the Tourmaline group. There is often a slight color change when the stone is moved from daylight to incandescent light—red to purplish-red, red to blue-pink, or red to peach. In general, the best colors to buy are pure red, hot raspberry-pink, or reddish-purple. As a rule, you don't want brown tones in the red.

Crystals are often flawed and cracked, so large clean material over 10 carats is rarer and more valuable. Clean stones over 15 carats are considered to be collector's gemstones. In general, rubellite's clarity is clean to included. The usual inclusions are irregular, thread-like cavities that run parallel to the length of the crystal and contain liquid or gas. They're often in tightly packed, mesh-type patterns. Rubellite also has gas-filled fractures and flat films with inclusions of hornblende, mica, apatite, and zircon.

Faceted rubellite often contains eye-visible inclusions, but, as long as the color is deep and saturated, the inclusions are accepted. Good color can hide inclusions, but if the inclusions are at the surface and interfere with the polish and luster, then that's a problem. Prominent white inclusions will devalue the stone.

In terms of cut, brilliant cuts and/or checkerboard cuts will show off the material best—they prevent the material from looking too dark and also help obscure inclusions. It's better to buy custom cuts, as the lapidary will have considered the material and planned the cut before commencing. These cuts tend to have better symmetry, proportions,

Gold multi-stone pink tourmaline pendant by Sushilla Done

The pendant features 13 tourmaline cabochons ranging in color from light pink to hot pink rubellite. They are bezel set in yellow gold and linked together.

Bi-color rubellite drop

This is a huge pear-shape gem measuring 40/34mm. It has a vibrant hot pink color with a green "watermelon" rind. It's extraordinary for its size.

Rubellite oval and cushion cabochons

This material came out of Mozambique in 2004. The parcel of cabochons had excellent color with good clarity. The hot pink has a pure hue without any brown tones.

and polish. As the crystals can be elongated, lapidaries often cut rectangular step cuts for less wastage. It's unusual to find large round cuts.

Heating rubellite after it has been cut intensifies the red color, and irradiating colorless tourmaline will produce red stones. Irradiated stones can fade when heated or exposed to bright light. As a rule of thumb, gemstones vary in tone and color, so if you see many stones that are all exactly the same color, then it's likely that they are irradiated. Most rubellite has a slight color change in different light sources, but irradiated material tends to lose this property, so the lack of color change can indicate treatment.

Sources include Myanmar, Brazil, Mozambique, Afghanistan, Madagascar, Kenya, and the USA.

Rubellite faceted square cushion

The stone measures 16/16mm, which is a large size for a faceted rubellite. The checkerboard or harlequin-cut crown brings life and light into the stone.

GEMMOLOGICAL INFORMATION

CRYSTAL SYSTEM
Trigonal, often hexagonal, shape. Crystals commonly have a long prismatic shape, heavily striated along the length, with flat ends.

MOHS HARDNESS 7.0–7.5

REFRACTIVE INDEX 1.603–1.820

SPECIFIC GRAVITY/DENSITY 3.01–3.06

LUSTER Vitreous

CHEMICAL COMPOSITION Complex borosilicate

COMMON TREATMENTS Heating, irradiation, acid treatment, and epoxy filling are all used for color, clarity, and improved durability.

OPTICAL PROPERTIES Chatoyance, color change, and pleochroism.

CUTTING AND STONE CUTS No cleavage and slightly brittle. Rubellite is pyroelectric; it can have an electrical charge when heated.

IMITATIONS/SYNTHETICS
Synthetic tourmaline is too expensive to produce, but synthetic spinel and dyed quartz are used to imitate rubellite.

NOT TO BE CONFUSED WITH...
Garnet, sapphire, ruby, spinel.

Panthère de Cartier bracelet (left)

This Cartier bracelet is fabricated in white gold and set with rubellite cabochons, emeralds, onyx, and diamonds.

Carved rubellite "secret" watch by Graff (right)

This is a rare and unusual timepiece. The 20.85ct hand-carved rubellite "hides" the dial while 19.35 carats of diamonds encrust the strap. This jewel showcases the expertise and talent of the lapidary, goldsmith, stone setter, and watchmaker.

Raw rubellite

Rubellite crystal in Muscovite matrix from the Malkhan pegmatite field in Russia. The prismatic tourmaline crystal is gem grade; it is fairly clean and has a good color.

PARAIBA TOURMALINE

Famous for its unmistakable neon-blue to green color, paraiba is a highly prized tourmaline. Mostly found in small sizes with small inclusions, it comes with a high price attached!

Paraiba tourmaline is quite a recent addition to the Tourmaline family, only appearing in the 1980s. The stones are set apart from other tourmalines by their vivid neon-blue to green to violet colors, and demand for them is huge, especially among Japanese buyers. A top-quality, 3 to 5-carat stone costs the equivalent of fine sapphire, at over $10,000 per carat. The price is driven by rarity.

Paraiba tourmaline belongs to the Elbaite tourmaline species and comes from the state of Paraiba in north-east Brazil. The crystals form as normal tourmalines, but under unique conditions: there are large amounts of the chemicals manganese and copper. It is the only tourmaline that has copper as a coloring agent. There is so much copper in a paraiba that there are pure metal copper inclusions in the crystals. Other inclusions are liquid- and gas-filled elongated cavities and hollow tubes that run parallel to the length of the crystal.

The full color range of paraiba is green-blue, blue-green, blue, and violet, but the blue and violet are the most in demand. Names such as "electric blue," "tanzanite blue," and "mint green" are used to describe these neon tourmalines. While it is possible to find beautiful, blue-green indicolites, the paraibas have a greater color saturation than other tourmalines.

Paraibas are always custom cut due to the scarcity and expense of rough material. They are frequently faceted in pears and ovals in small sizes up to 2 carats. Larger sizes are very rare. With paraibas, color is

Paraiba tourmaline and pearl temple gold pendant

A gold pendant set with a paraiba tourmaline cabochon and white diamonds. A cultured South Sea pearl has been mounted with a gold cap containing faceted paraiba tourmalines.

Paraiba tourmaline and diamond fern curl gold brooch by Zaffiro

Small, faceted paraiba tourmalines and white diamonds have been bezel set in 22kt granulated gold.

Brazilian paraiba tourmalines

The faceted stones are natural, unheated neon blue and turquoise with good clarity.

*African and Mozambique
paraiba-type tourmaline*

This African stone by R. Holt & Co. (left)
has an unusual blue color. It is probably
heat treated, which is the norm for
paraiba. Special and rare for its size,
the Mozambique tourmaline (right) is a
desirable neon turquoise.

GEMMOLOGICAL INFORMATION

CRYSTAL SYSTEM
Trigonal, often hexagonal,
shape. Crystals have a long
prismatic shape, heavily
striated along the length,
with flat ends.

MOHS HARDNESS 7.0–7.5

REFRACTIVE INDEX 1.603–1.820

SPECIFIC GRAVITY/DENSITY 3.05–3.11

LUSTER Vitreous

CHEMICAL COMPOSITION Complex
borosilicate with copper content

COMMON TREATMENTS Heating

OPTICAL PROPERTIES Chatoyance and
pleochroism.

CUTTING AND STONE CUTS No cleavage, but
slightly brittle. Paraiba is pyroelectric; it can
have an electrical charge when heated.

IMITATIONS/SYNTHETICS No synthetic
developed, but imitations such as synthetic
spinel exist.

NOT TO BE CONFUSED WITH... Synthetic
blue zircon.

more important than size and clarity. However, bear in mind that
many stones are treated; the majority of paraiba colored tourmalines
on the market have been heated to intensify the color.

The price of original Brazilian paraiba has been increasing year
on year, and these stones continue to be a solid investment. In terms
of other sources, there have been some vibrant, copper-bearing
tourmalines coming from Mozambique and Nigeria since 2008.
The African "Paraiba-colored" tourmalines are also expensive,
but not as costly as the original Brazilian paraibas. This offers
the possibility that there will be further finds of copper-bearing
tourmalines in the future, meaning more people can enjoy and
wear them. Paraibas have been used in designs by top jewelry
houses such as Tiffany, Cartier, and Theo Fennell.

Raw crystals

Paraiba-coloured tourmaline
crystals that have a nice clarity
and show the columnar crystal
shape with flat ends.

*Paraiba tourmaline
gold earrings by Jean
Scott-Moncrieff*

Earrings set with turquoise
paraiba cabochons bezel set
in brushed gold.

VERDELITE, CHROME TOURMALINE, BI–COLOR TOURMALINE, DRAVITE, AND SCHORL

Look out for the rare chrome tourmalines, which can rival emeralds or tsavorite garnets with their intense color. Plus there's the unmistakable parti-colored watermelon tourmaline, with its pink core and green "rind."

VERDELITE, also known as **GREEN TOURMALINE**, has a large color range, from pastel green to an intense emerald green to "peridot green." The best greens often display two color directions—blue-green from one direction and yellow-green from the other. Some green tourmalines are very dark and oily; these are cheap.

Verdelite is found in Kashmir (India), Afghanistan, Brazil, and Namibia.

CHROME TOURMALINE is an intense green, colored by chromium at the point of the crystal's composition. Vanadium sometimes occurs in chromes as well. A 4-carat "chrome" is cheaper than an equivalent tsavorite or emerald, so can be a good choice of stone. However, chromes command a higher price than green or blue tourmalines. Medium to dark tones are preferred—not too dark, though, so check the color in daylight and incandescent light.

Chrome tourmaline has Type II clarity, so some inclusions do occur. Ideally, look for a clean stone with medium saturation and good cutting, which is essential for color and brilliance. Chromes are easy to find below 2 carats, but 3.5 carats upward is more difficult. If the stone is larger than 3 carats, ask for a certificate. Tanzania is the only source.

Bi-colored crystal
It is common to have a colorless zone between colors in a tourmaline crystal. This image also shows the heavy striations that run the length of the crystals.

Tourmaline color range
A fine row of multi-colored faceted tourmaline beads showing the tremendous color range of tourmaline. The colors are pure and the cutting is good quality.

*Verdelite, chrome
and dravite*

From left: Verdelite
tourmalines, chrome
tourmaline, and dravite.

Tourmaline crystals are frequently color zoned along the length of the crystal and also concentrically. It's common to see three or four colors in crystals. The zoning in a watermelon tourmaline is the result of a shift in the chemistry of geothermal fluid as the crystal forms—manganese produces a pink core, then iron enters the solution to give the green outer rim of the "watermelon." Often there is a colorless zone between colors. Because of the changing water chemistry, it's rare to get very clean stones and the transition zone normally has imperfections. Check for flaws close to the surface, as they can weaken the stone.

BI-COLOR TOURMALINE, also known as **WATERMELON TOURMALINE**, is found in Brazil, East Africa, and Madagascar.

DRAVITE ranges in color from orange-yellow to golden brown to dark brown. It's rich in magnesium and exhibits strong dichroism. Dravite is found in Sri Lanka, the USA, Canada, Mexico, Kenya, Brazil, and Australia.

SCHORL is iron-rich tourmaline that occurs as opaque prismatic crystals. It was used in English Victorian mourning jewelry. Found in Brazil and Madagascar, it has a low value.

GEMMOLOGICAL INFORMATION

CRYSTAL SYSTEM Trigonal. Hexagonal outline with long prismatic crystals that are heavily striated along the length.

MOHS HARDNESS 7.0–7.5

REFRACTIVE INDEX 1.603–1.820

SPECIFIC GRAVITY/DENSITY Verdelite 3.05–3.11; chrome tourmaline 3.08–3.11; bi-color tourmaline 3.05–3.06; dravite 3.06; schorl 3.11–3.12

LUSTER Vitreous

CHEMICAL COMPOSITION Complex borosilicate

COMMON TREATMENTS Heating, irradiation, acid treatment, and epoxy filling of hollow tubes.

OPTICAL PROPERTIES Pleochroism, chatoyance, and color change.

CUTTING AND STONE CUTS No cleavage, but slightly brittle. The stones are pyroelectric; they can have an electrical charge when heated.

IMITATIONS/SYNTHETICS No synthetics. Synthetic spinel and quartz are sometimes used to imitate chrome tourmaline.

NOT TO BE CONFUSED WITH... Sapphire, topaz, emerald, tsavorite garnet.

*Bi-colored tourmaline
(watermelon), 200 carats*

A polished slice of tourmaline crystal showing a pink core and blue rind. It's an amazing specimen taken from a crystal measuring 2¹/₂in (65mm) wide. It shows the trigonal crystal structure and prismatic habit.

ANDALUSITE

Andalusite gives itself away with its strong pleochroism of green, brown, and red directions of color. This gem is unusual and beautiful, but has been sadly overlooked.

Andalusite does not belong to a species, but there are a couple of opaque varieties of this gem: chiastolite and viridine. It is plentiful in its opaque form, but transparent, facet-grade material is rare and large, clean, well-cut stones over 5 carats are valuable.

The colors of andalusite are pinkish-red, reddish-brown, rose-red, whitish, yellowish, violet, and greenish. The pleochroism is usually red, yellow, and green, but Brazilian material is olive-green to flesh-red. It can show multiple colors at one angle. When light enters the stone it is parted into three sections, each containing a section of the visible spectrum. It is one of a handful of birefringent (doubly refractive) crystals that have this property. Veils and rutile needles are the common inclusions, but some liquid inclusions with hematite flakes are found in Brazilian material.

The best cuts for andalusite are shapes with a long axis: ovals, marquises, and cushions. With these cuts, the stone shows one color at the center and a darker color near the ends. The lapidary can decide which color is seen through the table. It's possible to blend the colors in round or square cuts like a mosaic. Ultimately, the aim is to produce a pleasing mix of colors.

Andalusite has good durability and is perfect for rings. Jewelry settings need to be open to allow light to strike the stone at many angles to display the pleochroism. There has been greater interest in the stone in recent years, so there is more material on the market.

The original source of andalusite is Castile-La Mancha, in central Spain (not Andalusia). Brazil, the USA, Belgium, Myanmar, Canada, Australia, Sri Lanka, and Madagascar are other sources.

GEMMOLOGICAL INFORMATION

CRYSTAL SYSTEM
Orthorhombic. Crystals tend to be prismatic, striated, and square in cross section. Also thick, columnar, and massive form.

MOHS HARDNESS 6.5–7.5

REFRACTIVE INDEX 1.629–1.690 (birefringent)

SPECIFIC GRAVITY/DENSITY 3.13–3.17

LUSTER Matte, sub-vitreous, vitreous. Transparent to opaque.

CHEMICAL COMPOSITION Aluminum silicate. Andalusite is polymorphous with kyanite and sillimanite—these have the same chemistry as each other but different crystal habits.

COMMON TREATMENTS Untreated. If Brazilian material is heated, it can change color from olive-green to pink.

OPTICAL PROPERTIES Birefringence, trichroism, and rare cases of chatoyance.

CUTTING AND STONE CUTS Cleavage distinct in one direction. Slightly brittle. Avoid ultrasonic cleaners, as they can shatter the liquid inclusions.

IMITATIONS/SYNTHETICS None, as too difficult to imitate due to pleochroism.

NOT TO BE CONFUSED WITH... Chrysoberyl, tourmaline, sphene, smoky quartz.

Andalusite faceted cushion

The faceted cushion clearly shows the red and green color directions that andalusite has and is excellent for identification. The red direction runs the length of the stone and the green is across the width.

Brazilian andalusites

This shows the color range of Brazilian material as a result of the dichroism. The stones weigh approximately 1.50 carats each.

IOLITE

Also known as cordierite, among others.

—

The trichroism of iolite makes it an easy gemstone to identify. It's a deep purple-blue through the table, but grayish, yellowish, or clear when viewed from the side.

Iolite has several names, including cordierite, Viking stone (the Vikings used iolite as a polarizing filter to find the sun on a cloudy day), dichroite, and "water sapphire." The last two names refer to its pleochroism.

The colors of iolite are sapphire-blue to violet-blue and brownish, yellowish, and gray. The deep violet-blue color rivals that of tanzanite. It can be found in smaller calibrated sizes, plus large single sizes which have a much higher value. Iolite does have some inclusions, but it's possible to find eye-clean material. It can exhibit aventurescence: a metallic glitter from inclusions of hematite and goethite—this is called bloodshot iolite.

Iolite was initially discovered in 1813, but the first significant find of large transparent material was in 1996 in Palmer Creek, in the USA. Other sources are India, Australia, Brazil, Canada, Madagascar, Myanmar, Namibia, Sri Lanka, and Tanzania.

The lapidary needs to orientate the trichroic gem correctly for the best color and make sure that it is not cut too deep, otherwise the gem will become virtually opaque and inky, nearly black. Sometimes the cutter will intentionally cut iolite shallow to lighten the tone. It's usually cut with step cuts to allow light into the back of the stone and enhance the color. Traditional cuts are octagons and ovals.

Iolite is a good-looking and affordable alternative to blue/purple sapphire and tanzanite. Its durability makes it suitable for women's and men's jewelry.

Faceted iolite

An unusually large iolite with a fine color and clarity. It is an intense purplish-blue when viewed through the top. From the side, the color is light gray to colorless. This is a result of the pleochroism that iolite is known for and is the easiest way to identify this gemstone.

GEMMOLOGICAL INFORMATION

CRYSTAL SYSTEM Orthorhombic. Short prisms.

MOHS HARDNESS 7.0–7.5

REFRACTIVE INDEX 1.542–1.578

SPECIFIC GRAVITY/DENSITY 2.58–2.66

LUSTER Oily to vitreous

CHEMICAL COMPOSITION Magnesium aluminum silicate

COMMON TREATMENTS None

OPTICAL PROPERTIES Trichroism and rare cases of asterism and chatoyance.

CUTTING AND STONE CUTS Good cleavage, so cut with care. Requires correct orientation of three color directions. Do not heat or use ultrasonic cleaners.

IMITATIONS/SYNTHETICS None

NOT TO BE CONFUSED WITH... Blue sapphire, tanzanite, spinel, garnet, kyanite.

—

Rough "cobbed" iolite for cutting

This stone has been prepared for cutting by removing any matrix and badly flawed areas. This image shows the purple color direction that would show through the top of the cut gem.

QUARTZ

Also known as rock crystal.

Quartz is one of the most commonly mined minerals and also widely available. Clear quartz or rock crystal is commonly found in antique beads and jewelry, and can be identified by the wear on the facets.

Quartz is a huge species and occurs in all mineral environments, being a constituent of many rocks. It's one of the most varied of all minerals, occurring in different forms, habits, and colors, and it has more names than any other mineral.

The Quartz species is divided into two groups–macrocrystalline (single) transparent crystals that can be faceted, such as amethyst and smoky quartz, and there is cryptocrystalline quartz, an aggregate of tiny interlocking crystals, which can be opaque or translucent, such as chalcedony. The compacted microscopic crystals make this type of quartz an excellent material for carving, as it holds detail very well.

Quartz is allochromatic, so is colorless in its pure form (rock crystal), but it can be found in purple, yellow, pink, brown, black, gray, green, orange, blue, red, and milky white colors. It can also be multi-colored and banded. Colored quartz can be identified by its color zoning.

Historically, quartz has been used for cameos and intaglios for centuries. It was used by the Stuarts, Georgians, and Victorians, and in Art Nouveau and Art Deco jewelry. Quartz has also been used for lamps, lenses, the manufacture of glass, and for precision tools such as pressure gauges. It also has electronic uses in the computer industry.

GEMMOLOGICAL INFORMATION

CRYSTAL SYSTEM Trigonal. Hexagonal prisms with pyramidal/pointed ends and striations perpendicular to the length. It is often twinned.

MOHS HARDNESS 7

REFRACTIVE INDEX 1.54–1.55

SPECIFIC GRAVITY/DENSITY 2.65

LUSTER Macrocrystalline quartz is transparent to opaque, with a vitreous luster. Cryptocrystalline quartz is translucent to opaque, with a waxy to dull luster.

CHEMICAL COMPOSITION Silicon dioxide

COMMON TREATMENTS Heating, irradiation, dyeing, and stabilizing.

OPTICAL PROPERTIES Pleochroism, asterism, and chatoyance.

CUTTING AND STONE CUTS Indiscernible cleavage with conchoidal fracture. Step cuts and mixed cuts are common.

IMITATIONS/SYNTHETICS Glass and synthetic imitations

NOT TO BE CONFUSED WITH... Clear topaz, clear zircon, clear goshenite, colorless sapphire, diamond.

Stuart crystal earrings
c.1680-1690 (above left)

These historic earrings are set with transparent flat-topped rock crystal to hide a cypher behind the stone, which is a crown on a hair background. They were worn to show support for the monarchy after the execution of Charles I in 1649, a rather risky action to take.

Quartz point (left)

Clear quartz point showing the hexagonal crystal habit of quartz with pointed pyramidal ends. This is a clean crystal suitable for cutting.

Quartz faceted briolettes (left)

Long, faceted briolettes like this are not easy to
cut and drill, as there's a risk of snapping the piece
as it's being worked. While quartz is not the most
brilliant or durable of gems, these briolettes will still
give a good show and withstand the wear.

Victorian pendant (above)

A faceted quartz pendant has been mounted with
a carved smoky quartz beetle with brass legs. The
Victorians were fascinated by the natural organic
world and liked to include it in their jewelry.

The most important source of clear quartz is Brazil, but it can also
be found in the Swiss and French Alps, Madagascar, Russia and the
USA.

Quartz is not very durable and does not wear terribly well.
It is softer than other colorless gems, which means it can be scratched,
and the facet edges may become worn over time. It is commonly
treated. Macrocrystalline quartz is heated or irradiated, while
cryptocrystalline material is dyed, heated, or stained. It may also be
impregnated or coated with wax or clear resin to enhance the color,
luster, and stability of the material.

Synthetic rock crystal has been produced since 1950 and is used
in the manufacture of watches.

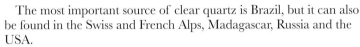

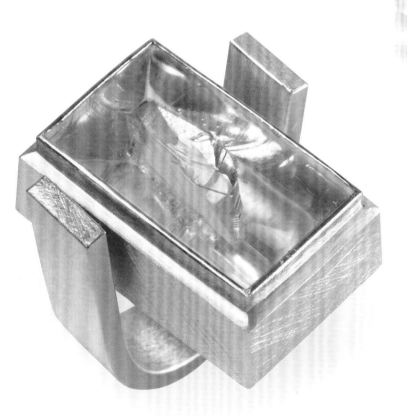

*Carved flower (above left) and
dandelion-cut quartz (above right)*

The quality of the carving and detail of this frosted
hand carved quartz flower cut (above left) make it
a charming piece. I discovered this unusual faceted
dandelion cut (above right) in South Africa.

*24kt gold and silver rock crystal
ring by Josef Koppmann*

The luster and warm tones of the gold leaf set off
the neutral colors of the brushed silver and clear
quartz in this contemporary ring.

AMETHYST

Purple-colored amethyst is plentiful in inexpensive silver jewelry. It is the most popular of the quartzes and the most valuable of the species. It was popular with Georgian, Victorian, and Arts and Craft jewelers.

Amethyst is macrocrystalline quartz; the crystals occur in purple, violet, lilac, and mauve colors in varying saturation. The more intense the color, the more valuable the gem material. Pale, cloudy amethyst is usually used for beads and carvings. Amethyst was popular in the 18th and 19th centuries, and was often foiled in jewelry to improve its appearance.

Amethyst is dichroic, with bluish-purple or reddish-purple directions. The color is caused by iron impurities and also by exposure to natural radiation. Often the color and tone of amethyst are related to the source. Deposits of a fine, deep, reddish-purple color were found in the Russian Urals; it was called Siberian amethyst. This is expensive now, as it's largely been mined out. Brazil produces a very fine pinkish-purple color; Canadian amethyst has a violet color; and amethyst from Uruguay is a deep purple-blue. African amethyst tends to be more deeply colored than Brazilian. Some amethyst can fade over time, depending on the source.

Other sources are Sri Lanka, India, Madagascar, the USA, Germany, Namibia, and Zambia.

Natural bi-colored crystals called ametrine can occur; they are part amethyst and part citrine. The crystals are yellow-orange and violet. Ametrine is found in Brazil and Bolivia, and it is very popular and sought after.

Large, clean crystals of amethyst can be found easily, but it is common to have uneven color distribution or zoning in the crystal. The lapidary has to take this into account when cutting gemstones. Typical inclusions are "tiger stripes" caused by parallel liquid-filled canals, thumbprints, and feathers (internal breaks).

GEMMOLOGICAL INFORMATION

CRYSTAL SYSTEM Trigonal. Hexagonal system with pyramidal/pointed ends. Color darkens at the tip of the crystal.

MOHS HARDNESS 7

REFRACTIVE INDEX 1.54–1.55

SPECIFIC GRAVITY/DENSITY 2.65

LUSTER Macrocrystalline quartz is transparent to opaque, with a vitreous luster.

CHEMICAL COMPOSITION Silicon dioxide

COMMON TREATMENTS Heating produces yellow citrine and prasiolite (green amethyst).

OPTICAL PROPERTIES Pleochroism. Bi-color crystals called ametrine.

CUTTING AND STONE CUTS Indiscernible cleavage with conchoidal fracture. Step cuts and mixed cuts.

IMITATIONS/SYNTHETICS Glass and synthetic imitations.

NOT TO BE CONFUSED WITH... Zoisite, iolite, scapolite, kyanite, fuorite, spinel, cubic zirconia.

Raw stone (left)

Section of a geode showing lots of small amethyst crystals. The color is often concentrated toward the pyramidal end of the crystal.

Amethyst faceted square cut (top) and green amethyst (left)

The untreated amethyst (top) displays top saturated color, whereas the treated one (left) changes from purple to green when heated.

Amethyst drop earrings by Josef Koppmann
Koppmann lays 24kt gold onto the silver and then gives the silver surfaces a brushed finish. The color of the faceted drops are a light lavender amethyst.

A large amount of amethyst is treated to deepen the purple color. It is also commonly heated to turn it into "green amethyst" (or prasiolite) and citrine. The Montezuma mine in Minas Gerais, in Brazil, produces amethyst that turns into green prasiolite when heated. Amethyst is also irradiated to produce lemon quartz/lemon citrine.

Amethyst can be cut as a faceted stone as well as a cabochon and beads. It is a good stone for carving and there are intaglios dating back to Ancient Roman times. It is suitable for all types of jewelry, but the gem will gradually wear over time. Amethyst is imitated by glass and hydrothermal synthetics.

Arts and Crafts amethyst pendant
This simple 9kt gold amethyst pendant from the 1900s is a typical design from the Arts and Crafts movement. It has a handmade appearance, it uses an inexpensive gemstone, and has a Celtic design.

Amethyst ametrine beads
Natural ametrine beads from Brazil, which produces much of the ametrine on the market. Natural crystals are bi-colored (both yellow and purple) and nice material is not that easy to find.

CITRINE

Citrine comes in a range of yellows, from gentle golden tones to hot orange and red-brown colors. Usually, natural citrine has a light golden color and most other colors are treated.

This yellow variety of quartz is colored by the presence of ferric iron. The majority of citrine on the market is heated amethyst, so fine natural material is rare and can be valuable. Treated citrine tends to have an orange-reddish color, with the exception of lemon quartz, which is irradiated. Over the years, citrine was used to imitate yellow topaz, so many dealers still call it yellow or Brazilian topaz, which are misnomers. The prices of the two gems are very different.

There are a couple of fine natural citrines available: palmeira citrine and Madeira citrine. The prices are much higher for these types of citrine.

Palmeira citrine has an intense amber-orange color and is named after its location or source—Palmeira, in southern Brazil.

Madeira citrine is named after the color of Madeira wine from the Madeira Islands—a rich, golden-orange to reddish-brown color. Madeira is the most valuable of all the citrines.

The leading producer of natural citrine is Brazil and the largest deposit of fine material is in the state of Rio Grande do Sul. The Serra mine produces approximately 660 pounds (300kg) of citrine a month. Rio Grande citrine has a very beautiful and intense reddish-brown color; it often contains fine, needle-like inclusions that give it a translucent, "sleepy" appearance.

GEMMOLOGICAL INFORMATION

CRYSTAL SYSTEM Trigonal. Hexagonal system with pyramidal/pointed ends. Color darkens at the tip of the crystal.

MOHS HARDNESS 7

REFRACTIVE INDEX 1.54–1.55

SPECIFIC GRAVITY/DENSITY 2.65

LUSTER Macrocrystalline quartz is transparent to opaque, with a vitreous luster.

CHEMICAL COMPOSITION Silicon dioxide

COMMON TREATMENTS Heating and irradiation of amethyst produces citrine.

OPTICAL PROPERTIES None

CUTTING AND STONE CUTS Indiscernible cleavage with conchoidal fracture. Step cuts and mixed cuts.

IMITATIONS/SYNTHETICS Glass and synthetic imitations.

NOT TO BE CONFUSED WITH… Yellow topaz, orthoclase, yellow sapphire, scapolite, heliodor, hessonite garnet, chrysoberyl, spessartite garnet, tourmaline.

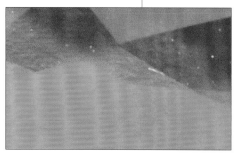

Raw stone (bottom right)

This rough material looks like golden citrine of a good quality. The color is evenly spread and the clarity looks good, so it would be cut into cabochons or carved.

Rio Grande (left), lemon (above), and natural golden (top) citrine

The usual color of citrine is seen in the pale golden yellow of the natural golden stone (top). The sharp color of the lemon citrine (above) is a sign of irradiation, whereas the rutile needle inclusions of the Rio Grande (left) give it a translucent appearance.

Madeira citrine (left)

A lovely old stone that has not been treated. It has a great tawny color with some subtle zoning.

Pair of Palmeira citrine faceted rounds with checkerboard cut (above)

This is natural Brazilian material with a warm golden brown color.

Necklace of lemon citrines by Daphne Krinos

The center-drilled lemon citrine beads are mounted on a necklace of black oxidised silver. The beads are simply polished with a crystal shape.

Citrine also has the usual quartz inclusions of liquids, zebra stripes, and negative crystals. You don't want to see inclusions or color zoning in the gem, so faceted citrine should, ideally, be eye-clean. Durability is good, but the stone can rub over time and large temperature changes can fracture it.

Reddish-orange citrine is produced when amethyst is heated to a temperature of 878°F (470°C). To achieve a darker red-brown color, citrine requires a temperature of 1,032°F (1,000°C). If smoky quartz is heated, it changes to a light- to medium-yellow citrine. These heat treatments are stable and permanent.

Synthetic quartz is grown for industrial purposes, but some hydrothermal material becomes synthetic citrine.

The best sources of citrine are Brazil, Spain, Madagascar, Russia, the USA, Myanmar, Namibia, and Bolivia.

18kt white gold citrine ring by Emma Farquharson

A cocktail ring with a square step-cut citrine that has been set into heavy architectural prongs, allowing side views of the lovely amber-colored stone.

ROSE QUARTZ AND SMOKY QUARTZ

Much rose quartz is an included pale pink color, but it can also be a very beautiful, translucent, peach-pink color that glows. Smoky quartz can be found in colors that range from light golden brown to nearly black. It is an inexpensive gemstone.

ROSE QUARTZ occurs in pink and peach colors, ranging from light to medium to dark tones. It is usually translucent and is found in a massive form, which is carved, cabbed, or cut into beads. The material is often cloudy or cracked because of its brittle nature. In 1987, it was discovered that microscopic, fibrous, dumortierite inclusions produced both the haze and color of rose quartz. Any transparent material is faceted. Asterism occurs due to the needle-like inclusions of dumortierite in the material. Star material comes mainly from Madagascar. Rose quartz is dichroic, with deep pink and pale pink directions.

The color of rose quartz can be intensified by applying concave cuts and cutting in large sizes. Rose quartz was used for intaglio seals by the Ancient Romans, as the material could be incized.

The best material is from Brazil and Madagascar, but other sources are India, Russia, Sri Lanka, the USA, and Spain.

Transparent pink quartz or pink crystalline quartz is very rare and is different from rose quartz, as it forms in a different environment. Well-formed crystals occur in Brazil (Minas Gerais) and specimens sell for very high prices. However, the material is sensitive to light and radiation. Pink quartz can be bright pink to purplish pink, while rose quartz tends to be evenly colored pink to peach.

Rose quartz and sapphire pendant by Zaffiro

A rich 18kt gold pendant set with a 12/9mm oval pale rose quartz cabochon, which is surrounded by faceted sapphires and diamonds.

Rose quartz rough material (far left) and tumbled pebbles (left)

The hazy clarity of the material is typical for rose quartz cutting rough and the depth of color is good. It also seems to be free of cracks.

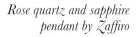

Rose quartz faceted oval

The color of this exceptional rose quartz is an intense, translucent peachy pink, which is accentuated by the large size of the stone and the dumortierite inclusions.

Smoky quartz buff-top faceted oval

It takes millions of years to achieve the deep brown color of smoky quartz through natural radiation, but it can be achieved artificially in an autoclave, in a very short amount of time.

SMOKY QUARTZ is found in igneous and metamorphic rocks, such as granite, as these contain traces of radioactive elements whose radiation produces the distinctive color of smoky quartz. Coloration requires a temperature of 122°F (50°C) as well as radiation, so higher mountain regions produce the better color because they are cooler than the valleys below.

Smoky quartz has a brown to golden brown to black color, which is caused by the radiation and traces of aluminum. The color of smoky quartz appears long after the crystals have grown. It's estimated that it takes several million years for a crystal to assume a deep brown color in a granite of average composition. Artificial irradiation in the presence of iron is used on synthetic quartz to form synthetic smoky quartz. Natural clear quartz is also irradiated to get a brown color. In general, you can't spot irradiation unless the crystals are nearly black.

Some smoky quartz is sensitive to UV light, like amethyst, and will become pale when in sunlight for a long time. It does not have as much color zoning as amethyst, but the color is still more saturated at the tip of the crystal. It is dichroic and shows yellow-brown to red-brown when viewed from different directions. Sometimes smoky quartz is called smoky topaz by traders, which is a misnomer.

Fine smoky quartz material is found in the Swiss Alps and Brazil. It often contains rutile needles. Large, clear crystals weighing as much as 660 pounds (300kg) can be found. Other deposits are found in Madagascar, Mozambique, Australia, Scotland, and the USA.

GEMMOLOGICAL INFORMATION

CRYSTAL SYSTEM Trigonal. Hexagonal system with pyramidal/pointed ends. Color darkens at the tip of the crystal.

MOHS HARDNESS 7

REFRACTIVE INDEX 1.54–1.55

SPECIFIC GRAVITY/DENSITY 2.65

LUSTER Macrocrystalline quartz is transparent to opaque, with a vitreous luster.

CHEMICAL COMPOSITION Silicon dioxide

COMMON TREATMENTS Heating and irradiation.

OPTICAL PROPERTIES Pleochroism and asterism.

CUTTING AND STONE CUTS Indiscernible cleavage with conchoidal fracture. Step cuts and mixed cuts.

IMITATIONS/SYNTHETICS Glass and synthetic imitations.

NOT TO BE CONFUSED WITH… Rose quartz not to be confused with kunzite, morganite, pink grossular garnet, pink scapolite; smoky quartz not to be confused with andalusite, dravite tourmaline, topaz, hypersthene, chrysoberyl, obsidian, brown diamonds.

Raw stone (left)

A very nice cluster of Brazilian smoky quartz points. The color and clarity are better closer to the point. It shows the quartz crystal habit very well.

Hand-cut smoky quartz beads

This is a gorgeous row of fine natural Brazilian smoky quartz; the beads have a lovely golden tone and are all slightly different.

QUARTZ WITH INCLUSIONS

Gemstones consisting of "quartz with inclusions" have become hugely popular in recent years and prices have shot up. Identification is fairly simple—if the stone is colorless and transparent, and also contains needles, platelets, or flakes, then it's likely to be quartz. Inclusions usually devalue a gemstone, as they can spoil the transparency and stability of the gem. In the case of quartz, however, the inclusions can give added value to the stone and are sought after as a mineral specimen.

Included quartz is something of a time capsule. The inclusions are often fragile minerals that are soft or occur as delicate fibers and needles that would normally be destroyed or damaged. But they survive inside the quartz. The macrocrystalline quartz grows around and envelopes the other minerals, capturing them forever.

Rutile is the mineral name for natural acicular (needle-like) crystals of titanium dioxide. They have a metallic luster and occur as inclusions in clear quartz. Rutile quartz is also known as sagenite or Venus hair stone; the color of the needles can be gold, green, brown, or copper. A rutile hematite starburst is the "Holy Grail" of rutile quartz. A six-sided, black hematite crystal acts as an alignment point for the rutile needles and they form a star pattern.

GEMMOLOGICAL INFORMATION

CRYSTAL SYSTEM Trigonal. Hexagonal system with pyramidal/pointed ends.

MOHS HARDNESS 7

REFRACTIVE INDEX 1.54–1.55

SPECIFIC GRAVITY/DENSITY 2.65

LUSTER Macrocrystalline quartz is transparent to opaque, with a vitreous luster. Cryptocrystalline quartz is translucent to opaque, with a waxy to dull luster.

CHEMICAL COMPOSITION Silicon dioxide

COMMON TREATMENTS None

OPTICAL PROPERTIES Chatoyance

CUTTING AND STONE CUTS Indiscernible cleavage with conchoidal fracture. Step cuts and mixed cuts, cabochons, and beads.

IMITATIONS/SYNTHETICS Glass and synthetic imitations.

NOT TO BE CONFUSED WITH... Sunstone/aventurine feldspar, aventurine quartz, rutile topaz in rare cases.

Earrings of oxidized silver with tourmalinated quartz and diamonds by Daphne Krinos

The black oxidized silver bezel settings and the angular top section of the earrings mirror the shapes and angles of the black tourmaline crystals inside the clear quartz. The diamonds add little highlights among the oxidized silver.

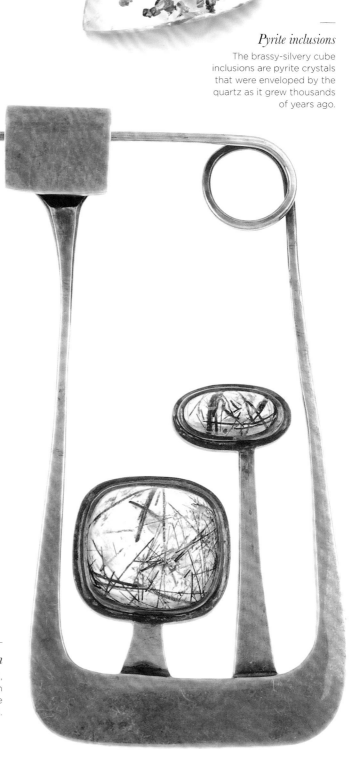

Pyrite inclusions
The brassy-silvery cube inclusions are pyrite crystals that were enveloped by the quartz as it grew thousands of years ago.

Gem silica (left)
A sought-after stone, gem silica is a mix of the delicate gemstones chrysocolla and malachite inside quartz. It displays turquoise and green, yet has the durability of quartz.

Quartz can also contain gold or silver deposits, iron minerals such as goethite and pyrite, and moss-like chlorite inclusions. Amethyst can often contain thin red flakes or black platy crystals of hematite. It's possible to find trapped liquid inclusions of water or oil, or to see negative crystals (hollow ghost-like forms within the quartz). Edenite quartz contains green needles and, unusually, it can display green growth lines inside the quartz. Gem silica is a particularly valuable quartz gemstone. Microscopic inclusions of the beautiful, turquoise-colored mineral chrysocolla are captured safely by the quartz crystal.

Cutting quartz of this nature requires some care; the needles shouldn't reach the surface of the stone as this can affect durability. Ideally, the quartz crystals need to be clear, free of cloudiness and cracks, so that the inclusions are not hidden or obscured by other inclusions. Certain cuts can be very effective with rutilated material; a simple prism cut will mirror and reflect a single "needle" multiple times, creating a fascinating gemstone.

The best material of this type comes from Brazil, but it's also found in Madagascar, South Africa, India, Sri Lanka, Germany, and Switzerland.

Tourmalinated quartz brooch, Fellows private collection
A charming vintage Swedish brooch, hallmarked 1961, fabricated of silver and tourmalinated quartz cabochons. It's an abstract landscape design with naive tree motifs that use the tourmalinated quartz to represent the growth of the trees.

AVENTURINE QUARTZ AND CAT'S EYE QUARTZ

Aventurine quartz can be identified by its translucent green-blue or orange-brown body, and the display of glittering aventurescence. Chatoyant or cat's eye quartz is one of only a handful of chatoyant gems used in jewelry. It's important to use the full name of "cat's eye quartz" or "chatoyant quartz" to avoid confusion with other chatoyant stones such as chrysoberyl.

AVENTURINE QUARTZ belongs to the cryptocrystalline group of the Quartz species and occurs in brown, peach, red, blue, green, and yellow. It has sparkly inclusions of small reflective crystals of different colors and is translucent to opaque. Aventurine quartz is composed of interlocking macrocrystalline quartz grains with grains of other color-imparting minerals. Grains of muscovite (fuchsite) mica inclusions will produce a green stone that has an iridescent green-blue sheen. Pyrite, hematite, and goethite inclusions will give the stone a brown color with sparkling golden inclusions.

The mica, hematite, and goethite inclusions produce what is called aventurescence. The level of aventurescence depends on the density and size of the metallic inclusions, as does the body color of the cabochon.

The material often has light and dark color zones or banding. It has a grainy texture in its rough state, but displays a soft or dull vitreous luster when polished. The quartz is commonly cut as cabochons, slabs, or beads.

The main sources of aventurine quartz are Austria, Brazil, India, Russia, the USA, Japan, and Tanzania.

There is a simulant on the market called goldstone, which imitates both aventurine quartz and aventurine feldspar (sunstone). It contains copper spangles, which are small triangular and hexagonal shapes of copper held in glass.

Be careful, as green aventurine quartz is sometimes sold as jade to unsuspecting tourists in China. Exercise caution!

GEMMOLOGICAL INFORMATION

CRYSTAL SYSTEM Trigonal. Hexagonal system with pyramidal/pointed ends. Cryptocrystalline occurs in massive form.

MOHS HARDNESS 7

REFRACTIVE INDEX 1.54–1.55

SPECIFIC GRAVITY/DENSITY 2.65

LUSTER Cryptocrystalline quartz is translucent to opaque, with a waxy to silky luster.

CHEMICAL COMPOSITION Silicon dioxide

COMMON TREATMENTS None

OPTICAL PROPERTIES Pleochroism and chatoyance.

CUTTING AND STONE CUTS Indiscernible cleavage with conchoidal fracture. Cabochons and beads.

IMITATIONS/SYNTHETICS Glass and synthetic imitations.

NOT TO BE CONFUSED WITH... Aventurine quartz not to be confused with malachite, Sunstone/aventurine feldspar, amazonite, jade; cat's eye quartz not to be confused with chrysoberyl cat's eye, sillimanite, scapolite.

Gold aventurine quartz cufflinks

These good-looking cufflinks are set with deep green aventurine quartz, which is off-set nicely by the 14kt yellow gold bezel settings. The hallmarks identify them as Austrian and they measure 13.4/10.5mm.

Aventurine quartz trillion cab by R. Holt & Co.

Small fuchsite mica inclusions give this stone its green color and iridescent sheen. This particular stone doesn't display much aventurescence, but it does vary from stone to stone.

From left to right: Green cat's eye quartz, hawk's eye, and tiger's eye

All three stones display chatoyance; the cat's eye has a good white eye down the center, whereas the other two exhibit shimmering waves and rays across the surface.

CAT'S EYE QUARTZ occurs both in massive cryptocrystalline form and also as macroscopic quartz crystals. The colors are gray-green, yellow, white, red, blue, brown, and black.

Tiger's eye has a waxy and fibrous appearance that produces chatoyant "rays," which occur as a result of oxidized iron inclusions. Hawk's eye also reflects small rays of chatoyant light, which shimmer on the surface.

The cat's-eye effect is produced by asbestiform fibrous mineral inclusions or tube-like cavities in parallel orientation. The quartz grows around or envelopes the fibrous minerals, which are inclusions of crocidolite-blue asbestos. The inclusion produces a cat's-eye effect.

Each of the stones displays a different color depending on the inclusions that are present. Cat's eye quartz often has a grayish-yellow translucent color due to the crocidolite and hornblende inclusions. It also displays a silky luster.

Tiger's eye is black with iron-oxide staining, which gives it yellow and golden brown stripes. Hawk's eye forms when crocidolite changes to quartz; however, the original blue-gray or blue-green color of crocidolite remains.

The main sources of cat's eye quartz are Sri Lanka, India, Australia, the USA, and Brazil.

Tiger's eye and hawk's eye slabs are mined in South Africa.

Raw stones

Unpolished green aventurine quartz (top) and unpolished tiger's eye (bottom).

Cat's eye (left) and tiger's eye and hematite cabochon (right)

On the left, it's possible to see the parallel fibers that produce the chatoyance in this black cat's eye quartz. On the right, an example of minerals becoming mixed; this stone clearly shows areas of the metallic gemstone, hematite, with the yellowish-brown tiger's eye banding.

CHALCEDONY, BLUE CHALCEDONY, CARNELIAN, AND CHRYSOPRASE

The chalcedonies give us beautiful translucent stones in vibrant colors. The lavender-blue of chalcedony, the hot red-orange of carnelian, and the apple-green of chrysoprase have appeared in jewelry since Ancient Roman times.

Chalcedony in its broad sense is a group of stones within the Quartz species that are fibrous cryptocrystalline quartz. It is an excellent material for carving and jewelry-making. Chalcedony is a solid color rather than banded or patterned, but it is never transparent or completely opaque. The colors of chalcedony are due to the presence of metallic impurities such as iron, nickel, and copper during the crystallization process. The porosity is high, so the stones are frequently dyed.

CHALCEDONY in its narrow sense is a lovely translucent stone that's bluish-white to gray to lavender-blue. It is a solid color, rather than banded, and is found in the lining of geodes and as crusts. Certain sources produce the best colors.

BLUE CHALCEDONY includes Mohave blue and Mount Airy blue, medium-blue chalcedonies from California and Nevada in the USA. African blue from Namibia is blue-gray to nearly pure blue in color, with light to medium to dark tones. The most valuable chalcedony is holly blue from Oregon; it's blue with a pink to lavender tone. There is also a lilac chalcedony from Turkey that can fade slightly in sunlight.

CARNELIAN occurs in yellow-orange, reddish-orange, and orange-brown colors, which are semi-opaque to translucent. It can have a uniform color or be banded. The color is due to the presence of iron oxide as a coloring agent. It is heated to improve the color and make it more red. In India, carnelian is placed in the sun to change the brown tints to a red color. A great deal of carnelian is actually dyed chalcedony from Brazil and Uruguay.

GEMMOLOGICAL INFORMATION

CRYSTAL SYSTEM Trigonal. Hexagonal prisms with pyramidal/pointed ends and striations perpendicular to the length.

MOHS HARDNESS 6.5–7.0

REFRACTIVE INDEX 1.54–1.55

SPECIFIC GRAVITY/DENSITY 2.58–2.65

LUSTER Cryptocrystalline quartz is translucent to opaque, with a waxy to vitreous luster.

CHEMICAL COMPOSITION Silicon dioxide

COMMON TREATMENTS Heating, dyeing, and stabilizing.

OPTICAL PROPERTIES None

CUTTING AND STONE CUTS No cleavage with conchoidal fracture. Cut as cabochons and slabs.

IMITATIONS/SYNTHETICS Glass and synthetic imitations.

NOT TO BE CONFUSED WITH… Chrysoprase is not to be confused with imperial jade, grossular garnet.

Carnelian, blue chalcedony, and chrysoprase
The red-orange, unheated carnelian cabochon shows color zoning—typical of chalcedony. For the size of the blue chalcedony, the color is evenly spread but there are a few cloud-like inclusions tucked away. The navette chrysoprase cabochon was cut from excellent Australian material, so the color is an intense apple green that won't fade.

CHRYSOPRASE has been used as a decorative stone for centuries and can be seen in Ancient Greek and Roman jewelry. It is a stunning gemstone and has the highest value of all the chalcedonies. It's a pure apple-green color, which is due to the presence of nickel. Depending on the source, it can fade in sunlight. The best material is from Queensland, Australia, and this doesn't fade. The material can be nearly opaque to nearly transparent, and has a medium tone. When chrysoprase is very fine, it can look like imperial jade. Occasionally, there are "cloud" inclusions in the material, which affect its translucency. Other sources are the Russian Urals, the USA, Brazil, and Austria.

14kt gold and chrysoprase pin from "La Belle Epoque," c.1910

An exquisite brooch displaying very fine workmanship. It is comprised of high-quality translucent chrysoprase and "taille d'épargne" (a technique of etching onto metal).

Carnelian carved ring c.1960 *(right)*

This bullet-shaped vintage ring carved from natural carnelian has small diamonds set around the circumference in a narrow band of 18kt white gold.

Raw carnelian, blue chalcedony, and chrysoprase

Typical raw chalcedony that is a natural color can occur as crusts, in veins amongst matrix, or in botryoidal form. It's tightly knit, so perfect for carving material.

AGATES

The banded stripes of agate are distinct, but tonally gentle—creams, reddish-browns, grays, soft blues, and black are the natural colors. Sadly, nearly all agate mined since the 1900s will have been enhanced for color.

Excavations have shown that agates were used by the Ancient Egyptians over 3,000 years ago—it's one of the oldest minerals to be worked. Much banded agate comes from agate geodes, which are rock cavities with internal agate crystal formations or concentric banding. Agate also forms in cavities in volcanic rocks. It is the distinct banding that distinguishes agate from the chalcedonies. The bands take on different colors according to the impurities present—silica-rich fluids give color to the bands. White quartz crystals commonly cover the surface of the agate. The colors are frequently enhanced with dye.

GEMMOLOGICAL INFORMATION

CRYSTAL SYSTEM Trigonal. Hexagonal prisms with pyramidal/pointed ends and striations perpendicular to the length.

MOHS HARDNESS 6.5–7.0

REFRACTIVE INDEX 1.54–1.55

SPECIFIC GRAVITY/DENSITY 2.65

LUSTER Cryptocrystalline quartz is translucent to opaque, with a waxy to dull luster.

CHEMICAL COMPOSITION Silicon dioxide

COMMON TREATMENTS Dyeing and stabilizing

OPTICAL PROPERTIES None

CUTTING AND STONE CUTS Indiscernible cleavage with conchoidal fracture. Cut as slabs and cabochons.

IMITATIONS/SYNTHETICS Glass and synthetic imitations

NOT TO BE CONFUSED WITH... Onyx or sardonyx.

Botswana agate

Clean monochrome agate with concentric banding and a crystalline quartz center. This was a geode that was sliced in half, but agate can also occur in rock cavities.

Antique agate necklace

This row of translucent agate beads dates to the Victorian era. Rows of banded agate such as this are currently in high demand.

Banded cabochon oval (top)

This is an antique cabochon that is undyed, so it displays natural browns, whites, and blacks. The waxy luster and distinct curved banding make it easy to identify.

There is a huge variety of agates available. Botswana agate, scenic agate, thunderegg agate, dryhead agate, landscape agate… They are all interesting and beautiful stones that make great pieces of jewelry.

Agate was hugely popular in the Victorian era, as much was mined in Scotland. It is possible to find natural, undyed banded agate and carnelian from the 19th century, but it is highly sought after. The price of natural dark brown/black and white banded agate has increased hugely over the last few years.

Agate was collected from Idar-Oberstein, in Germany, from 1548. The main deposits currently are in Brazil and Uruguay, as well as Mexico, Madagascar, Italy, Egypt, India, China, and Scotland.

Agate and chalcedony (see page 102) are frequently dyed, because they are so porous and the dye takes well. Organic dyes are commonly used; however, these are not lightfast and will fade in sunlight or during tumbling of rough.

The better "dyes" are aqueous (water) chemical solutions, as they can dye rough material prior to cutting and are light- and tumble-fast. In general, the colors from chemical coloration are more natural and subtle. Chemicals color gemstones naturally via impurities such as copper, nickel, chromium, manganese, iron, and cobalt. As these metal traces are found naturally in gems, chemical coloration is not really considered to be unnatural.

The gem materials need to be porous to take a dye. They will have minute connected spaces internally, so the dye substance needs to have small molecules. The chemical dyes penetrate the spaces easily, but the organic dyes have larger molecules, which gives only a superficial coloration, so the dyeing has to take place once the gemstone has been cut.

To check for dye, look for dye pockets between layers or boundaries in any fractures. Dye will show up like mosaic markings running through the fractures.

Banded agate

These slabs were found at an antique fair and re-cut. The color and banding are striking and well defined.

Undyed red banded agate

Banding is colored by the presence of silica-rich fluids in different concentrations.

Arts and Crafts agate pendant

This lovely pendant dates to the early 1900s, when the Arts and Crafts and Art Nouveau movements were popular and inexpensive gemstones were preferred to diamonds and sapphires. The gray and white agate cabochons are set in silver.

MOSS AGATE, DENDRITIC AGATE, AND FIRE AGATE

These are three very distinct gemstones from the Quartz species. They are all chalcedonies with inclusions that are very appealing. Two look as though organic matter has intergrown into the gem, while the third could be confused with an opal.

MOSS AGATE is translucent and is colorless to white to light gray. It is composed of chalcedony with dark, moss-like formations or inclusions. These inclusions are green, red, or brown due to green hornblende, green chlorite, and some manganese impurities. Moss agate is usually cut as slabs to show off the inclusions. This is a rarer and more sought-after variety of chalcedony and can have a moderately high value. Moss agate looks plant-like. This "plant matter" is actually inorganic traces of iron or manganese, which gain access to the crystallizing chalcedony as solutions from nearby rocks. The impurities crystallize inside the agate/chalcedony, seeping through the fine surface fractures and cracks. The main sources are India, China, and the USA.

DENDRITIC AGATE is a colorless to whitish quartz with black, brown, and sometimes reddish-brown dendritic crystals. The word dendrite is derived from a Greek word for "tree-like," as the stone appears to be organic due to the plant-like inclusions. Cutting dendritic agate can be tricky as the dendrites form at different depths within the material, so, in order to reveal an interesting dendrite cluster, the material has to be ground down to remove layers of chalcedony. This can leave an undulating or uneven surface. This material can contain quite a lot of internal cracks, so check that it's stable.

The best source is Brazil. Other sources are China, India, Australia, Uruguay, Madagascar, Mexico, Mongolia, and Namibia.

GEMMOLOGICAL INFORMATION

CRYSTAL SYSTEM Trigonal. Hexagonal prisms with pyramidal/pointed ends and striations perpendicular to the length. It is often twinned.

MOHS HARDNESS 7

REFRACTIVE INDEX 1.54–1.55

SPECIFIC GRAVITY/DENSITY 2.65

LUSTER Macrocrystalline quartz is transparent to opaque, with a vitreous luster. Cryptocrystalline quartz is translucent to opaque, with a waxy to dull luster.

CHEMICAL COMPOSITION Silicon dioxide

COMMON TREATMENTS Heating, irradiation, dyeing, and stabilizing.

OPTICAL PROPERTIES Pleochroism, asterism, and chatoyance.

CUTTING AND STONE CUTS Indiscernible cleavage with conchoidal fracture. Step cuts and mixed cuts are common.

IMITATIONS/SYNTHETICS Glass and synthetic imitations

NOT TO BE CONFUSED WITH... Dendritic agate not to be confused with moss or dendritic opal; fire agate is also not to be confused with opal.

Moss agate (left) and dendritic agate (above)
Examples of rough material in natural green moss agate and natural dendritic agate; the latter shows black dendrite crystals within white translucent agate (quartz).

Antique moss agate earrings
Charming moss agate beetle earrings, which are part of a set including a carved pendant in moss agate. They date from the Victorian era, c. 1870–1885, when there was great interest in the natural world, in particular the study of entomology.

Agate variations

Left: Brown moss agate slab, 1in (25mm) in diameter. Right: High quality dendritic agate pear shape, approximately 1¼in (30mm) long.

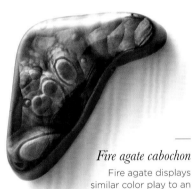

Moss agate earrings by Daphne Krinos

Trillion slabs of green moss agate in red iron stain or iron oxide are held in place by frames of black oxidized silver. The gemstones have been cut as thin slabs so that light travels through the translucent material when they hang from the ear.

Fire agate cabochon

Fire agate displays similar color play to an opal, in this case producing bright greens and oranges on a brown body. The iridescence is caused by the interference of light on internal layers of iron oxide within the chalcedony.

Dendritic agate and diamond pendant, Fellows private collection

Rose-cut diamonds surround an oval panel of fine dendritic agate. Dendritic agate can be difficult to cut, as often the dendrites are at different depths within the agate.

FIRE AGATE is not actually an agate, like dendritic agate; instead, it's a chalcedony with a layered composition. It is rare and unique among the agate or chalcedony species because of this layered internal composition. It exhibits the optical effect called iridescence, which is caused by interference and light diffraction. As light passes through the layers, it splits into spectral colors to produce a colorful effect. The thin layers inside fire agate consist of orange-brown limonite or goethite (iron oxide) inclusions. The limonite is overgrown by layers of silica (chalcedony) and when polished reveals iridescent color play, with orange, yellow, red, blue, green, and, occasionally, violet colors. Fire agate usually has botryoidal (grape-like) bubbles included in the interior, which are revealed when it's cut and polished.

The main sources are California, Arizona, and Mexico.

FOSSILIZED WOOD, FOSSILIZED CORAL, JASPER, AND SARDONYX

Chalcedony can form pseudomorphs from organic materials such as wood and coral. Pseudomorphs can also occur with opal—wood, shells, and belemnites have turned into silica opal (see page 151).

FOSSILIZED WOOD is normally found in cabochon and slab form, and the wood-grain inclusions make the gem fairly easy to spot. The organic wood is chemically replaced by a mineral substance. Petrified or silicated wood is wood that has been transformed completely into chalcedony. In Arizona, the Petrified Forest National Monument is an ancient forest that has been transformed and the remains can be seen in huge silicified logs. The original shape and appearance remain intact, but they consist of chalcedony. The cabochons can be found in a mix of browns, reddish-browns, greens, and dark browns.

Sources of fossilized wood are found in Arizona in the USA.

FOSSILIZED CORAL is ancient coral in which the coral has been replaced by agate, preserving the coral skeletons and leaving flower-like patterns. The colors include reds, browns, creams, golden yellows, and grays. The distinct "flower" patterns together with the gentle colors are reminiscent of 1950s textiles. Fossilized coral is cut as cabs and slabs. In Tampa Bay, Florida, there are areas of silicified coral that date to the Piocene or lower Miocene Age—5 to 10 million years ago. Although also known as coral agate, fossilized coral doesn't have banding and so is not really an agate.

Fossilized wood cabochon

A typical fossilized, or silicated, wood cabochon from Zimbabwe. It displays the appearance of wood but it has actually pseudomorphed into a mineral—chalcedony.

GEMMOLOGICAL INFORMATION

CRYSTAL SYSTEM Trigonal. Hexagonal prisms with pyramidal/pointed ends and striations perpendicular to the length.

MOHS HARDNESS 6.5–7.0

REFRACTIVE INDEX 1.54–1.55

SPECIFIC GRAVITY/DENSITY 2.65

LUSTER Cryptocrystalline quartz is translucent to opaque, with a waxy to dull luster.

CHEMICAL COMPOSITION Silicon dioxide

COMMON TREATMENTS Dyeing

OPTICAL PROPERTIES None

CUTTING AND STONE CUTS Indiscernible cleavage with conchoidal fracture.

IMITATIONS/SYNTHETICS Glass and synthetic imitations

NOT TO BE CONFUSED WITH... None

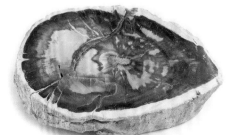

Fossilized coral earrings with red spinel and Tahitian pearls by Zaffiro

The coral used in these drop earrings was found in the seabed of the Bering Sea, and is thought to be 140 million years old.

Raw stone

A cross-section of a fossilized wood log. Identification is straightforward as the wood inclusions are so clear. It's composed of cryptocrystalline quartz and is opaque with a waxy luster.

Fossilized coral

Fossilized coral is a pseudomorph and is found in old seabeds. The patterns are a cross-section of branched coral, which are colored by impurities; they look like textiles from the 1950s.

Jasper necklace

A simple beaded necklace of jasper, showing the variety of different patterns, colors, and shapes that occur with this gemstone. Each piece of Jasper is unique, yet the cost is very affordable.

JASPER should really be considered as a chalcedony, but because of its grainy structure it's usually placed in a group by itself. It comes in an array of colors and patterns; it can be multi-colored, striped, spotted, or flamed. It contains up to 20 percent foreign materials, which determine its color, streak, and appearance.

SARDONYX is a blend of sard and onyx; it has the straight white bands of onyx and the brown-red to orange-red colors of sard.

Onyx is a layered stone with a black base and white upper layer, usually with parallel banding. It is similar to agate, but has straight bands rather than curved ones. It can be brown and white, and occasionally unicolor.

Sard is a brownish-red variety of onyx. It's a solid-colored chalcedony and the color can be patchy.

All the above stones are used for cameos, inlay work, carvings, and beads. They are stained or dyed to improve their color. Black onyx is predominantly dyed black agate. It is possible to find natural black agate from Brazil if you don't want a dyed stone.

Raw stone

Common red jasper rough is in plentiful supply and is found worldwide. It is either cut into cabochons or slabs, or is carved.

Onyx pear-shaped cabochon

This cabochon contains the typical black, brown, and white banding of onyx, which tend to be fairly straight rather than curved like banded agate.

Group of three jasper cabochons

Jasper can be found in most colors and in many varieties or patterns with a host of names. These colorful cabochons include landscape jasper on the left and orbicular jasper at the top.

ZIRCON

Sadly zircon is not a well-known gem, which is a shame as it has a great deal to offer. It can be identified by the double refraction, adamantine luster, high brilliance, and high density.

I've found that many buyers confuse zircon with the man-made diamond simulant, cubic zirconia, so it's not really appreciated as a gemstone! Zircon has a lovely color range of earthy tones, including golden brown, reddish-brown, cinnamon, sherry, green, golden yellow, orange-red, and blue. "Hyacinth zircon" refers to yellow-red to red-brown colors. It's an allochromatic stone, so the colors come from impurities. Pure colorless zircon has been used to imitate diamonds for many years, as it has an adamantine luster and high brilliance. However, unlike a diamond, zircon will show signs of wear and tear on its facet edges over time. In addition, the high density and birefringence (double refraction) indicate that it's not a diamond. The birefringence produces the optical effect of doubling the back facets.

Zircon has a number of other properties that make it an interesting stone. Red and blue stones have strong pleochrism, for example. Zircon can also contain radioactive thorium and uranium, which break down the crystal structure. These stones are called "low zircon" and tend to be green.

Common inclusions are zoning, an uneven color distribution, angular, skeletal-like tension fissures, liquid inclusions, needles (often in green stones), and healing cracks. Some untreated zircon can have a cloudy or smoky appearance, but the majority of material is clean. Most zircon is faceted, but it is possible to get a cat's-eye effect due to long parallel, or needle, inclusions, so this will be cut as a cabochon.

GEMMOLOGICAL INFORMATION

CRYSTAL SYSTEM
Tetragonal. Short, stocky, four-sided prisms with a square cross section and double pyramidal ends. Alluvial pebbles.

MOHS HARDNESS 7.5

REFRACTIVE INDEX 1.810–2.024 (very high). Birefringent.

SPECIFIC GRAVITY/DENSITY 3.93–4.73 (weighs heavy)

LUSTER Resinous to adamantine (like a diamond)

CHEMICAL COMPOSITION Zirconium silicate

COMMON TREATMENTS Heating brown material to 1,472–1,832°F (800–1,000°C) turns the color to colorless or blue. UV and sunlight can produce changes in heated stones.

OPTICAL PROPERTIES Birefringence and chatoyance. Pleochroism is distinct on red and blue zircons.

CUTTING AND STONE CUTS Brilliant cuts due to the brilliance in the stone, step cuts, and mixed cuts. Indistinct cleavage, but can be brittle.

IMITATIONS/SYNTHETICS Glass and synthetic spinel is used to imitate blue stones.

NOT TO BE CONFUSED WITH... Spinel, green sapphire, chrysoberyl, tourmaline, blue topaz, garnets.

Zircon gold ring by Zaffiro, Etrusco collection
This ring is set with an intense forest green zircon weighing 5.90cts. The gem is set in 22kt granulated gold with a double split twist band. It is a good-looking zircon that's been cut to maximize the gem's numerous optical properties.

Faceted zircon (top)
In zircon, birefringence causes a doubling of the back facets, so there appear to be twice as many facets.

Raw stone
Brown zircon crystal with a short, chunky, four-sided prismatic habit that has a square-ish cross section.

The sizes are mixed: blues and greens occur in the 1 to 10-carat range; yellows and oranges are usually up to 5 carats; and reds/purples are in smaller sizes.

Cutting zircon can be difficult, as it's brittle. It's usually cut into brilliant cuts to display and maximize the luster and fire. There is a "zircon cut," which uses eight extra facets around the pavilion to produce more brilliance and dispersion.

Brown zircon is commonly heated to colorless and blue (called starlite). Blue zircon is very popular; approximately 80 percent of zircons sold are blue. In terms of pricing, red and green zircon have collector's values, while colorless and blue stones sell the best and so have a higher price!

The main sources are Sri Lanka, Myanmar, Cambodia, Thailand, Vietnam, Kampuchea, Australia, Brazil, Nigeria, Tanzania, and France.

Pearl and blue
zircon brooch by Lang

Baroque pearls have been used for the petals. The single claw-set blue zircon was probably heated for color, as blues are the most popular and expensive zircons.

Zircon varieties

Clockwise from top: Golden zircon faceted oval, treated blue zircon faceted round cut, natural blue zircon faceted cushion, and green zircon faceted cushion.

Tuscan garden series earrings by Zaffiro
Earrings set with blue zircons and diamonds.

PYROPE AND ALMANDINE GARNET

These are well-known varieties of garnet and were hugely popular in the 18th and 19th centuries. There is plenty of antique jewelry to be seen with dark red garnets cut as rose cuts or carbuncles.

The use of red garnet dates back thousands of years—it was used by Egyptian pharaohs for decorative and ceremonial purposes, while Ancient Romans wore garnet rings and traded in garnets. Garnet is a large, inter-related species with the main varieties being almandine, spessartite, grossular, andradite, pyrope, and uvarovite garnets. Garnet is rarely pure; it is common to have a mix of varieties. Pyrope and almandine share the same physical properties, but pyrope has a magnesium content and almandine an iron one.

PYROPE comes from the Greek word *pyropos*, meaning "fiery"; the stones are brilliant due to the high RI. Pyrope is found in volcanic rock and alluvial deposits, and is often an indicator of diamond-bearing rock. The usual color is blood-red due to iron and chromium impurities, and it resembles ruby. Pyrope can have a brown tint and, if from Switzerland or South Africa, it may be lighter red.

The crystals are generally small and rounded. Pyrope is cut in small sizes, as large stones tend to go black. On the whole, the material is eye-clean and cut as both cabochons and faceted stones. The high density makes the gems weigh heavy. There are no treatments, but fakes can be found in the Czech Republic.

GEMMOLOGICAL INFORMATION

CRYSTAL SYSTEM Cubic with high symmetry. Crystals occur as rhombic dodecahedrons.

MOHS HARDNESS 6.50–7.50 (almandine); 7.25 (pyrope)

REFRACTIVE INDEX 1.76–1.83 (almandine); 1.72–1.76 (pyrope)

SPECIFIC GRAVITY/DENSITY 4.0 (almandine); 3.8 (pyrope). Dense stones.

LUSTER Vitreous

CHEMICAL COMPOSITION Iron aluminum silicate (almandine); magnesium aluminum silicate (pyrope)

COMMON TREATMENTS None

OPTICAL PROPERTIES Almandine can exhibit asterism (four-ray star). Brilliant stones due to high RI. Attracted to neodymium magnets.

CUTTING AND STONE CUTS No cleavage, but can be brittle. Cut as faceted stones, carbuncle cabochons, and rose cuts.

IMITATIONS/SYNTHETICS None

NOT TO BE CONFUSED WITH... Ruby, spinel, rubellite tourmaline.

Pyrope garnets (top)
Two faceted ovals showing the usual red garnet that everyone knows and loves.

Victorian garnet and gold bracelet
This is an example of Victorian Etruscan designs, which were influenced by the Ancient Romans. The pyrope garnet cabochon has been carbuncled and foiled to allow light through the stone.

Raw stone
The orderly faces of the garnet crystals belong to the cubic crystal system.

Pyrope was originally found in Bohemia (Czech Republic), but is now no longer mined commercially there. Sources are now the USA (Arizona), South Africa, Madagascar, Sri Lanka, Argentina, Australia, Brazil, Myanmar, Scotland, Switzerland, Tanzania, and China.

ALMANDINE is one of the most common of the Garnet species. It can be brownish-red, orange-red, and purplish-red due to the presence of iron. Almandine is a darker red than pyrope garnet, and can appear nearly black. It can be opaque to sub-translucent, and it's very rare to find gem-grade translucent to transparent material. It has a modest value unless it is large, transparent, and gem grade.

Common inclusions for almandine are needle-like crystals of rutile and hornblende that can give it a translucent "sleepy" look. There are also small, black mineral inclusions. Almandine was often hollowed out as a carbuncle as the color was so dark. Brilliant cuts will boost the light in a dark stone. There's no cleavage but it can be brittle, which means that facet edges can chip.

Almandine is sourced worldwide.

Faceted almandine garnet
Nearly 15mm in diameter, this purplish-red almandine is large for a garnet. This garnet's RI is quite high, so you'll get a brilliant gemstone.

Raw stone
A well-shaped single almandine garnet crystal in a rhombic dodecahedron habit. Garnet is a dense gemstone, so it weighs heavy.

Georgian garnet and pearl gold stomacher
An interesting piece of jewelry; stomachers were bodice ornaments that were pinned over the abdomen. This is made of gold, set with Bohemian almandine garnets and natural river pearls.

RHODOLITE GARNET

Rhodolite garnet is a good-looking gemstone. It has a beautiful, intense, raspberry-red color with great brilliance and life. Check for rutile needle inclusions, as this will help identify rhodolite from other similar colored stones.

The word rhodolite is derived from the greek word *rhodon*, meaning "rose-colored." Rhodolite garnet is a superior gem to the dark red garnets and is therefore more valuable. It is not a specific garnet subgroup in itself, but it describes garnets with a rose or pink "rhododendron" color. The first deposit was found in North Carolina in the USA in the late 1890s.

Rhodolite garnet's composition is a mix of pyrope and almandine garnets—approximately two parts pyrope and one part almandine. Rhodolite garnet can be identified by its color: a rose- or raspberry-red, purplish-pink, or red with no brown tones. However, a simple way to identify rhodolite is the use of a strong neodymium magnet. Rhodolite is attracted to the magnet because it contains high concentrations of iron and manganese chemicals.

The clarity of rhodolite is generally very good, but it does contain rutile needle inclusions that can produce a hazy effect. Large sizes are rare and 10 carats-plus is very rare.

One of the best sources is Tanzania, which produces larger "clean" sizes. Sri Lanka mines beautiful "rose garnets," which are very similar to rhodolite garnet, with fabulous purplish-red colors. Other sources of rhodolite garnet are Sri Lanka, Zimbabwe, Brazil, Myanmar, China, Kenya, Madagascar, Mozambique, South Africa, and the USA.

Rhodolite is suitable for all types of jewelry. In the 19th century, the Russian jeweler, Fabergé, created rhodolite garnet brooches set with diamonds and rubies. In the 1900s, Paulding Farnham, a designer at Tiffany & Co., created an Iris flower brooch using rhodolite garnets, diamonds, and green demantoid garnets. The jewelry designer Chaumet also used rhodolite garnets in his "Chaumet est une fête" collection.

Rhodolite could be mistaken for rubellite (red/pink tourmaline), but the rutile inclusions and the pleochroism in rubellite are good indicators of its identity. It is also a dense, heavy stone, while rubellite is not. Rhodolite can be used as an alternative to ruby—it is not heated or treated, it's much cheaper, and there are also no ethical concerns.

GEMMOLOGICAL INFORMATION

CRYSTAL SYSTEM Cubic, high symmetry. Crystal shape is rhombic dodecahedron.

MOHS HARDNESS 6.5–7.5

REFRACTIVE INDEX 1.77–1.82 (high brilliance due to high RI)

SPECIFIC GRAVITY/DENSITY 3.93–4.30 (dense stone)

LUSTER Vitreous

CHEMICAL COMPOSITION Iron aluminum silicate

COMMON TREATMENTS None

OPTICAL PROPERTIES Contains rutile needles, so often has silk (the reflection of light off the needles). Attracted to neodymium magnets.

CUTTING AND STONE CUTS Indiscernible or no cleavage. Can be slightly brittle. Can be faceted or cut as a cabochon.

IMITATIONS/SYNTHETICS None

NOT TO BE CONFUSED WITH... Spinel, rubellite tourmaline, ruby.

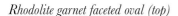

Rhodolite garnet faceted oval (top)

A lively Sri Lankan rhodolite garnet, which is sometimes called a rose garnet. The stone is very clean and it has a typical saturated raspberry color.

Raw stone

An uncut pinkish-red rhodolite garnet aggregate. Density is high, so garnet will weigh heavier than other gemstones.

Rhodolite garnet and diamond platinum
cocktail ring—estate jewel by Lang
A handmade ring *c*.1950s, set with a 4.59ct faceted
cushion-shaped rhodolite garnet that has an
intense raspberry-red color and good clarity.

SPESSARTITE GARNET

Also known as mandarin garnet.

Spessartite garnet possesses two properties that make it easy to spot—the "Fanta-Orange" color and exceptional brilliance. While there are several orange to orange-red gemstones, they don't have the "life" of spessartite garnet.

Spessartite garnet (often known as mandarin garnet) is a relative newcomer to the jewelry scene, only really appearing from 1991 onward. It is an idiochromatic stone—the chemical that gives it the red-orange color, manganese, is part of its chemical composition. The red color is a result of the presence of iron. The pure orange and red-orange materials from Namibia are the most valuable colors.

Clean, transparent spessartite garnet is rare; it is frequently included with tremolite or tirodite fibers and needles, which give the stone a translucent "sleepy" look. The gem can also contain feather-like or lace-like liquid droplets, plus negative crystals and crystal inclusions. It's easy to confuse spessartite garnet with hessonite garnet, which has a similar color and clarity. Medium-sized stones up to 2 carats are easy to find, but if you are looking for 4 to 5 carat-plus

Spessartite garnet and diamond earrings, Fellows private collection (top)

A stunning pair of faceted red-orange spessartite garnets with small brilliant-cut white diamonds pave set around the central stones.

GEMMOLOGICAL INFORMATION

CRYSTAL SYSTEM Cubic system which has the highest symmetry in the form of cubes, octahedrons, or pentagonal/rhombic dodecahedrons (12-sided crystals with diamond-shaped facets).

MOHS HARDNESS 6.5–7.5

REFRACTIVE INDEX 1.79–1.82 (it can be difficult to get an RI reading, as spessartite garnets are over the range of the usual contact liquid used).

SPECIFIC GRAVITY/DENSITY 4.1–4.2 (heavy stone)

LUSTER Vitreous (bright and lively)

CHEMICAL COMPOSITION Manganese aluminum silicate. (It can be identified by its high range of magnetic susceptibility—in other words, it's attracted to magnets.)

COMMON TREATMENTS None

OPTICAL PROPERTIES Brilliance is very good as a result of its high RT and vitreous luster.

IMITATIONS/SYNTHETICS None

NOT TO BE CONFUSED WITH... Chrysoberyl, amber, topaz, hessonite garnet, fire opal, Madeira citrine, orange tourmaline, zircon.

Faceted trillion mandarin garnet

Large faceted mandarin garnet (spessartite) from Namibia. It's a stunning gemstone that has great purity and intensity of color. The inclusions are less important than the color and size of the stone. This stone is large, weighing over 11 carats.

18kt gold Sirena earrings by Milena Kovanovic

The warm orange-brown spessartite garnet pears are off-set beautifully by the cornflower blue sapphires.

Varieties (above)

Clockwise from top left: Reddish-orange spessartite garnet faceted oval, orange mandarin garnet cushion cabochon with typical inclusions, and brownish-red spessartite garnet faceted oval.

Mineral specimen of spessarite garnet crystals

The crystals are very small and not suitable for cutting. The typical rhombic dodecahedron habit can just be seen and this identifies it as spessartite garnet.

gems with good clarity and color, they will be difficult to source and command correspondingly high prices.

This type of garnet was originally found in a Bavarian mountain range in Spessart, Germany, in the 1880s, but wasn't really used in early jewelry. The fine gem-grade mandarin material, discovered in Namibia in 1999, renewed interest in the stone. Spessartite garnet can also be found in East Africa (Mozambique, Tanzania, Kenya) and there are deposits in China, Brazil, Myanmar, Kashmir (Pakistan), the USA, and Sri Lanka. The best orange material comes from Namibia.

Spessartite is sturdy and tough, and relatively easy to cut as there's no cleavage. The gem is often cut with extra facets to show off its great brilliance, with ovals, trillions, and cushions being the usual cuts. As it has a high specific gravity, size is a consideration when designing jewelry because large pieces will weigh heavy.

Spessartite garnet has been used by top jewelry houses such as Cartier, Bulgari, and Christian Dior in both faceted and cabochon forms. It is a stone that you can buy with confidence, as there are no synthetics or imitations currently on the market.

GROSSULAR HESSONITE AND TSAVORITE GARNETS

Grossular hessonite is also known as grossularite hessonite.

Here are two fine garnet gemstones. Hessonite has an apricot to rich orange-brown color range with treacle-like inclusions. Tsavorite comes in smaller sizes, but makes up for it with an intense emerald-green color that few gemstones possess.

Grossular garnet, or grossularite, is a group name for closely related vari-colored garnets belonging to the Garnet species. None of the gems is red and the group is allochromatic—pure grossular is colorless. The colors include white, pink, green, yellow, orange, brown, purple, and gray. The grossular garnets are lively gemstones with good durability and a pretty color range. They are suitable for all types of jewelry. Hessonite and tsavorite are the two gems most used for this purpose.

HESSONITE was used by the Ancient Romans for carved cameos and intaglios. It is a transparent garnet with an attractive color range that's produced by iron or manganese impurities. Hessonite is nearly always color zoned. Common inclusions are fingerprints (healed fractures), small crystals such as zircon, growth lines, and two-phase inclusions. Under the microscope, the stone has a granular appearance that looks like swirling treacle. This comes from inclusions of diopside crystals. Hessonite originating from Tanzania has inclusions of actinolite and apatite.

Hessonite is found in the gem gravels of Sri Lanka in an orange-brown color up to 100 carats in weight, while Quebec is producing quality hessonites up to 25 carats. In general, however, "clean" stones come in smaller sizes. Other sources are Madagascar, Brazil, Russia (Siberia), and the USA.

GEMMOLOGICAL INFORMATION

CRYSTAL SYSTEM Cubic or isometric system. Crystals with good symmetry and often twinned. Crystals often show striations that are similar to trigons found on diamonds.

MOHS HARDNESS 6.5–7.5

REFRACTIVE INDEX 1.72–1.80

SPECIFIC GRAVITY/DENSITY 3.65

LUSTER Resinous to vitreous

CHEMICAL COMPOSITION Calcium aluminum silicate

COMMON TREATMENTS None

OPTICAL PROPERTIES Good brilliance due to the high RI.

CUTTING AND STONE CUTS No cleavage, but can be brittle. Grossular garnets are quite dense stones, so large pieces will weigh heavy.

IMITATIONS/SYNTHETICS Synthetics exist but are rarely seen.

NOT TO BE CONFUSED WITH... Hessonite garnet not to be confused with spessartite garnet, chrysoberyl, dravite tourmaline, topaz; tsavorite garnet not to be confused with peridot, emerald, green tourmaline, zircon, diopside.

Raw stone

Aggregate of some very nice hessonite crystals showing symmetry (cubes and octahedrons), good color, and clarity. There are heavy striations similar to the trigons on diamonds.

Hessonite garnet faceted round cut (left) and cushion

The round cut is a warm apricot and contains acicular (needle) inclusions and small mineral crystals. The cushion is a very clean orange-red stone that only has some minor crystal inclusions.

*Hessonite garnet
faceted oval (left)*

This rich, red-brown
hessonite garnet from Sri
Lanka has a grainy, treacle-
like appearance when viewed
through a loupe.

*Madison tsavorite and
diamond gold ring by
Emma Chapman*

A handmade one-off ring
using a 7/3mm faceted
marquise-cut tsavorite in a
vintage design. The ring has
an oxidized silver and gold
carved shank.

Faceted tsavorites

Tsavorite is one of the most
important and valuable gems
of the garnet species, These
stones have some needle
inclusions but good color.

Raw stone

Tsavorite garnet crystals from
the Merelani Hills, Arusha
region, Tanzania. The color
is a sought-after deep green
tone and the crystals display
good symmetry because
garnet belongs to the cubic
crystal system.

TSAVORITE is a rare stone that only came onto the market in the
1960s when it was found on the border of Kenya and Tanzania.
It is transparent and the finest color is an intense medium green,
but the color can range from lighter yellowish-green to a dark green.
It is colored by chromium and vanadium impurities.

Tsavorite does have moderate inclusions, but it's possible to source
fine material that's eye-clean. It's a brilliant stone with a vitreous
luster, but is only found in small sizes. Three carats-plus is rare and
it's very hard to find large gem-grade pieces. The prices have been
increasing steadily for good-quality stones. It's a viable alternative to
emerald—it's robust and brilliant, and has fewer inclusions than
emerald and a saturated color.

The main source is the Tsavo region of Kenya. Other sources are
Tanzania, Pakistan, Italy, South Africa, Russia, Mexico, Canada,
and the USA.

DEMANTOID GARNET AND COLOR–CHANGE GARNETS

Demantoid garnet is hard to ignore due to its diamond-like luster, exceptional fire, and a brilliance greater than a ruby or sapphire.

Color-change garnets are among the few gemstones with this optical property. Always check the color of a stone in both daylight and incandescent light.

DEMANTOID GARNET is the most valuable gem of the Garnet species. It belongs to the Andradite group of garnets. It is always green, ranging from a mid-yellowish-green (from ferric iron) to a deeply saturated emerald green (from chromium impurities). Usually, the more intense the green, the more valuable the stone, but the slightly lighter green stones display much more fire, so are more colorful!

Demantoid is a rare stone that comes in small sizes up to 2 to 2.5 carats. Usually oval and round shapes are cut, as these minimize wastage and they'll often be "diamond cut" to maximize the brilliance and fire.

One of the best ways to identify demantoid garnet is the horsetail-like inclusions, which are fine, hair-like inclusions of byssolite and chrysotile asbestos. These inclusions help with identification of the stone, so are not regarded negatively.

Demantoid was discovered in the Russian Urals in 1853 and the material is highly prized. In 1996, deposits were found in the Green Dragon Mine in Namibia and in 2003 Madagascar started producing demantoids. There have been some sightings in Afghanistan, Italy, Iran, China, Korea, Zaire, and the USA.

GEMMOLOGICAL INFORMATION

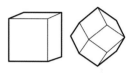

CRYSTAL SYSTEM Cubic or isometric system. Crystals with good symmetry, usually rhombic dodecahedrons (12 sides with rhombic faces).

MOHS HARDNESS 6.5 (demantoid garnet); 7.0–7.5 (color-change garnets)

REFRACTIVE INDEX 1.88–1.94 (demantoid garnet, which has a very high RI and so has more brilliance than ruby and sapphire); 1.73–1.81 (color-change garnets)

SPECIFIC GRAVITY/DENSITY 3.7–4.2 (heavy stones)

LUSTER Vitreous to adamantine (demantoid)

CHEMICAL COMPOSITION Calcium iron silicate/calcium chromium silicate (demantoid garnet); manganese aluminum silicate (color-change garnets)

COMMON TREATMENTS None

OPTICAL PROPERTIES Excellent brilliance due to high RI. Demantoid garnet has a higher dispersion that exceeds diamond, so has tremendous fire. Color-change properties.

CUTTING AND STONE CUTS Indistinct cleavage, but can be brittle.

IMITATIONS/SYNTHETICS Synthetic color-change stones

NOT TO BE CONFUSED WITH... Demantoid garnet not to be confused with peridot, chrysoberyl, grossular garnet, emerald, tourmaline; color-change garnets not to be confused with alexandrite, color-change sapphire.

Victorian demantoid garnet and diamond double-heart brooch, c.1880

Each heart of the brooch is set with a demantoid garnet to the center of an old, brilliant-cut diamond surround. There is a diamond-set ribbon-bow surmount. The estimated total of demantoid garnets is 3.3 carats; the diamonds are estimated at a total of 1.1 carats. All are set in silver to a yellow-gold mount; gross weight 4.15 grams.

Deep emerald green and lighter green demantoids (left)

The lighter green will exhibit the greatest fire, but the deeper green is the more desirable color.

COLOR-CHANGE GARNETS are other rare and valuable members of the Garnet species. They change color depending on the light source. This effect is not pleochroism. These stones have two light transmissions instead of one. Usually, a red gem will appear red because it absorbs all frequencies of light except red. In the case of color-change gems, they absorb all frequencies except blue and red. Therefore, the stone will appear blue or green when the light source is rich in the blue wavelength (daylight) and red when the light source is rich in the red wavelength (incandescent light).

The color change is dramatic and is often better than the one found in alexandrite, for example. Usually the garnet is brown-green to bronze in daylight and pink/red in incandescent light. In Sri Lanka, the stones change from blue-grayish-green in daylight to reddish-purple in incandescent light. In 1999, Madagascan color-change garnets were discovered that are blue in daylight and purple in incandescent light—this was the first time blue garnets were commercially available!

Sources are East Africa (Umba Valley, Tanzania), Sri Lanka, Madagascar, Norway, and the USA.

Color-change garnet

On the left, in daylight, the stone is green and on the right, in incandescent light, it is reddish-brown.

Rough demantoid crystals in matrix

The crystals are a deep green color and have good symmetry. Demantoid garnet has a high vitreous to adamantine luster.

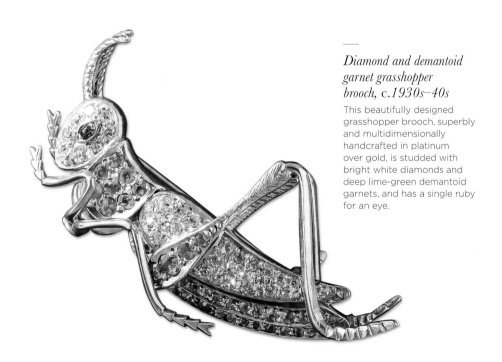

Diamond and demantoid garnet grasshopper brooch, c.1930s–40s

This beautifully designed grasshopper brooch, superbly and multidimensionally handcrafted in platinum over gold, is studded with bright white diamonds and deep lime-green demantoid garnets, and has a single ruby for an eye.

JADEITE

A fine, translucent, emerald green has been set as the "Holy Grail" of jadeite; however, there is a range of other colors that are just as beautiful. Jadeite's mottled coloration, greasy to vitreous luster, and lightly dimpled surface will help you identify the gem.

Jadeite is a gemstone species containing two related gems—jadeite and nephrite (see page 124). Jadeite is the more valuable, rarer gem and has a wider color range than nephrite. Jadeite occurs in white, green, lilac-pink, white, brown, red, black, orange, and yellow. It's an allochromatic species. In the 18th century, Burmese "Imperial Jade" was introduced as a gemstone and has been the most important and valuable color ever since. It is an emerald-green color due to chromium impurities and can have small, black chlorite inclusions. The best material is translucent to nearly transparent, and it can sell for more per carat than diamonds.

Jadeite is found as boulders with rough brown crusts. It is common to have opaque material and it is usually mottled in color—for instance, green and lavender will be mixed in one piece of rough. It's rare to have one solid, even color in jadeite and this is often an indicator of dyeing. It is a porous stone; once cut and polished, it can have a dimpled surface that shows the pores. The main sources of jadeite are Myanmar, Guatemala, Japan, and California.

There is a related gemstone called Maw Sit Sit (or jade albite), which is composed of fine emerald-green jadeite, albite feldspar, and black chlorite inclusions. It is sourced in Myanmar.

Because of the value of jadeite, in particular the imperial green and lavender, it is commonly treated to improve color, luster, and stability. There are three basic grades: Types A, B, and C.

Type A means the jadeite has only been coated with wax. This is traditional and accepted in the trade; it doesn't have an impact on the value. The jadeite is dipped in molten wax to fill any surface-reaching pores and fractures.

GEMMOLOGICAL INFORMATION

CRYSTAL SYSTEM Monoclinic. Tiny interlocking granular pyroxene crystals make this excellent carving material.

MOHS HARDNESS 7

REFRACTIVE INDEX 1.66–1.68

SPECIFIC GRAVITY/DENSITY 3.33

LUSTER Greasy to vitreous

CHEMICAL COMPOSITION Sodium aluminum silicate.

COMMON TREATMENTS Waxing, acid treatment, and dyeing.

OPTICAL PROPERTIES Opaque to translucent

CUTTING AND STONE CUTS Slabs, cabochons, and carvings

IMITATIONS/SYNTHETICS Glass, dyed quartzite, and aventurine quartz.

NOT TO BE CONFUSED WITH... Chrysoprase, aventurine quartz, hydro-grossular garnet.

Art Deco jadeite, diamond, and ruby bracelet from Bentley and Skinner (below)

This 1920s design is comprised of six plaques of green jadeite that have been carved in a floral design. The plaques are interspersed with ruby and diamond-set links.

Fine natural jadeite cabochons (top)

The green jadeites are an intense green, which is sought after, and the lavender color is an attractive shade that is not too pale.

Jadeite ring in 18kt white gold by R. Holt & Co.

A simple double-claw ring featuring a fine, translucent, green jadeite cabochon that has an even coloration and is not enhanced.

Jadeite bead necklace

Good-quality polished oval beads of translucent green, lavender, and butterscotch jadeite. This trio of colors is unusual but very attractive.

Maw Sit Sit cabochon

This 43mm diameter cabochon has a fine jade color, which is most sought after. The black chlorite inclusions are a normal occurrence with this variety.

Type B means the jadeite has been bleached and waxed. It is soaked in hydrochloric or sulfuric acid to remove oxidation staining and lighten the color. It is then waxed. Sunlight and heat can cause the treated jade to discolor over time, and also make the material brittle.

Type C includes all the above treatments, plus dyeing. The dye usually fades over time, because it's exposed to heat and light.

It is possible to see the dye using a microscope or spectroscope, but full disclosure from the dealer should be made prior to purchase. This is a gemstone that requires some checking, so be careful.

Jadeite cabochons

A set of jadeite cabochons showing its wide range of natural colors. It's white in its pure form and is colored by chemical impurities.

NEPHRITE

Also known as green stone.

Nephrite is viewed as the poorer cousin to jadeite, but is still an excellent fine-grained carving material. Made famous as a jewelry stone by the Russian jeweler, Fabergé, it can be identified by the spinach-green color and greasy luster.

The word nephrite is derived from the Greek word for "kidney," which was a reference to the various medicinal properties attributed to jade. Nephrite has a smaller color range than jadeite and is more common. The most well known is the iron-rich, spinach-green color, but there are also magnesium-rich, white or cream and gray-brown to black colors. Green is the most valuable, but Russian white and Wyoming black are also sought after. Green chatoyant (cat's eye) nephrite occurs in Russia.

In 1863, nephrite was classified as a separate stone to jadeite. Nephrite is a fibrous aggregate variety of tremolite and actinolite. It is a calcium magnesium iron silicate, whereas jadeite is composed of granular pyroxene crystals. Nephrite is slightly softer than jadeite, but is considered stronger due to the denser structure. It also has a lower level of luster than jadeite; nephrite is classified as having a greasy to resinous luster, while jadeite is vitreous. Nephrite has a lower specific gravity, even though it's more compact, and is considered tougher than steel. It is generally opaque, but can have some degree of translucency. It is cut as cabochons, beads, and intricate carvings, much of which comes from China, one of the most important cutting centers for jade.

The main sources of nephrite are New Zealand, Russia, the USA, Australia, Canada, Brazil, China, Taiwan, and Zimbabwe. New Zealand produces fine material, which is found as rocks and pebbles along its shores. The Maoris have worked with nephrite for centuries, using it to make tools, weapons, and jewelry.

GEMMOLOGICAL INFORMATION

CRYSTAL SYSTEM Monoclinic structure; an intergrown fine fibrous aggregate.

MOHS HARDNESS 6.0–6.5

REFRACTIVE INDEX 1.60–1.627

SPECIFIC GRAVITY/DENSITY 2.90–3.03

LUSTER Dull, greasy, vitreous

CHEMICAL COMPOSITION Calcium magnesium silicate

COMMON TREATMENTS Coated, impregnated, and dyed.

OPTICAL PROPERTIES Translucent to opaque. Chatoyance rarely.

CUTTING AND STONE CUTS No cleavage. Excellent carving material; holds detail well. Can be scratched.

IMITATIONS/SYNTHETICS Dyed glass.

NOT TO BE CONFUSED WITH… Jadeite, aventurine quartz, bowenite, serpentine, quartzite, chrysoprase.

Carved nephrite jade leaves

This exquisite pair of nephrite jade ivy leaves was hand carved in Germany approximately 50 years ago. The leaves have so little depth to them and demonstrate the incredible strength of nephrite.

Raw stone (right)

Nephrite jade occurs worldwide in locations from Canada to Russia, and New Zealand. Spinach green is the most important color, but white and black nephrite can also occur. It has a denser structure and lower luster than jadeite.

Wyoming jade from the USA is good dense material that has a deep, even color and also cuts well, while the Lake Baikal region in Russia produces a fine spinach-green nephrite. Nephrite from British Columbia, in Canada, is also a good carving material and has a lovely color.

On the whole, nephrite is not treated as much as jadeite and there's no grading system. However, it is still coated or impregnated with wax to improve stability and luster. Nephrite is dyed less than jadeite, possibly because it has a more compact structure that doesn't take dye as well. Nephrite also doesn't achieve the prices of jadeite.

Carved nephrite jade bear

This bear is a simple but very effective design. With the minimum of detail, the heft and the movement of the bear as it catches a salmon is captured. The carving also shows the high polish that's possible with nephrite.

Navette cabochons

Rare nephrite jade with chatoyance (cat's eye) that originates from Russia.

KUNZITE

Kunzite is recognizable for its attractive pink-lilac color and for the distinct pleochroism; there are three color directions. It can also be identified by the large, clean gemstones.

There are two gem-quality varieties of the Spodumene species: kunzite and hiddenite. Kunzite is a widely available pink gemstone and hiddenite is a rare light to emerald-green collector's gem.

The most important jewelry stone is kunzite, which occurs in light pink to saturated pink, lilac to lavender, and light violet to pink-violet colored by manganese impurities. The most common is a light to medium pink-lilac color. The deeper pinks are usually treated for color.

The prismatic crystal structure gives kunzite its distinct pleochroism: pink, violet, and colorless, or colorless and two shades of body color. Kunzite is sensitive to light, so fading is a problem. I was offered some Pakistani material that was a beautiful color a couple of years ago. I was suspicious, so I left it out on my table in my south-facing living room and it lost its color within two days. The color of pink-lilac kunzite can fade gradually over time and especially so if it's been enhanced. It's reported that the natural kunzite from Pala, in California, is stable.

Kunzite comes in large sizes up to 20 carats-plus and large natural stones with a good color are valuable to collectors. On the whole, these are very clean stones, but can contain aligned tubes, fractures, and fibrous inclusions that run parallel to the length of the crystal.

Kunzite is a troublesome stone for cutters because of the perfect cleavage, brittle fracture, and pleochroism. It has to be orientated

GEMMOLOGICAL INFORMATION

CRYSTAL SYSTEM Monoclinic. Prismatic tabular habit with striations parallel to the length of the crystal. The deepest color is at the ends of the crystal.

MOHS HARDNESS 6.5–7.0

REFRACTIVE INDEX 1.66–1.68 (birefringent)

SPECIFIC GRAVITY/DENSITY 3.15–3.21

LUSTER Vitreous

CHEMICAL COMPOSITION Lithium aluminum silicate (kunzite has industrial uses due to the lithium content).

COMMON TREATMENTS Irradiation and heating.

OPTICAL PROPERTIES Light-sensitive, so the color fades. Birefringence. Strong pleochroism—trichroic.

CUTTING AND STONE CUTS Perfect cleavage and brittle. Heat-sensitive and avoid ultrasonic cleaners. Common cuts are emerald cuts and step cuts, plus rounds and ovals.

IMITATIONS/SYNTHETICS None

NOT TO BE CONFUSED WITH... Pink morganite, pink tourmaline, pink sapphire, pink spinel. Usually kunzite's softness and large sizes make it easy to identify.

Faceted kunzite

This faceted pear-shaped kunzite is natural Brazilian material; it has long, fibrous tubular inclusions and needles running along the length of the stone.

Kunsite, peridot, and rubellite ring

Rectangular-cut pink kunsite and green peridot, oval and circular-cut rubellite, brilliant-cut diamonds, white enamel, 18-karat gold, and platinum.

Kunzite pendant by Zaffiro, Jacqueline collection

The pendant is set with a large pear-shape kunzite (10.94ct) and diamonds in granulated 22kt rose gold. Kunzite is more suited to a pendant than a ring because of its brittle nature.

Kunzite scroll ring by David Webb, Colors collection

Cushion-cut kunzite, brilliant-cut diamonds, hammered 18-karat gold, and platinum.

Faceted kunzite

Kunzite is pleochroic, so when this stone is viewed from the top it is a medium pinkish-violet color, but when it is viewed from the sides it is colorless to pale pink. This helps identify kunzite.

Raw stone

Rough kunzite crystal showing prismatic crystal habit with deep striations. Often the color is deeper at the ends of the crystal.

to show the best color, but its cleavage also has to be considered. The lapidary can find that as he/she polishes the stone, fine layers of material lift off due to the cleavage plane. Many cutters in the West don't want to work with it.

Kunzite is irradiated and heated to achieve deeper tones; often both processes are performed, but still the color can be unstable. Fading can occur if you wear the stone in daylight, so some jewelers recommend that kunzite jewelry should be kept for night-time use only!

Kunzite was first comprehensively described by G.F. Kunz, a mineralogist from the USA, in 1902. The sources are Afghanistan, Pakistan, Brazil, Sri Lanka, the USA, Madagascar, Myanmar, Canada, Russia, Mexico, and Sweden.

Hiddenite

Hiddenite is the rare sister stone to kunzite. The color is light to emerald green. This stone has good clarity barring some needle-like inclusions, which are typical for this gem.

TANZANITE

By far the most important gem from the Zoisite species is tanzanite, the color of which can match a deep blue sapphire. It is a transparent stone, which is violet to blue or purple. Blue has a slightly higher value than violet. Medium-dark tones are sought after, but some people like the very intense, deep blue-violet color. The color identifies it, as does the pleochroism and color shift; it is more violet in incandescent light and blue in daylight.

Tanzanite is birefringent (or doubly refractive) and displays strong pleochroism. Crystals show blue, red-violet, and yellow-green or purple, blue, and slate-gray. Typical inclusions are fingerprints, healed cracks, growth tubes, and minerals such as actinolite, graphite, and staurolite.

Most tanzanite starts off a reddish-brown and is heated to approximately 932°F (500°C) to change the color to blue. Sometimes heating occurs naturally underground or after mining. As a result, heating does not affect the value. Most certifying bodies state that heat treatment is undetectable, but it should be assumed.

Cutting tanzanite is not straightforward because of the perfect cleavage. It is also soft and brittle. The dispersion is low and it's not a particularly brilliant gem, so it needs to be cut in brilliant cuts and trillions to improve the "life."

The color of tanzanite is graded AAA, AA, A, ranging from a very intense blue-violet to a lighter-toned purple-violet. The prices change accordingly. It has been featured in financial newspapers as an investment stone due to its rarity—there is (currently) only one deposit/source. At this time, there is no difficulty sourcing tanzanite; there is a plentiful supply of all grades and most sizes, except large, clean pieces which are rarer and more valuable.

GEMMOLOGICAL INFORMATION

CRYSTAL SYSTEM Orthorhombic. Crystals are flattened rhombic prisms.

MOHS HARDNESS 6.5

REFRACTIVE INDEX 1.69–1.70 (birefringent)

SPECIFIC GRAVITY/DENSITY 3.10–3.38

LUSTER Vitreous and pearly on cleavage surfaces.

CHEMICAL COMPOSITION Calcium aluminum hydroxysilicate

COMMON TREATMENTS Assume that all tanzanites are heated.

OPTICAL PROPERTIES Birefringence. Distinct pleochroism (dichroic or trichroic). Rare chatoyance. Color shift between daylight (blue) and incandescent light (violet).

CUTTING AND STONE CUTS Perfect cleavage. Uneven or conchoidal fracture. Avoid ultrasonic cleaners and keep away from heat and chemicals.

IMITATIONS/SYNTHETICS Cubic zirconia "tanzanite" and synthetic forsterite. There is no synthetic tanzanite at this stage.

NOT TO BE CONFUSED WITH... Blue sapphire, iolite, amethyst, kyanite.

Blue cabochon
A beautiful, deep blue cabochon tanzanite showing healed cracks and fingerprint inclusions, which are common in cabochon material. But even with inclusions, this is still a lovely stone.

Faceted tanzanite (left)

This is an intense AAA
cushion. It may look like a
blue sapphire here, but the
color shift makes it more
violet in incandescent light.

*Silver tanzanite pendant
by Sushilla Done*

Rose-cut tanzanites of different shapes
and in various shades of purple have been
bezel set and linked together to form an
articulated pendant.

The Tanzanian gemstone was first recorded in 1967 and the gem
was launched onto the market by Tiffany and Co., in the USA, who
created a tanzanite-based collection of jewelry. It is only suitable for
"occasional" rings or pendants and earrings, as it can't withstand
much wear and tear.

The other gemstones in the Zoisite species include green transparent
zoisite, which is a rare collector's gem. Anyolite (or ruby in zoisite) is a
chrome-rich green zoisite in massive form that contains black
hornblende and opaque ruby. It's commonly used for carving and
cabochon material. Sources are Tanzania and Kenya. Thulite is a pink
to red massive material that is colored by manganese. Again, it is used
for carving and cabochons. Sources are Norway, Australia, Italy, and
the USA.

Raw stone

This raw tanzanite has a good
color but is not gem grade
or suitable for cutting. These
crystals are flattened rhombic
prisms.

Cubic zirconia tanzanite

There are tanzanite imitations
on the market, some of
which are being sold as
natural tanzanite. Cubic
zirconia tanzanite is much
denser than tanzanite,
so it feels very heavy.

Ruby in zoisite cabochon

An example of the poor
relation to tanzanite, ruby in
zoisite is always opaque and
has low value. It was primarily
used for carving, but is
occasionally used in jewelry.

PERIDOT

Also known as olivine and chrysolite.

Peridot is a well-known green gemstone; it is the gem-quality material from the mineral olivine. It is an idiochromatic stone; it is always green, as iron (the coloring agent) is part of its chemical composition. Peridot has a range of green tones, from a light yellowish-green to an olive green to a brownish-green. The most sought-after and valuable color is deep, intense green with an olive tone. It's been calculated that the best color of peridot needs to have an iron content of less than 15 percent and include trace elements of nickel and chromium, which contribute to the color.

It has high birefringence (double refraction), which can help with identification. It also has a distinctive oily-greasy luster. The birefringence distinguishes peridot from other green stones. When you view the stone through the table facet, it's possible to see the doubling up of the lower facets in the pavilion. On the whole, peridot has good transparency at smaller sizes, but some large stones can appear slightly cloudy from inclusions and impurities. The most distinct inclusions are disk-like "lily pads," which are diskoidal cracks with dark chromite crystals at the center. Other inclusions are Ludwig needles, which are inclusions of Ludwigite crystals (not rutile crystals) and denote Pakistan origin. There are also healing cracks and small, rounded fluid droplets. Large, good-quality "clean" stones are rare and fine pieces are valuable.

One of the most important sources of peridot was the volcanic Zabargad Island (St. Johns Island) in the Red Sea. Peridot forms deep in the Earth's crust in magma and rises to the surface via volcanic activity. St. Johns was mined for 3,500 years and the Crusaders brought peridot to Europe in the Middle Ages. The best sources these days are Myanmar (Mogok) and Pakistan/Afghanistan. Other sources

GEMMOLOGICAL INFORMATION

CRYSTAL SYSTEM Orthorhombic. Short compact prisms that are vertically striated.

MOHS HARDNESS 6.5

REFRACTIVE INDEX 1.640–1.710 (birefringent)

SPECIFIC GRAVITY/DENSITY 3.27–3.48

LUSTER Greasy to vitreous

CHEMICAL COMPOSITION Magnesium iron silicate (idiochromatic)

COMMON TREATMENTS None

OPTICAL PROPERTIES Asterism—four or six rays are rare. Birefringence. Chatoyance rarely.

CUTTING AND STONE CUTS Indistinct cleavage, but brittle.

IMITATIONS/SYNTHETICS Synthetic spinel and sapphire constructed to imitate. Garnet glass doublets. Green foil was once placed behind peridot to improve color and brilliance.

NOT TO BE CONFUSED WITH... Verdelite/green tourmaline, chrysoberyl, zircon, grossular garnet.

Peridot cabochon oval

Being a cabochon, it has some inclusions—mainly healed cracks and water droplets.

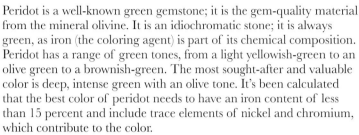

Peridot faceted cushion (top)

This is a fine Burmese peridot with a lovely color—there are no brownish tones and it is a pure hue.

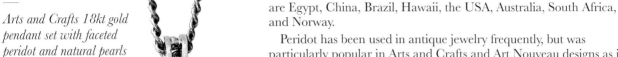

*Arts and Crafts 18kt gold
pendant set with faceted
peridot and natural pearls*

A lovely pendant that shows
typical design motifs of Arts
and Crafts jewelry in the early
20th century. Cheaper stones
were used by the jewelry-
makers and peridot was very
popular.

are Egypt, China, Brazil, Hawaii, the USA, Australia, South Africa,
and Norway.

Peridot has been used in antique jewelry frequently, but was
particularly popular in Arts and Crafts and Art Nouveau designs as it
was an inexpensive gemstone. It featured in Suffragette jewelry to
represent the colors of the movement—green, purple, and white.
Peridot was green, purple was amethyst, and white was pearl.

There are no specific problems with cutting peridot as it has
indistinct cleavage, but it is a softer stone at 6.5 Mohs and can be
brittle. It's commonly cut as faceted stones, cabochons, and beads. It
has no resistance to acid, so be careful when using cleaning products.

Raw stone

This doesn't show the
prismatic crystal habit
but the color is bright, if
slightly yellow. There is some
cloudiness and cracks.

PREHNITE

Prehnite is a lovely, translucent apple-green color that can have striking inclusions. It is usually found in cabochon form; however, new faceting material is now coming onto the market.

This is not a newly discovered gem; it's been around for over 200 years. It was named in 1788 in honor of a Dutch Colonel, Hendrik von Prehn. Prehnite is usually pale green to dark green to yellow- to brown-green. Also, it can more rarely be gray, blue, orange, white, and colorless depending on the impurities present. These types are sought after by collectors. Prehnite's typical apple-green tone is quite unique; few other gemstones have that color.

Single crystals are uncommon; usually prehnite occurs as aggregates with radiating fan-like, globular, or stalactitic forms. In China, prehnite is referred to as "grape jade" owing to the nodular or botryoidal formations that resemble bunches of grapes. Size-wise, it's possible to find some interesting large cabochons, but faceted material is in small sizes.

Prehnite has some distinct inclusions that help with identification. Often there are black tourmaline needles (crystals), as well as epidote inclusions. These are yellow-green to black and are long, slender translucent crystals. There are also reddish-brown inclusions with fractures radiating outward, so check the cracks for stability.

Unfortunately, this is another challenging stone for the cutter! It has distinct cleavage and an irregular fracture, so it chips easily. It also contains cracks that can break if a lot of pressure is placed on them. Prehnite is also very sensitive to heat, so care needs to be taken as it can actually give off water when heated.

In Africa new finds of faceting prehnite are being mined in large quantities, while in Canada exciting new deposits of individual prehnite crystals have been found. This is going to make the gemstone more available, well-known, and popular.

Prehnite cabochon

This cabochon is recognizable for its color and translucency; it appears to have an inner glow. The stone has yellow-green epidote inclusions, which are common.

GEMMOLOGICAL INFORMATION

CRYSTAL SYSTEM
Orthorhombic. Columnar, tabular crystals and aggregates. Colorless, "brick- shaped" crystals.

MOHS HARDNESS 6.0–6.5

REFRACTIVE INDEX 1.611–1.669 (birefringent)

SPECIFIC GRAVITY/DENSITY 2.82–2.94

LUSTER Vitreous to pearly/waxy

CHEMICAL COMPOSITION Basic calcium aluminum silicate

COMMON TREATMENTS None

OPTICAL PROPERTIES Birefringence. Rare chatoyant stones from Australia. Transparent to translucent.

CUTTING AND STONE CUTS Cleavage good, but chips easily. The material is not easy to facet as it has internal cracks. Cut as facet, cabochons, and carvings.

IMITATIONS/SYNTHETICS None

NOT TO BE CONFUSED WITH... Peridot, jade, apatite, serpentine, hemimorphite. Peridot is harder and more transparent than prehnite, while jade is deeper in color and less transparent.

Inclusions (left)

The 30mm diameter cabochon contains many needle-like inclusions of tourmaline crystals, which are usual and help identify it.

Raw stone

Vivid yellow-green prehnite botryoidal crust, sometimes called grape jade in China because of the grape-like formation.

KYANITE

Also known as cyanite and disthene.

Royal-blue kyanite has been used to imitate fine blue sapphire, but the color distribution and pronounced pleochroism clearly identify the stone as kyanite.

The name kyanite is derived from the Greek word *kyanos*, meaning "deep blue." Gem-quality kyanite can actually be pale to deep blue, gray, green, yellow, pink, and white. "Sapphire blue" is the desirable color and zoning or streaks are not viewed as a flaw. Kyanite typically has an uneven color distribution, with deeper blue areas within the crystal. There are also white streaks, blotches, or a lack of color on the long axis.

There is pronounced pleochroism; the color directions are violet-blue, colorless, and cobalt-blue. This also occurs with green crystals. Kyanite frequently has inclusions of graphite, quartz, pyrite, hematite flakes, and rutile fibers. Internal stress cracks and horizontal striations run parallel to the length of the crystal. Gemstones have been cut up to 20 carats in weight, but the maximum for a clean faceted stone is approximately 5 carats.

Kyanite is anisotropic (it has two hardness values); the softer direction is parallel to cleavage planes and the harder is perpendicular to cleavage planes. The habit of color streaking and blotching is a result of the dual hardness.

Nepal is currently one of the finest sources of gem-grade kyanite. Kenya is also producing fine faceting material in a teal color and Brazil has good-quality rough. Other deposits are found in Myanmar, Tanzania (orange crystals), and Mozambique. Alluvial crystals are found in Canada, India, Australia, the USA, and Kenya.

Cutting kyanite is very challenging; it requires careful orientation of the crystal. The lapidary also has to adjust speed and pressure as he/she cuts and polishes due to the dual hardness. The three color directions and the color zoning in the crystal all have to be taken into account, as well as minimizing the inclusions.

Kyanite marquise cabochons
The zoning of these cabochons helps to identify them.

GEMMOLOGICAL INFORMATION

CRYSTAL HABIT Triclinic. Crystals are bladed, flattened, and elongated prisms and also fibrous massive.

MOHS HARDNESS 4.0–4.5 and 6.0–7.0 (anisotropic)

REFRACTIVE INDEX 1.71–1.75 (moderately birefringent)

SPECIFIC GRAVITY/DENSITY 3.53–3.68 (heavy stone)

LUSTER Vitreous to pearly on cleavage plane.

CHEMICAL COMPOSITION Aluminum silicate. Forms in aluminum-rich metamorphic rocks and in association with talc, hornblende, albite, and quartz. Kyanite is a polymorph of andalusite and sillimanite. These have the same chemical composition, but different crystal structures.

COMMON TREATMENTS Occasional oiling to enhance the luster.

OPTICAL PROPERTIES Transparent to translucent. Moderate birefringence. Chatoyance. Pleochroism. Color change. Some fluorescence and color zoning.

CUTTING AND STONE CUTS Perfect cleavage with splintery fracture. Cut as faceted gems and cabochons—ovals and pears preserve most weight. Sharp corners can "fray."

IMITATIONS/SYNTHETICS None, but kyanite has been used to imitate sapphire.

NOT TO BE CONFUSED WITH... Blue sapphire, topaz, spinel.

Silver kyanite ring by Emma Chapman, Lotus Flower collection

The ring is set with a sapphire-blue faceted kyanite. It might look like a sapphire, but it doesn't have the hardness or the brilliance common to sapphire.

Raw stone

This shows the common kyanite crystal habit flattened with elongated prisms. It has a good color, with inclusions of pyrite, graphite, and hematite.

MOONSTONE AND AMAZONITE

The Feldspar species is known for the many optical effects exhibited by the gems, which makes them popular stones.

Feldspars are the most common minerals on the surface of the planet; in fact, approximately 60 percent of the Earth's crust is composed of this species. The Feldspar species is comprised of two groups: the orthoclase feldspars and the plagioclase feldspars. Orthoclase is derived from the Greek word for "break straight," referring to the fact that the gemstones in the group have perfect cleavage at a near 90-degree angle. The orthoclase group consists of moonstones, amazonite/microcline, and transparent gem-grade orthoclase. The other Feldspar group of plagioclase feldspar gems includes labradorite and rainbow moonstone (see page 140), and also oligoclase/sunstone (see page 142).

The transparent gem orthoclase is either colorless or yellow, and has a vitreous luster. It occurs as columnar crystals and tabular prisms. Common inclusions are internal stress/cleavage cracks. Yellow orthoclase is colored by the presence of iron and is usually cut as a step cut or emerald cut because of its brittle nature. Cat's eyes do occur occasionally. Orthoclase is mainly cut for collectors. The sources of orthoclase are Sri Lanka, Myanmar (yellow and colorless facet grade), Madagascar, and Germany.

Faceted yellow orthoclase and Sri Lankan blue moonstone

This yellow orthoclase is a very large collector's stone. The Sri Lankan gem has a good blue schiller and the highest value of the moonstone group.

GEMMOLOGICAL INFORMATION

CRYSTAL SYSTEM Monoclinic with a prismatic habit.

MOHS HARDNESS 6.0–6.5

REFRACTIVE INDEX 1.518–1.527

SPECIFIC GRAVITY/DENSITY 2.56–2.62

LUSTER Vitreous

CHEMICAL COMPOSITION Potassium aluminum silicate

COMMON TREATMENTS Dyeing

OPTICAL PROPERTIES Stones have adularescence (white/blue schiller). No pleochroism or dispersion. Can have asterism and chatoyance.

CUTTING AND STONE CUTS Perfect cleavage. The conchoidal uneven fracture makes the stone brittle. Stones can rub and fray at corners. Material can often be cracked.

IMITATIONS/SYNTHETICS Adularescent synthetic spinel exists.

NOT TO BE CONFUSED WITH... Milky quartz or chalcedony, glass imitations, some opals.

Rough moonstone

Gray, peach, and white moonstone rough material displaying adularescence. This is fairly clean material and doesn't have many cracks running through it.

Set of seven oval moonstones

This shows the natural color range of moonstones— reds, green, ochre, browns, and peach. They are quality stones with no cracks and a good schiller. The material comes from India.

MOONSTONE is the most well-known gemstone from the orthoclase group and is a potassium feldspar. The color range of moonstone is colorless, white, green, peach, brownish, reddish, and gray to black. It is either translucent or transparent.

Moonstone exhibits a bluish to milky white sheen as you move the gem, which is caused by the reflection of light inside the stone. This "sheen" is called adularescence or schiller. It occurs because moonstone contains two minerals—orthoclase and albite—which are initially intermingled. However, as the newly formed mineral cools, the intergrown minerals separate out into stacked alternating layers of orthoclase and albite. These are microscopic layers of approximately 0.5 microns thick. As light travels between the layers there is interference and the light disperses, producing the optical effect known as adularescence. The light seems to hover or shimmer across the surface of the stone, giving it an attractive and mysterious glow that appears to move as you turn and tip the stone. The thin albite layers give the stone a blue color, while the thicker layers produce a white schiller.

In 1997, in Southern India, a new green moonstone was discovered and named "parrot green." It exhibited adularescence, and was also pleochroic with a yellow direction. Parrot moonstone is a bright, vivid green and is translucent to opaque. It is different to the fine transparent green moonstone that can also be found.

Common inclusions in moonstone are centipedes, which are tiny tension cracks and parallel cleavage fractures. Moonstones also contain healing cracks and crystal inclusions. Cheaper moonstone material can be heavily layered and cracked. Most colored moonstones are found in large sizes. Fine blue moonstone is available between 1 and 10 carats, but large, good-quality, 20- to 30-carat stones are rare and expensive.

Green moonstone beads

It's not easy to find green moonstone beads at this size and quality; they have a good schiller and a subtle, natural gray-green color. They will look fabulous made into a necklace.

Green moonstone and Sri Lankan blue moonstones

The green moonstone has good clarity, a fabulous "inner light," and a star. The blue moonstone cabochon (left) has a milky translucency and a great blue schiller. The second blue gem (right) shows the layering that occurs inside moonstone; it causes the interference of light, which produces the optical effect, adularescence.

Blue moonstone signet ring by Judith Crowe

A Burmese blue moonstone with two brilliant-cut light yellow diamonds mounted in platinum.

Blue moonstone necklace

A stunning four-row necklace of faceted blue moonstone beads with an 18kt white gold clasp. The cutting and gem material are first-class—the beads are all in a uniform shape and the blue schiller is intense.

To display the adularescent optical effect best, the lapidary needs to cut the moonstone with a convex polished surface. Moonstone requires fairly strong curvature to exhibit the schiller, which needs to be centered on the cabochon and seen from all angles. Polished and faceted spheres are very good at displaying the intense blue and silvery schiller, so moonstone works well in bead form. Inclusions tend to interfere with the adularescence, so look for clean material.

Moonstone is usually cut as an oval cabochon, but it is possible to find more interesting shapes such as cushion- and loaf-shaped cabochons that display the schiller well. Avoid cuts that are too flat or shallow, as this will affect the optical effect. Blue moonstone can be faceted, despite its perfect cleavage and brittle nature, to produce a combination of brilliance plus schiller. However, the faceted gems are more fragile, and facet edges can become scuffed or chipped over time. Moonstone is often carved as well.

The most valuable moonstone has a colorless body with a strong blue schiller. Transparent green moonstone can also be stunning and exhibit chatoyance, so it has a value. White, gray, yellow, brown, and peach moonstones are beautiful, but are less sought after and cheaper in price. In general, the quality factors for moonstone are purity, an even saturation of color, good clarity, and an absence of cracks or inclusions. The stone should have an intense schiller that covers the stone as you move it. The cut should display the optical effect to best effect.

Moonstone has appeared in jewelry through the centuries; it was especially popular in the Victorian era and can also be found in Arts and Crafts designs of the early 1900s. The main sources are Myanmar (Mandalay region, including the Mogok Valley), Sri Lanka, Madagascar, India, Brazil, Tanzania, and the European Alps.

Raw moonstone

Gray rough moonstone showing layered and cracked material, which would be difficult to cut. There are also cleavage cracks arising from the perfect cleavage of moonstone.

Gold moonstone ring by Catherine Mannheim

An 18kt gold ring set with blue moonstone. The high dome of the cabochon is typical of moonstone cutting, as it intensifies the optical effects. The brushed finish of the gold emphasizes the gemstone's schiller—a high polish would compete with the adularescence.

Gold moonstone earrings by Zaffiro

Earrings set with a trefoil of moonstone cabochons, weighing 7.23cts. The stones are set in granulated 22kt gold with an 18kt post.

*Green moonstone
and diamond ring
by David Webb*

This gold and platinum ring
is set with a moonstone
cabochon, which is clasped
by brilliant-cut diamonds.

*Blue moonstone
earrings by
Catherine
Mannheim*

A pair of round
checkerboard-cut
blue moonstones
set in brushed 18kt
yellow gold with
gold drop sections.
The checkerboard
cut gives the
subtle moonstone
cabochons some
sparkle.

*Moonstone pendant by
Zaffiro Classic Collection*

Rainbow moonstones, small
diamonds, and alexandrites
are combined in this rich 22kt
granulated gold pendant.

Pair of amazonite 18/18mm cushion cabochons

These Brazilian amazonite cabochons are a sought-after blue-green color with a distinct silky luster that helps to identify them.

AMAZONITE is a popular gemstone from a Feldspar variety called microcline, which has the same chemical composition as moonstone and orthoclase (i.e. potassium aluminum silicate), but it has a triclinic crystal structure. Amazonite has a characteristic gray to green to yellow-green to blue-green color, which is due to small amounts of lead and/or iron impurities. It is often mottled with white in an even pattern. The most desirable color is a saturated and evenly distributed blue-green. It is usually found as opaque massive material and has a vitreous to silky luster. Amazonite is cut as cabochons or carvings, and found in a range of sizes. It is slightly fragile and can lose its polish quite easily. The main sources of amazonite are India, the USA, Canada, Russia, Madagascar, Tanzania, and Namibia. It could be confused with jadeite, chrysoprase, serpentine, or turquoise.

Amazonite beads, approximately 8mm diameter

Very nice-quality amazonite beads that are translucent and have an intense natural color that is mottled with white. This mottling is common to amazonite, as is the silky sheen.

LABRADORITE, SPECTROLITE, RAINBOW MOONSTONE, AND ANDESINE LABRADORITE

The Plagioclase Feldspar species includes a group of four stones that are very popular with jewelry-buyers—labradorite, spectrolite, rainbow moonstone, and the enhanced andesine labradorite.

LABRADORITE was first discovered in 1770 in Labrador, Canada. It reveals an intense play of colors when moved in the light. So unique is labradorite's color-play that the description "labradorescence" was chosen to describe the effect, which is a result of light being diffracted within the layers of the stone. The color of the schiller can range from a blue-green sheen to a whole spectrum of colors in a high-grade stone. Labradorite's body color is dark gray to gray-black, colorless, or orange-red to brownish. The material can be opaque to transparent. The gem's layered structure produces colorful iridescence and adularescence, which is a white to bluish light that moves over the stone in a similar way to that of moonstone.

The best labradorite material shows either a pure, intense, royal blue or the full spectrum of colors in its color-play. It also displays aventurescence, a glittering or sparkling optical effect that is caused by light hitting mineral platelet inclusions (composed of hematite, pyrite, or fuchsite mica) inside the stone.

Labradorite can be full of inclusions or nearly transparent, but interestingly, the inclusions are a good thing in this case! Very clean material produces a simple blue schiller, but more included labradorite will show a greater spectral iridescence. So, the better clarity gives less color, while the included material will show full labradorescence. The main sources of labradorite are Canada, Finland, and Madagascar.

GEMMOLOGICAL INFORMATION

CRYSTAL SYSTEM Triclinic crystal system. Single crystals are rare; the gem is usually found as a solid aggregate.

MOHS HARDNESS 6.0–6.5

REFRACTIVE INDEX 1.56–1.57

SPECIFIC GRAVITY/DENSITY 2.62–2.75

LUSTER Vitreous

CHEMICAL COMPOSITION Calcium sodium aluminum silicate

COMMON TREATMENTS Andesine labradorite is color-enhanced.

OPTICAL PROPERTIES Adularescence, labradorescence, and iridescence. The aventurescence is due to metallic inclusions. The layered structure causes interference of light and results in color-play.

CUTTING AND STONE CUTS Perfect cleavage and slightly brittle. The stones can rub and scuff.

IMITATIONS/SYNTHETICS None

NOT TO BE CONFUSED WITH... Moonstone, fire agate, aventurine quartz.

Group of 15mm diameter labradorite checkerboard cuts

These were cut in a good grade of material (often cheaper labradorite cabochons are heavily flawed and full of cracks).

Slab of labradorite and labradorite oval cabochons

The cutting and polishing of this slab is not good, but the price is low. The cabochons are better; they are almost transparent with a blue and orange schiller.

Adila labradorite pendant by Emma Chapman

A simple design using a labradorite drop cabochon and a small faceted rainbow moonstone.

Raw stone

A section of labradorite rough material. The layered structure causes interference of light and produces a form of color-play known as labradorescence.

SPECTROLITE comes from Finland and is a rare variety of labradorite. It has a beautiful, spectral color-play that ranges from intense blue to purple hues to orange/amber.

RAINBOW MOONSTONE is also known as "Madagascan moonstone." However, it is not from the moonstone family. It is a fine, almost transparent gemstone with an intense blue schiller and metallic luster.

ANDESINE LABRADORITE has a pink to red body color that displays adularescence. The stone is commonly enhanced for color.

On the whole, these gemstones are suitable for most types of jewelry but, ideally, labradorite ring stones should have a protective setting. Labradorite is usually cut as cabochons or carved, but it is also sometimes faceted. Unfortunately, due to its hardness and perfect cleavage, the facets will get rubbed and chipped over time. Try to avoid stones with sharp, right-angled corners because they will fray and scuff.

Cluster of spectrolite cabs

The marquise has cracks, but the color range of the schiller is good. The ovals show yellow, amber, and blue iridescence.

Andesine labradorite set in gold studs by R. Holt & Co. and andesine oval cab

These stones make for great earrings. The cab (right) has a lovely sheen.

SUNSTONE

Also known as aventurine feldspar and oligoclase.

Sunstone is a good-looking, gem-grade feldspar that glitters with inclusions. It has a host of optical effects, exhibiting chatoyance, asterism, and aventurescence.

Sunstone can be pink-red, red-brown, and orange-red. The gemstone ranges from opaque to translucent and sometimes transparent.

Sunstone commonly contains metallic inclusions of goethite, pyrite, and hematite (Oregon sunstone has copper inclusions) that refract light between the crystal layers to produce an iridescent effect as the stone is moved. This is called aventurescence or schiller. The intensity of this optical effect depends on the size of the inclusions; smaller platelets produce a simple sheen over the stone, while larger inclusions appear as floating, spangled metallic platelets.

Plagioclase feldspars have perfect cleavage and tend to be brittle; they pick up scuffs and sharp corners become frayed. The layered composition can make it tricky to cut. When faceted, sunstone usually has large, flat facets to maximize the color and reflections off the metallic inclusions. Opaque material is cut as cabochons and beads.

Often sunstone can exhibit asterism (four-ray stars) and chatoyance (cat's eyes). In general, it is a low- to medium-priced stone for the cabochons, but transparent red material has a much higher price.

Sunstone occurs in India, Canada, Madagascar, Norway, Russia, and the USA (Oregon, North Carolina, Utah).

Sunstone can be vulnerable to damage when set in jewelry, so it needs a protective setting. Don't use ultrasonic cleaners.

Sunstone cabochon

The body is clear with red, green, and orange metallic platelets of pyrite, hematite, and goethite.

GEMMOLOGICAL INFORMATION

CRYSTAL SYSTEM Triclinic crystal system. Single crystals are rare; the gem is usually found as a solid aggregate.

MOHS HARDNESS 6

REFRACTIVE INDEX 1.54–1.55

SPECIFIC GRAVITY/DENSITY 2.64

LUSTER Vitreous

CHEMICAL COMPOSITION Calcium sodium aluminum silicate

COMMON TREATMENTS Not treated or dyed.

OPTICAL PROPERTIES Aventurescence, chatoyance, and asterism (four-ray star).

CUTTING AND STONE CUTS Perfect cleavage and slightly brittle.

IMITATIONS/SYNTHETICS There is a man-made stone called "goldstone." There is also artificial aventurescent Italian/French poured glass with copper inclusions.

NOT TO BE CONFUSED WITH... Aventurine quartz, orthoclase moonstone.

Faceted sunstone

This is a fine orange-red transparent sunstone weighing 3 carats, which is the typical size of this material. It has good clarity, with no aventurescence.

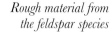

Rough material from the feldspar species

This is a solid aggregate; an opaque (heavily included) orange color with a metallic schiller. The softness and perfect cleavage can make it difficult to cut.

SUGILITE

Found in lilac, plum, magenta, reddish-purple, and grape-jelly purple, sugilite is a colorful addition to the "gem library" for jewelry makers. Only discovered in the 1970s, sugilite was officially classified as a rare gem in 1980, which immediately increased its value.

Not part of a group or species, gem-quality sugilite was first found in a manganese mine in South Africa. The manganese gives sugilite its pink-purple color, and the host rock provides black inclusions.

With sugilite, color equals grade—a uniform intense purple is the most valuable. A mottled appearance is acceptable, but light areas lower the value. It is generally opaque to occasionally translucent with patches, veins, and layers. The layering can contain hair-line cracks, making cutting difficult. Sugilite has indistinct cleavage, giving it good wearability—it is usually carved, cut into cabochons and beads, or slabbed for inlay work. It can be found in large sizes, with 10 carats-plus being common.

Other names include sugilite jade, purple turquoise, wesselite, royal azel, cybeline, lavulite, and royal lazelle.

Dark colors can be lightened by heating and sugilite is sometimes dyed to enhance the purple color. Imitation sugilite also occurs.

In general, sugilite is a medium-priced stone. It's not widely known, but has been used by Christian Dior who produced a "Queen of Sugilite" ring and used sugilite as dials on their watches. Bulgari also made a sugilite ring.

As it is fairly durable, sugilite can be cleaned with soap and water, as long as the soap is washed off. It is stable under normal light and heat. Avoid ultrasonic cleaners.

Sugilite can be sourced in South Africa (Wessels Mine), Australia (New South Wales), Tajikistan, Italy, and Canada (Quebec).

Raw stone
Sugilite aggregate showing color bands and patches plus black inclusions from host rock. The material can be opaque to translucent and can be carved, slabbed for inlay work, and cabbed.

GEMMOLOGICAL INFORMATION

CRYSTAL SYSTEM Hexagonal. Single hexagonal crystals are very rare; it is usually found in massive form, which is quite tough. Sugilite is often mixed with chalcedony, so its hardness can vary.

MOHS HARDNESS 5.5-6.5

REFRACTIVE INDEX 1.544-1.611

SPECIFIC GRAVITY/DENSITY 2.74-2.80

LUSTER Vitreous, resinous, or waxy

CHEMICAL COMPOSITION Potassium sodium lithium iron manganese aluminum silicate. Sugilite belongs to the cyclosilicate group of minerals.

COMMON TREATMENTS Heating and dyeing.

OPTICAL PROPERTIES None

CUTTING AND STONE CUTS Cabochon cuts, inlay work, and beads. Translucent material is sometimes faceted. Check rough material for fine cracks.

IMITATIONS/SYNTHETICS Yes

NOT TO BE CONFUSED WITH... Amethyst, tanzanite, iolite, sodalite, haroite.

Natural sugilite material showing different qualities and cuts
From left, a light color; the middle stone shows surface texture and coloration, while the stone on the right shows good-quality, intense purple color.

OPALS

Opals are a large family of non-mineral gemstones containing many different varieties that are covered in the next few pages. However, there are certain topics that apply to all opals such as how color-play occurs and is valued, which are discussed here.

Color is assessed on body color and color-play. The background color is caused by the suspension of impurities within the silica spheres. Color-play is assessed on the ratio of iridescent opal compared to background, the intensity, the dominant hues (red is highly valued), and pattern. If the entire spectrum of color shows, then that's highly valued. If the colors are milky and light, then the value reduces. An opal can display one or two colors, or the whole spectrum.

Rotate the stone through 360 degrees to see if there are dead patches with no color— dead patches affect the value. Large patches of color are viewed as having a higher value than pinpoints.

Clarity and the quantity of inclusions are also assessed. Common inclusions in opals are sand, non-opal spots, healed fractures, black potch "webbing" (areas of black common opal that lie between the colors), and areas of sandstone. Fine, black potch webbing between the color zones is not seen as a flaw in opals.

Cutting opal is a challenge, as crazing can occur at random. This often happens when the opal is removed from damp conditions and then allowed to dry out too quickly. It can also occur if an opal is suddenly exposed to intense light or to vibration during cutting and polishing. The lapidary has to assess the direction of the color-play in the material, map out the placement of inclusions, maximize the rough, and then avoid crazing! Ethiopian opals have a tendency to craze during cutting.

Opals have appeared in jewelry from the Middle Ages onward. The opal mines of Hungary were used by Europeans for centuries, but Australia has been the main producer since 1800. Other opal producers are Czechoslovakia, the USA, Mexico, Brazil, and Ethiopia.

Opal has also been imitated for centuries; opalite glass was being used from the 1700s. More recently, in 1974, John Slocum in the USA developed a silicate glass imitation, but this lacked the silky, flat color patches of natural opal. It looks almost crumpled under magnification. In 1973, a colorful Gilson imitation opal that had a mosaic-like structure when looked at under magnification was developed in a laboratory in France. There are also inexpensive polystyrene latex imitation beads and cabochons on the market.

Doublets have been available since 1860. These are a composite stone in which a thin layer of natural opal is cemented onto a base of potch opal, glass, dyed black chalcedony, or plastic. Triplets are also manufactured; these are similar to doublets, but have a dome of rock crystal or glass to cover the layer of opal.

A selection of different opals

From the top: Semi-black opal, black opal, precious white opal, fire opal, fossilized shell opal, and yowah wood opal.

Raw Ethiopian opal

Ethiopian Welo opal rough, translucent light material with matrix. Opal is non-crystalline and has massive form.

PRECIOUS OPAL

The term precious opal covers those stones with an iridescent color-play. The term common or potch opal is used for opaque opals that have no iridescence. Color-play is caused by the internal structure of opal; it is a three-dimensional lattice of tiny silica spheres that diffract the light as it travels through the lattice. The size of the spheres affects the color range—the larger and more ordered the spheres, the greater the color range. Small spheres produce blue, as blue has the shortest wavelength. Large spheres have a longer wavelength, so red appears, which is the most valued color. If the spheres are all one size and are uniformly arranged through the stone, then the opal displays just one color. If there's an orderly arrangement of small spheres in one area, medium-sized in another area, and large in another, then segments of color will appear in the color-play, like a harlequin. Random sizes of spheres will scatter all the colors equally, but can lead to a milky "potch" appearance.

GEMMOLOGICAL INFORMATION

CRYSTAL SYSTEM Amorphous; opal is not a crystalline mineral.

MOHS HARDNESS 5.0–6.5

REFRACTIVE INDEX 1.37–1.52

SPECIFIC GRAVITY/DENSITY 1.98–2.50 (low)

LUSTER Vitreous, waxy to resinous

CHEMICAL COMPOSITION Hydrated silica gel. Has a water content of up to 21 percent from its aquatic origin.

COMMON TREATMENTS Impregnating/stabilizing with wax or resin, smoking, heat and sugar treatment, and coating.

OPTICAL PROPERTIES Iridescence, opalescence/color-play, and chatoyance.

CUTTING AND STONE CUTS Opals are fragile stones, so cutting requires care. Stabilized material should improve durability.

IMITATIONS/SYNTHETICS Glass, Gilson opals, synthetic opals, composite opals—both doublets and triplets.

NOT TO BE CONFUSED WITH... Labradorite, ammonite, moonstone, mother of pearl.

18kt gold drop earrings with Andean opal by Jean Scott-Moncrieff
This opal was specially cut.

Opal doublet
A doublet is a composite opal where a layer of opal is cemented to a base of potch opal or agate.

Gold fire opal and diamond cocktail ring, Fellows private collection
An oval faceted orange-red fire opal surrounded by brilliant-cut white diamonds.

BLACK OPAL

The top opal of the group is the black opal—it commands the highest prices. It can be recognized by the dark body, which is either opaque or translucent and shows off the bright color-play. Beware of treated black opals and synthetics.

There are very few sources of high-quality black opals in the world—they are rarer than precious white opals. Nearly all the world's supply of black opal is mined in New South Wales, Australia, with the best and most famous deposits being from Lightning Ridge. It is also found in the Mintabie District and Andamooka Ranges in South Australia. Outside Australia there are sources in the USA (Nevada) and Ethiopia.

Ethiopian black opals are usually enhanced, and just don't have the same quality as Australian opals. They're quite fresh on the market, so their longevity remains to be seen. The impact of the treatment processes is also not yet fully understood. Australian black opal is normally untreated, but the Ethiopians darken light-colored stones by using an old smoking method that allows carbon to penetrate the opal deeply, making the color darker. There is another "reported" treatment, which uses a combination of heat and sugar. The stones are soaked in a sugar solution, then immersed in sulfuric acid and slowly heated to darken the body color. Coating also occurs, as does impregnation with a polymer resin, wax, or oil, which stabilizes the opal and hides any cracks and fissures in a damaged stone.

A black precious opal will always have a dark background: either solid opaque or dark gray, and transparent or translucent. The body color can be dark blue, dark green, or gray-black. The most common colors in the color-play of black opals are yellow, blue, and green. Violet, red, and orange are rarer, and the most valuable and sought-after colors. The average weight of black opal is 7 to 8 carats; 10 carats becomes harder to source, with 15 carats-plus being rare.

Australian black opals contain small traces of iron oxide and carbon elements. This combination of trace elements gives the opal the darkened body that produces a much brighter reflection of colors. Most black opals have some potch opal left on them, as this helps deepen the body tone and in turn enhance the color-play. They have a pearly to resinous to wax-like to vitreous luster.

In general, because black opal is so expensive, the rough material will be maximized, so most stones have a free-form shape. They are normally cut with low domes, as the color "bars" (areas of color-play) are thin and the color-play isn't deep.

Black opal cushion

Good-quality black opal with a dark, semi-opaque body color and blue and green color-play across the whole stone. It was re-cut from a larger broken stone, which must have been tremendous.

GEMMOLOGICAL INFORMATION

CRYSTAL SYSTEM Amorphous; opal is not a crystalline mineral. Crystal habit massive.

MOHS HARDNESS 4.5–6.5

REFRACTIVE INDEX 1.37–1.47

SPECIFIC GRAVITY/DENSITY 1.97–2.22 (low)

LUSTER Vitreous, waxy to resinous. Pearly.

CHEMICAL COMPOSITION Hydrous silicon dioxide gel. Has a water content of up to 21 percent from its aquatic origin. Normal water content is 6 to 10 percent.

COMMON TREATMENTS Impregnating/stabilizing with wax or resin, smoking, heat and sugar treatment, and coating.

OPTICAL PROPERTIES Iridescence and opalescence/color-play.

CUTTING AND STONE CUTS Opals are fragile stones, so cutting requires care. Brittle, conchoidal fracture.

IMITATIONS/SYNTHETICS Glass and Gilson opals, synthetic opals, composite opals—both doublets and triplets.

NOT TO BE CONFUSED WITH... Labradorite, ammonite, moonstone, mother of pearl.

Raw stone

The image shows many small black opal fossilized shells in clay matrix. See opal pseudomorphs (pages 150–151).

Black opal and diamond pendant,
Fellows private collection

An 18kt gold pendant with heart-shaped black opal surrounded by brilliant-cut diamonds with diamond bail. The opal is good quality, displaying reds, purples, and blues. Made in the 1980s.

Selection of black
opals (below)

From top: 8.55ct Australian black opal; 4.21ct Australian black opal; large black antique black opal that has a pasty patch in its center due to aging.

Opal and diamond brooch
by Bentley and Skinner

This Art Deco opal and diamond brooch has a central oval panel containing a mosaic of opal, onyx, and hardstone. It depicts a seascape at sunset. The outer border is set with rose-cut diamonds.

PRECIOUS WHITE OPAL AND CRYSTAL OPAL

PRECIOUS WHITE OPAL is less dramatic than black opal, but more affordable and available. A good stone can have great color-play, with a range of pinks, yellows, greens, and blues. It is a translucent to opaque crystal, with a light white or beige body color. Precious white opal is more common than precious black opal, and can be found in calibrated cuts and sizes. It doesn't have the drama of black or boulder opal (*see page 150*), but can still be very beautiful. However, poor-quality material is common and the stones can be pale and pasty with faint color-play. Antique pieces of jewelry often contain white opals, but look out for those that have dried out and are full of fine cracks. A darkened or enclosed setting will improve the color-play on precious white opals, and also protect them. Designers frequently put a row of durable diamonds around a precious opal in order to protect it from knocks.

GEMMOLOGICAL INFORMATION

CRYSTAL SYSTEM Amorphous; opal is not a crystalline mineral.

MOHS HARDNESS 5.0–6.5

REFRACTIVE INDEX 1.37–1.52

SPECIFIC GRAVITY/DENSITY 1.98–2.50 (low)

LUSTER Vitreous, waxy to resinous

CHEMICAL COMPOSITION Hydrated silica gel. Has a water content of up to 21 percent from its aquatic origin.

COMMON TREATMENTS Impregnating/stabilizing with wax or resin.

OPTICAL PROPERTIES Iridescence, opalescence/color-play, and chatoyance.

CUTTING AND STONE CUTS Opals are fragile stones, so cutting requires care. Stabilized material should improve durability.

IMITATIONS/SYNTHETICS Glass and Gilson opals, plus synthetic white and black opals.

NOT TO BE CONFUSED WITH... Labradorite, ammonite, moonstone, mother of pearl.

Precious white opal carved mice

These are unusual carvings from Germany using precious white opal with fire opals for the eyes. The color-play is not great, but it would have been too expensive to use high-quality material and carving precious opal is a risky business.

Ethiopian crystal opal in matrix

The seller tried to cut this opal, but it crazed immediately; the material became milky and cracked. Apparently a lot of this Ethiopian material behaves that way.

Faceted crystal opal oval (left)

The cutter has done a fine job to facet this crystal opal. It's a very subtle, pure stone; when you first look at it, you don't see much color—but as you move it ghostly blues and pinks appear within the gem.

CRYSTAL OPAL is usually a clear, transparent material with color-play that is visible in the interior of the stone. A fine piece is lovely; it has the purity of water with floating colors that mysteriously appear as you move the stone, then change, disappear, or reappear within the body of the crystal.

It is widely accepted that a dark background or mat is necessary for viewing crystal opals and that they should be set in an enclosed setting for the best color.

Sources are Australia, the USA (Nevada, Idaho, Oregon, California), Canada (British Columbia), Ethiopia, the Czech Republic, Slovakia, Hungary, and Honduras.

Cutting opal is a challenge, as crazing can occur at random. This often happens when the opal is removed from damp conditions and then allowed to dry out too quickly. It can also occur if an opal is suddenly exposed to intense light or to vibration during cutting and polishing. Uncut opals are often stored in water to reduce the risk of crazing. The lapidary has to assess the direction of the color-play in the material, map out the placement of inclusions, maximize the rough, and then avoid crazing! Ethiopian opals have a tendency to craze during cutting.

Custom cuts maximize the color-play and are used with black opal and boulder opal. Large, free-form pieces are common, because opal has a low density and weighs light. However, the shape still needs to be symmetrical with a well-rounded dome to give the best color. Stones that are too thin or too deep can cause setting issues; solid opals need some depth to keep them stable and durable.

Opals need to stay hydrated, so should be kept in a cool, dark place away from sunlight and heaters. It's a good idea to keep a damp cotton-wool ball inside the box with the opal, as dehydration leads to cracks. Opals are also sensitive to sudden temperature changes, chemicals, and rough handling. Never use an ultrasonic cleaner, as the vibration can open up a crack.

Opal brooch by Bentley and Skinner

Exquisite precious white opal and diamond flower brooch c. 1860. An old-cut diamond is set in the center, with five petals containing oval opals with borders of grain-set diamonds.

Precious opal, 10mm diameter round

Australian precious opal with very nice green and blue color-play that covers the whole stone. The photo makes the body look very orange, but in normal light the orange is more subtle and the green and blue color-play is dominant.

PRECIOUS BOULDER OPAL AND YOWAH WOODS

More robust than precious white opals and black opals, boulder opals can be identified by the matrix that's attached to the crystal. "Yowahs" are fascinating opals because they preserve the look of wood in great detail.

BOULDER OPAL is precious opal from Australia. It is found in cracks in, or as coatings on, ironstone or sandstone boulders. Boulder opal has a layer of host rock, and so is a good choice for jewelry, including rings. It is also cheaper than the precious black and white opals, making it more accessible to buyers. Always check that a boulder opal has a good layer of crystal so that it will be durable. It is possible to confuse boulder opals with composite doublets and triplets because of the layered composition.

GEMMOLOGICAL INFORMATION

CRYSTAL SYSTEM Amorphous; opal is not a crystalline mineral.

MOHS HARDNESS 5.0–6.5

REFRACTIVE INDEX 1.37–1.52

SPECIFIC GRAVITY/DENSITY 1.98–2.50 (low)

LUSTER Vitreous, waxy to resinous

CHEMICAL COMPOSITION Hydrated silica gel. Has a water content of up to 21 percent from its aquatic origin.

COMMON TREATMENTS Impregnating/stabilizing with wax or resin, smoking, heat and sugar treatment, and coating.

OPTICAL PROPERTIES Iridescence, opalescence/color-play, and chatoyance.

CUTTING AND STONE CUTS Opals are fragile stones, so cutting requires care. Stabilized material should improve durability.

IMITATIONS/SYNTHETICS Glass and Gilson opals, synthetic opals, composite opals—both doublets and triplets.

NOT TO BE CONFUSED WITH... Labradorite, ammonite, moonstone, mother of pearl.

Nebula cuff by Zaffiro Etrusco Collection
The cuff is made of 22kt granulated gold on forged oxidized sterling silver. The large Australian boulder opal, measuring 19mm long, has strong blue color-play, which is off-set by the small brilliant-cut blue and white diamonds.

Fossilized opal shell (left) and boulder opal
An opal pseudomorph, it's possible to see the shell outline and form on the stone on the left. The boulder is a very fine opal, with intense turquoise and blue color-play.

YOWAH WOODS are pseudomorphs; the wood is replaced by crystal opal and yet retains the appearance and shape of the original organic matter. Australian deposits are interesting, as they lie in an area that used to be an ancient inland sea. So, shells and opal belemnites are very collectable. Belemnites are fossilized marine animals that lived in the earth's Jurassic and Cretaceous Periods and have changed to opal. The closest living relative is a squid or cuttlefish.

Arts and Crafts boulder opal and diamond in gold by F. Walter Lawrence

This opal pendant from the Art Nouveau era features a large oval boulder opal with blue and green color-play and two smaller matching opals.

Andamooka blonde boulder opal

This is a good example of Andamooka boulder opal. It has a thick layer of opal on top of the matrix, with beautiful color-play in red, lilac, purple, yellow, and blue in an unusual diagonal pattern.

Belemnite opal

A belemnite opal, which is a rare pseudomorph. The organic matter has been replaced by precious opal, but the opal has kept the shape of the Jurassic cuttlefish.

Mismatched pair of Yowah wood opals

More fascinating pseudomorph opals, these show the appearance of wood but are made of precious opal.

Raw stone

Precious opal on ironstone from Australia. Boulder is usually found as a vein or layer within the host rock and is then split open to reveal the opal layer attached to the matrix.

FIRE OPAL AND ANDEAN BLUE OPAL

The vivid orange color of fire opal helps with identification, but it can be confused with other gemstones such as mandarin garnet and carnelian. Andean opal has a distinct turquoise color, which is similar to that of chrysocolla and gem silica.

FIRE OPAL is colored by small traces of iron oxide and ranges in color from white to yellow, to orange, to red to brown. The more intense and saturated the color, the more valuable the stone. Red stones are valued more highly than orange stones.

Fire opal can be clean and transparent to milky and translucent. Good-quality material may have some minor color-play inside the stone, mainly flashes of green but occasionally some blue. The rough material occurs as kidney- and grape-shaped aggregates (reniform and botryoidal, respectively). The luster is sub-vitreous, and waxy to resinous. Chatoyance does occur rarely.

One of the most important sources is the state of Querétaro, in Mexico, which has been mined since 1835. The fire opals from this source can have a bluish or golden internal light/sheen and are called Mexican water opal or hydrophanous opal. Other sources of fire opal are the USA, Guatemala, Australia, Canada, and Brazil.

There is also a variety called jelly opal, which is transparent with a jelly-like appearance and a bluish schiller or sheen over the stone.

Fire opal is both faceted and cut as cabochons, but care needs to be taken when wearing faceted fire opal because it can be brittle. The facet edges will wear over time or chip, so it's a good idea to have a protective bezel or rub-over setting. Fire opal is frequently cured by drying it prior to cutting to reduce instability and make the stone less delicate. It needs to be kept cool during cutting and polishing to avoid dehydration and crazing. It is thought that if the source of the material is dry, then the stone will be more durable for cutting.

GEMMOLOGICAL INFORMATION

CRYSTAL SYSTEM Amorphous; opal is not a crystalline mineral.

MOHS HARDNESS 5.0–6.5

REFRACTIVE INDEX 1.37–1.52

SPECIFIC GRAVITY/DENSITY 1.98–2.50 (low)

LUSTER Sub-vitreous, waxy to resinous

CHEMICAL COMPOSITION Hydrated silica gel. Has a water content of up to 21 percent from its aquatic origin.

COMMON TREATMENTS Impregnating/stabilizing with wax or resin, smoking, heat and sugar treatment, and coating.

OPTICAL PROPERTIES Iridescence, opalescence/color-play, and chatoyance rarely.

CUTTING AND STONE CUTS Opals are fragile stones, so cutting requires care. Stabilized material should improve durability.

IMITATIONS/SYNTHETICS Synthetic fire opals

NOT TO BE CONFUSED WITH... Labradorite, ammonite, moonstone, mother of pearl.

Fire opal rough material
The color and clarity are mixed; whiteish areas that are opaque with sections that are a translucent deep orange.

Cabochon fire opals
Clockwise from top right: Orange jelly opal with purple-blue schiller; fine fire opals—red-orange pear and red oval; and two rare chatoyant orange fire opals.

Fire opal and diamond ring in gold by Daphne Krinos
This fire opal cabochon is enhanced by the 18kt yellow gold and the single bezel-set diamond acts as a highlight.

Fire opal faceted cushion (left)

A fine red fire opal, colored by iron oxide impurities. The color is intense and the opal has good transparency, making it desirable and valuable.

Patricia series pendant by Zaffiro

The pendant is set with a deep turquoise Peruvian opal (15.01ct) and small white and black diamonds in 22kt granulated gold.

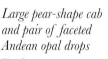

Andean blue opal drop earrings by Jean Scott-Moncrieff

These elegant earrings are made from 18kt and 22kt gold. The faceted Andean blues are set into rectangular collets, which intensify the color.

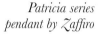

ANDEAN OPAL, from Peru, is popular due to its amazing vivid or neon turquoise color, which is the result of copper impurities, but it does not have color-play. It is translucent and often contains dendritic inclusions. Andean opal is commonly stabilized for cutting and is highly sensitive to heat. I have concerns about the color stability of Andean opal, as many of the stones that I've had cut have gradually discolored to a not-very-attractive greenish color over time.

Large pear-shape cab and pair of faceted Andean opal drops

The fine, intense turquoise color of these three stones is the color that's made Andean opal so popular and has made it so expensive now.

Raw stone

Blue opalite in matrix—a non-precious opal that is less valuable than black and white opals.

HEMATITE

Hematite's metallic luster is quite unique and, together with the high density and weight, there isn't another gemstone like it! The name comes from the Greek word for blood, referring to the fact that hematite looks red when thinly sliced. Hematite has been used as a red pigment in powdered form for many years.

Specular hematite has an opaque metallic appearance that also shows a red color when thinly sliced. It is the gem form of iron oxide. The thin crystals are red-brown in color, but hematite has a shiny silver appearance when it is worked and polished. Hematite is usually massive in form, but it's possible to find finer black rhombohedral crystals with iridescent surfaces. The term specular hematite refers to the shiny crystals and the fact that they were once used as mirrors.

Hematite is one of only a couple of gems that has a metallic luster. It has a very high specific gravity and is the densest gem available. It also has a high refractive index, so often can't be checked on a refractometer because the liquid range isn't high enough. Despite this, hematite is a soft stone that requires re-polishing from time to time in order to sharpen up the facet edges and improve its appearance. It needs to be kept away from other jewelry, as it is easily scratched.

There are various trade names for hematite. Iridescent hematite is a hematite-rich slate from Arizona that exhibits multi-colored surfaces, possibly due to long exposure on a mine dump. Rainbow hematite is a granular specular mass with high iridescence that comes from Minas Gerais in Brazil. Titano hematite is a titanium-rich variety. Specularite is a hematite aggregate with a glistening luster. Alaska black diamond is a misnomer, referring to the fact that this hematite resembles black diamonds. Iron rose, which comes from Switzerland and Brazil, is the name for a group of specular crystals that are arranged like a flower. Hematite also appears as kidney-shaped nodules.

The main hematite deposits are found in North America (Lake Superior and Quebec), Brazil, Venezuela, England, Germany, and Italy, where it's been mined since the time of the Ancient Etruscans. It has also been found on Mars! There is no shortage of hematite, so it is an inexpensive gemstone.

Hematite cabochon by R. Holt & Co.

A sizeable cabochon of 30mm diameter. The large size makes it heavy because of its high density. It has a bright, silvery high polish, displaying a distinct metallic luster, which identifies it.

GEMMOLOGICAL INFORMATION

CRYSTAL SYSTEM Trigonal. Platy habit and massive.

MOHS HARDNESS 5.5–6.5

REFRACTIVE INDEX 2.94–3.22 (high)

SPECIFIC GRAVITY/DENSITY 5.20 (weighs heavy)

LUSTER Metallic

CHEMICAL COMPOSITION Iron oxide

COMMON TREATMENTS Stabilizing to make the stone less crumbly.

OPTICAL PROPERTIES Iridescence

CUTTING AND STONE CUTS Very soft. Can be carved and faceted, but the edges and facets get worn.

IMITATIONS/SYNTHETICS Hematine is a magnetic synthetic. Hemalyke is a trade name for reconstituted material which is less brittle.

NOT TO BE CONFUSED WITH... Marcasite, pyrite.

Hematite 9mm diameter faceted beads

The faceted edges of the beads don't have the sharpness associated with harder gemstones and over time they will rub and scuff.

Raw material by R. Holt & Co.

Hematite rough is red and looks more like red jasper until you feel the weight. The color is due to the stone's iron oxide composition, which is effectively rust colored.

SCAPOLITE

Also known as wernerite.

Scapolite is not a well-known stone, but it is very attractive. There are two distinct types of the gem—one is a cat's eye and the other a faceted stone.

The brilliance and vitreous luster make scapolite a desirable gem; the colors are beautiful, especially the deep purples, while the soft pink cat's eyes are dramatic. The name comes from the Greek words *scapos* (meaning "rod") and *lithos* (meaning "stone"), so the name basically means "long stick"—a reference to the shape of the crystals.

The color range is colorless, white-pink, purple, bluish-gray, pale yellow, brown, orange-brown, golden yellow, orange-yellow, and gray to colorless. Yellow is a common color, so natural purple and violet stones are more expensive than yellow ones. Golden scapolite from Tanzania is darker and cleaner than Brazilian scapolite, so it has a higher value. Some purple stones are irradiated, so these need to be tested. Cat's eyes occur in pink and purple material, and are rare and valuable. Variations of composition, from sodium-rich to calcium-rich crystals, affect the color and properties of scapolite; there is a variety called rainbow scapolite, which displays iridescence unlike any other type. Another type of scapolite shows dramatic fluorescence and this is largely found in Quebec and Ontario.

Certain stones are pleochroic: violet stones show dark blue/lavender-blue directions and colorless/violet when viewed from different angles. Common inclusions are hollow tubes, needles, and platelets, which create optical effects. Hematite inclusions (small platelets) produce aventurescence in scapolite.

Sizes range from 10 to 12mm in diameter for pink cat's eyes and up to 8 carats for faceted purple stones.

Scapolite was discovered in North Myanmar in 1913 in fibrous white, pink, and violet material. In 1920, yellow deposits were found in Madagascar and then in 1930 material was found in Brazil. In 1975, deposits of rare purple crystals were found in Tanzania.

Perfect cleavage, chatoyance, and pleochroism make scapolite slightly challenging for cutters, but the effort can be worth it. Purity of color, saturation, a well-proportioned cut, and good clarity will give the stone a high value.

Faceted purple scapolite
This beautiful stone was bought 18 years ago from a Tanzanian source. It's now a valuable piece because it's a purple scapolite with an intense color, the clarity is excellent, and it's a large size.

GEMMOLOGICAL INFORMATION

CRYSTAL SYSTEM Tetragonal. Crystal habit is prisms that resemble sticks, but often a large, coarse material in massive form. Both crystals and massive form can be found in Brazil, Sri Lanka, Kenya, Canada, and Madagascar.

MOHS HARDNESS 6

REFRACTIVE INDEX 1.54–1.58 (varies according to location)

SPECIFIC GRAVITY/DENSITY 2.70

LUSTER Resinous to vitreous

CHEMICAL COMPOSITION Complex silicate

COMMON TREATMENTS Heated to change or improve the color. Also irradiated to change the color from yellow to purple, but this fades.

OPTICAL PROPERTIES Pleochroism in some stones. Chatoyance in pink and purple material, but this is rare. Fluorescence in Burmese, Tanzanian, and Quebec stones. Also displays iridescence, tenebrescence, and aventurescence.

CUTTING AND STONE CUTS Perfect distinct cleavage in two directions. Uneven conchoidal fracture. Has to be orientated correctly to cut a cat's eye.

IMITATIONS/SYNTHETICS Synthetics exist, but only for research purposes.

NOT TO BE CONFUSED WITH... Amblygonite, chrysoberyl, golden beryl, sphene, golden topaz, tourmaline, peridot, rose quartz.

Pink cat's eye (top) and violet cat's eye scapolite
The pink Burmese scapolite is of a large size with an excellent eye. In the violet cat's eye, it's possible to see the internal fibers that produce the white eye.

Raw stone
A partially crystallized Nigerian golden-yellow scapolite in a prismatic habit. It's a widely available color; the darker yellows are more valuable and African material is a deeper yellow than Brazilian.

CHROME DIOPSIDE AND STAR DIOPSIDE

Chrome diopside is a vivid chrome-green color and comes in small sizes of 2 carats and under. However, star diopside is very different; it is black and exhibits asterism (four-ray star).

Faceted diopside gemstones are usually bottle-green, brownish-green, or light green. The more iron-rich and magnesium-poor the gem, the darker the color until it's nearly black.

CHROME DIOPSIDE is not typical of most diopsides; the gemstone is a bright saturated green which is colored by chromium. The gem looks best when it is under 2 carats in weight, as the material often becomes too dark or strongly saturated when the stone is any bigger. The most desirable chrome diopside is medium to dark green, with good clarity and transparency.

Chrome diopside was marketed as an alternative to emerald and tsavorite by the Russian producers, but there's still not enough of a reliable supply to make commercial jewelry.

Another downside of chrome diopside is its poor durability. It has two directions of perfect cleavage, plus it can also scratch and break, as it has a hardness of only 5.5 Mohs. It is best used for earrings and pendants, so avoid setting it in rings and bracelets.

Russia (Eastern Siberia) has a good supply, but there are production problems due to the freezing weather and permafrost. It can only be mined there for six months of the year. However, Pakistan is now producing good-quality material, so there will be a more reliable source of chrome diopside. Smaller sources are Austria, Brazil, Myanmar, Canada, Finland, India, and Italy.

GEMMOLOGICAL INFORMATION

CRYSTAL SYSTEM Monoclinic with columnar crystals.

MOHS HARDNESS 5.5–6.5

REFRACTIVE INDEX 1.66–1.72

SPECIFIC GRAVITY/DENSITY 3.29 (heavy)

LUSTER Vitreous

CHEMICAL COMPOSITION Calcium magnesium silicate. Chrome diopside is an indicator mineral for diamonds; it often occurs in the same locations.

COMMON TREATMENTS Very rarely

OPTICAL PROPERTIES Asterism (four-ray star) from fibrous inclusions.

CUTTING AND STONE CUTS Faceted and cabbed. Step cuts and emerald cuts due to the fragile, brittle nature of the stone.

IMITATIONS/SYNTHETICS None

NOT TO BE CONFUSED WITH... Chrome tourmaline, emerald, demantoid garnet, tsavorite, hiddenite, black star sapphire (six-rays).

Raw stone

This chrome diopside monoclinic crystal has areas of better clarity and color zoning. Crystals commonly have a columnar habit.

A group of oval chrome cabochons

The smaller size shows the vibrant chrome-green color better, as larger stones tend to go very dark to nearly black. The cabs have some magnetite needle inclusions.

Chrome diopside cabochons (left)

The 8mm antique cushions were specially cut from Russian material. Most is faceted, as diopside has low brilliance compared to other green gemstones, so good-quality cabochons are hard to find.

Raw stone

Aggregate of star diopside rough crystals. Monoclinic crystal system, which has a moderately high density.

STAR DIOPSIDE also has two distinct directions of cleavage. The material contains needle-like inclusions that produce silk and asterism. Star diopside normally has one straight visible line of the star with a second weaker, wavy line. To show the four-ray star requires two directions of needle alignment. The cutter has to orientate the material correctly so that the direction of the needles or fibers and the base of the cabochon align on the same plane. The cutter also needs to ensure that the star is centered on the stone. The needles can be magnetite, and this induces slight magnetism, or they can be rutile and/or ilmenite. Star diopside is inexpensive for a star stone. The primary source for dark green to black star stones is Southern India.

There is one other stone called violane in the Diopside family. It has white, gray, light blue, lilac, and purple colors, and is normally cut into cabochons and beads. The primary source is Italy and the USA—it is rare.

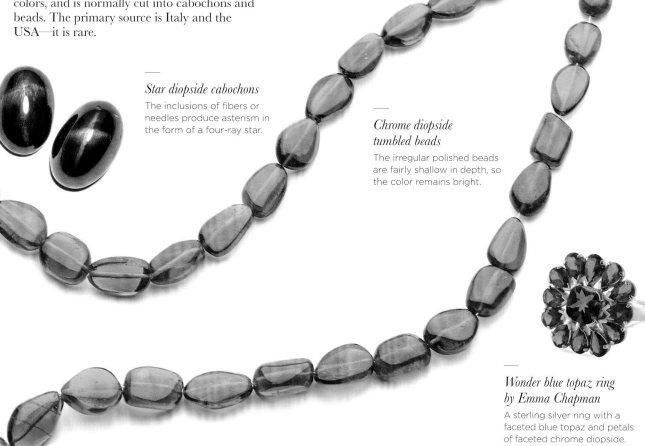

Star diopside cabochons

The inclusions of fibers or needles produce asterism in the form of a four-ray star.

Chrome diopside tumbled beads

The irregular polished beads are fairly shallow in depth, so the color remains bright.

Wonder blue topaz ring by Emma Chapman

A sterling silver ring with a faceted blue topaz and petals of faceted chrome diopside.

TURQUOISE

Turquoise has a distinct sky-blue to greenish-blue turquoise color and is usually opaque. It feels light in weight and often contains host rock or spider's web veins.

Turquoise was one of the first gems to be mined—Persian deposits have been worked for approximately 3,000 years and it was found in Tutankhamun's tomb in Egypt, which dates to 5500 BC. It was introduced into Europe during the 16th century via Turkey—hence the name.

The color range is intense sky-blue to blue-green to apple-green, depending on the amount of iron and copper in the composition. If the turquoise is interspersed with black, gray, or brown veins of the host rock or minerals, then it's often called turquoise matrix or spider's web turquoise. The most popular color is sky-blue, which is also called robin's egg blue and Persian blue.

Origin affects the color and durability of turquoise. Persian material from north-east Iran is a pure sky-blue or duck-egg blue. Persian material is very closely knit and doesn't require stabilizing. In the past, it was often engraved and inlaid with gold, and the carvings have survived for hundreds of years.

Turquoise from the USA often contains more iron, so it has a greenish color, but Sleeping Beauty turquoise from Arizona is an intense sky-blue. This is nearly mined out now, so the material is sought after.

Tibetan turquoise has become very popular and is a greener-colored variety. It is expensive and sold on the Internet, so be careful of misrepresentation.

Other sources are Mexico, Russia, China, Chile, Australia, Turkestan, Afghanistan, and Brazil.

Eilat stone (or pseudomalachite) is found in Eilat, Israel. This is a greenish-blue mix of chrysocolla, malachite, and turquoise with other copper minerals. Turquoise has a cryptocrystalline structure and this results in porosity; the gemstone is susceptible to body oils, solvents, and dirt, which alter the color, as does aging. Turquoise is opaque to semi-translucent. Size-wise, smaller stones

Persian cabochons

With exceptional color, this material is tightly knit so is suitable for carving, unlike most turquoise.

GEMMOLOGICAL INFORMATION

CRYSTAL SYSTEM Crystal habit is triclinic. Massive microcrystalline form in veins, and as nodules and crusts (botryoidal).

MOHS HARDNESS 6

REFRACTIVE INDEX 1.61–1.65

SPECIFIC GRAVITY/DENSITY 2.30–2.90

LUSTER Waxy to dull

CHEMICAL COMPOSITION Hydrated copper aluminum phosphate

COMMON TREATMENTS Stabilized with wax, plastic, or resin to make the stone less crumbly and maintain its looks.

OPTICAL PROPERTIES Nothing unusual

CUTTING AND STONE CUTS A fragile gemstone, with conchoidal fracture. Very porous, which can lead to fading and cracking. It is carved, cabbed, and cut in bead form. Extra care needs to be taken of turquoise jewelry, as it will absorb creams and perfumes. Gently wash off perspiration and cosmetics after wearing. Avoid ultrasonic cleaners.

IMITATIONS/SYNTHETICS Stained howlite, limestone, chalcedony, glass, and enamel. Also dyed magnesite, variscite, or glass. Lab-grown synthetic turquoise is on the market. In 1972, French company Gilson made imitation glass-based turquoise.

NOT TO BE CONFUSED WITH... Dyed howlite, dyed chalcedony, Andean blue opal, amazonite/microcline, glass imitations.

Rough turquoise with matrix

This shows a nodular microcrystalline form, which is common for turquoise.

Underside of Persian cabs

These stones have deliberately been left in their natural state so that they can be identified as natural material; not treated, reconstituted, or made of glass.

are plentiful, but large, 15-carat-plus pieces are more difficult to find. Common inclusions are metallic pyrite and calcite.

Turquoise is enhanced using oil, paraffin, colors, or copper salt. It is possible to check if turquoise is dyed using a small dab of acetone (nail-polish remover)—if the color comes off, then the stone is dyed. This won't happen if the turquoise has been coated or stabilized.

For decades, turquoise has been impregnated with wax, plastics, and polymers to enhance the durability, color, and luster. The Zachery treatment decreases the porosity, so the stone takes a better polish, and enhances the blue.

Since 2008, composite turquoise has been sold; powdered turquoise is bonded with a glass or plastic polymer and then colored to make a reconstituted material. Some of it has veins or a matrix composed of a gold-colored polymer with actual fragments that resemble pyrite or marcasite. One of the names for this composite is neolite.

Slabs and reconstituted cabochon
A pair of Chinese slabs in duck-egg blue with silvery inclusions. On the right is a reconstituted cabochon. It has been given spider's web inclusions and color so it is a desirable sky-blue.

Victorian serpent necklace, c.1850
The flexible, tapering, yellow-gold body of this fine Victorian necklace is formed of three rows of scale-like, collet-set turquoise cabochons. The head is decorated with rose-cut diamond brows, garnet eyes, and yellow-gold teeth. Approximate length: 16in (40cm); gross weight: 48.43 grams

LAPIS LAZULI

Used as a pigment for ultramarine oil paints for hundreds of years, lapis lazuli has a gorgeous deep or intense blue color. Lapis lazuli is one of the most important opaque blue gemstones in existence, and the name simply means "blue stone" in Arabic and Latin.

Lapis lazuli is a rock that is comprised of up to five different minerals, including lazurite, sodalite, hauyne, calcite, and pyrite. There is a 25 to 40 percent lazurite content, making the tone of the color vary from greenish-blue to violet-blue in medium to dark tones with low to high saturation. The blue comes from sulfur coloring agents. In general, lapis lazuli is an intense deep blue, with brassy, yellow pyrite inclusions, and spotted or striated with white calcite. If there are a lot of pyrite inclusions, then the lapis will take on a greenish color. However, the best color for lapis lazuli is an even and saturated blue with no pyrites.

Historically, the best lapis lazuli comes from Afghanistan, where it has been mined since the 7th millennium BC. The Ancient Egyptians used it alongside turquoise in the gold funeral mask of Tutankhamun.

The other sources of lapis lazuli are Russia and China (a pale blue color), the USA (California and Colorado have dark blue deposits), Chile, Myanmar, Tajikistan, India, and Pakistan.

Lapis lazuli cabochon

This cab has brassy pyrite and streaky white calcite inclusions. Lapis contains up to five different minerals, so it has various crystal systems and chemical compositions.

GEMMOLOGICAL INFORMATION

CRYSTAL SYSTEM Various. Lapis lazuli is found in boulders or within limestone.

MOHS HARDNESS 5.5

REFRACTIVE INDEX 1.50 (average)

SPECIFIC GRAVITY/DENSITY 2.80

LUSTER Vitreous to greasy

CHEMICAL COMPOSITION Rock containing lazurite and other minerals.

COMMON TREATMENTS Dyed and impregnated with wax or plastic for stability, color, and luster. Reconstituted.

OPTICAL PROPERTIES Nothing specific

CUTTING AND STONE CUTS Carvings and gemstones.

IMITATIONS/SYNTHETICS Lazurite imitations, as well as dyed magnesite, jasper, howlite, and sodalite.

NOT TO BE CONFUSED WITH... Zurite, sodalite, pietersite, hawk's eye quartz, charoite.

Burmese raw stone

A polished slice displaying parallel streaky inclusions of pyrites and calcite. It is commonly found in boulders and within limestone deposits.

24kt gold and silver cufflinks by Josef Koppmann

Rectangular lapis lazuli slabs mounted in a protective bezel setting.

Mary Rose lapis lazuli earrings by Milena Kovanovic

Oval lapis lazuli cabochons are set in gold-plated silver with a border of seed pearls.

There are a number of treatments for lapis lazuli, which have differing results. It is often dyed to improve the color, but the dye isn't particularly stable and so the stone fades. You can check for dyeing by wiping a cotton swab soaked with acetone (nail-polish remover) in a discreet area. If blue comes off, then the stone is dyed. Dye is used to disguise the white patches of calcite and then the lapis is coated with a colorless wax to stabilize the material, hide any cracks, and prevent the dye from rubbing off. Lapis lazuli is also heated to a red heat to intensify the color of pale blue material and so yield a fine, dark blue.

Imitations of lapis lazuli are plentiful, using stained and dyed minerals such as jasper, magnesite, howlite, and sodalite. Frenchman Pierre Gilson produced an imitation in the 1970s that had a similar composition to the natural material. In addition, there is a glass or paste imitation on the market which contains tiny inclusions of copper. Reconstituted lapis lazuli exists, in which powdered lapis is mixed with a PVA or glue-type substance and then re-formed into stones and beads.

Art Deco lapis lazuli and diamond stick pin by La Loche
This pin is mounted with a marbled lapis lazuli carving of a Buddha, which has a rose-cut diamond-set coronet.

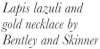

Lapis lazuli and gold necklace by Bentley and Skinner
A necklace of lapis lazuli round beads interspersed with frosted gold beads.

Lapis lazuli
This is very fine Afghan material, a saturated ultramarine blue that is evenly spread and free of inclusions. The best quality should be pure blue.

OBSIDIAN AND TEKTITE

Obsidian is a dark brown to black stone, which shows various optical effects as it is moved. It can have subtle green and purple banding, or a gold or silver metallic sheen.

Natural glass, or tektite, is formed from volcanic lava that cooled too quickly for crystallization to occur. It's not considered a mineral, as the composition is too complex and there's no crystal structure. It's been used since prehistoric times to make tools, weapons, masks, and mirrors. The sharp glass edge of obsidian provided arrows, blades, and scalpels.

OBSIDIAN can be black, gray, brown, orange, and, rarely, green, blue, or red. The dark body is due to the presence of iron and magnesium, and the color can be uniform, striped, or spotted. Often the dark color has speckled effects, which are caused by tiny gas bubbles. Banding is caused by the solidification of flowing lava—it cools at different rates, leading to banding.

Common types of obsidian are mottled (snowflake and peanut obsidian), banded or veined (mahogany or midnight lace), pebbles or nodules (Apache Tears), sheen and cat's-eye obsidian (gold or silver aventurescence), rainbow and flame obsidian (blue, violet, green, gold and silver iridescence from augitic pyroxene or magnetite crystal layers).

The inclusions can give a metallic sheen to the stone and internal bubbles or cristobalite crystals produce a snowflake appearance, hence snowflake obsidian. They also produce iridescence and color flashes. Other inclusions are acicular (needle-like) gas bubbles, teardrop-shaped bubbles, transparent rods of sillimanite (in Chilean material), and orange spessartite inclusions (also Chilean).

Deposits relate to volcanic activity. Sources are Hawaii, Japan, Java, Iceland, Hungary, Italy (Lipari Islands), Russia, Mexico, Ecuador, Guatemala, and the USA—Arizona and New Mexico (nodules called Apache Tears).

GEMMOLOGICAL INFORMATION

CRYSTAL SYSTEM There is no crystal system—it is amorphous. Its habit or shape can be tektites.

MOHS HARDNESS 5.0–5.5

REFRACTIVE INDEX 1.45–1.55

SPECIFIC GRAVITY/DENSITY 2.35–2.60

LUSTER Vitreous. Transparent to opaque.

CHEMICAL COMPOSITION Siliceous glassy rock, mainly silicon dioxide.

COMMON TREATMENTS None

OPTICAL PROPERTIES Chatoyance, aventurescence, and iridescence.

CUTTING AND STONE CUTS No cleavage, with conchoidal fracture. Polishes to a smooth, glassy finish. Tektites are faceted, but have no brilliance.

IMITATIONS/SYNTHETICS None

NOT TO BE CONFUSED WITH... Hematite, wolframite, jet, green diopsides, green moldavite.

Sheen obsidian cabochon by R. Holt & Co. (top)

This stone displays aventurescence; inclusions of tiny gas bubbles produce the sheen.

Raw black obsidian from Armenia (left)

This is common dark gray to black translucent obsidian that has been used as a mirror and a sharp cutting tool over the centuries. It is amorphous with a conchoidal fracture.

*24kt gold obsidian and diamond
necklace by Josef Koppmann*

Koppmann has paired intense black obsidian
with brilliant-cut white diamonds, embedding the
diamonds into each section of obsidian.

TEKTITE or natural glass was first found in 1787 in the Moldau River, in Czechoslovakia, so it was called Moldavite. This is the only locality in which tektites are found. Tektites are translucent and green to brown in color, with an uneven, rough outer skin that has a lumpy, scarred texture. Inclusions are round or torpedo-shaped with bubbles or swirls. The button shapes formed that way as they cooled.

The origin of tektites is uncertain; it's been suggested that they are either from outer space, melting as they passed through the Earth's atmosphere, hence the shape and texture, or that they are the result of a large meteorite hitting the ground, causing nearby rocks to melt and scatter, and form scarred deposits as they cooled.

Carved tektite, natural glass

A curious piece, this transparent tektite from
the Libyan desert has been hand carved into an
Egyptian scarab.

*Snowflake obsidian rough material
(left) and carving of a cat*

This variety of obsidian has internal bubbles or
cristobalite inclusions that produce the white
"snowflakes." It is widely available and inexpensive.

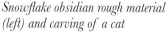

Rainbow obsidian

A fine specimen of rainbow obsidian,
displaying bands of yellowish-green and
purple-blue. The specimen has been cut
to show off the color and banding to best
effect.

SPHENE

Sphene always causes a stir—it has higher dispersion than a diamond and the resulting fire is unmistakable! As well as high dispersion and strong fire, sphene also has a rich body color. However, it is brittle and so not always ideal for jewelry. The color ranges from colorless to yellow to green to brown to blue to rose-red and black. The crystal is often color-zoned, so both buyers and cutters need to pay attention. The color correlates to the iron content—green and yellow stones are low in iron, while brown and blue gems are the result of a high iron content. Chrome sphene occurs when chromium impurities are present as the crystal forms: a gorgeous intense chrome sphene—sometimes called Mexican emerald—is found in the USA. Sphene is also titanium-rich, which is why it's called titanite (due to the titanium content). Deposits of a rare color-change sphene have been found in Afghanistan and Pakistan, but this is not readily available.

Sphene comes in large sizes, up to 20 carats, but the stones will be included. Typical inclusions are feathers, crystals, needles, fingerprints, and zoning. Sphene exhibits strong trichroism (pleochroism), showing three different color directions. It is also birefringent (doubly refractive), which means it's possible to see the doubling of the back facets in the pavilion. It has an adamantine luster as well!

The pricing of sphene depends on the color—yellow and brown stones are affordable, but greens become more expensive, especially the chrome-green stones.

Cutting sphene can be difficult. Aside from mapping the inclusions, the cutter also needs to plan the orientation for the best color, assess the cleavage planes, aim for correct proportions for the fire, and try to achieve an adamantine luster—it is very difficult to polish. Round brilliant cuts show the stone off well.

In most cases, it's not possible to check the refractive index of sphene as it's too high to get a reading using typical RI fluid.

The sources of sphene are Austria, Canada, Switzerland, Madagascar, Mexico, the USA, Sri Lanka, and Brazil. Deposits have also been found in Pakistan, Afghanistan, Burma, India, and Russia.

GEMMOLOGICAL INFORMATION

CRYSTAL SYSTEM Monoclinic. Wedge-shaped ends. Well-formed, flattened prismatic crystals and massive forms.

MOHS HARDNESS 5.0–5.5

REFRACTIVE INDEX 1.84–2.02 (brilliance and dispersion)

SPECIFIC GRAVITY/DENSITY 3.53

LUSTER Resinous and adamantine.

CHEMICAL COMPOSITION Calcium titanium silicate

COMMON TREATMENTS Heated for color enhancement.

OPTICAL PROPERTIES Moderate to strong pleochroism—pale yellow/brownish and yellow/orange-brown. High dispersion. Birefringence. Rare color change.

CUTTING AND STONE CUTS Heat sensitive. Ideally, stones should be faceted to show off the dispersion and birefringence. Difficult to polish. Distinct cleavage in one direction and conchoidal fracture.

IMITATIONS/SYNTHETICS None

NOT TO BE CONFUSED WITH... Grossular garnet, zircon.

Faceted sphene

An amber sphene displaying strong dispersion, acicular inclusions, and the doubling of back facets.

Faceted sphenes (top)

These yellow and green sphenes all display the gemstone's property of dispersion and fire.

APATITE

Apatite can have the color of a paraiba tourmaline, but it will be small and soft. Extra care needs to be taken in polishing and setting this gemstone—check for chips on the facet edges.

Apatites are bright stones with strong colors. They can be colorless, green, blue, brown, yellow, purple, violet, gray, and pink. Spanish apatite is called "asparagus stone" due to its light green color. Blue Burmese apatite is dichroic: one direction is colorless and the other is blue. Rare violet apatite comes from Germany, Portugal, and Maine, in the USA.

Apatite can be opaque to transparent. Typical inclusions in apatite are healed fractures and hollow growth tubes. These fibrous inclusions produce chatoyance or cat's eyes in a cabochon cut; they are rare and valuable. Blue apatite from Sri Lanka and Myanmar is chatoyant, while Brazil produces green cat's-eye stones. Tanzanian chatoyant apatite is so intense that it resembles the valuable chrysoberyl cat's eyes. The discovery of neon blue-green fluorapatites in Madagascar has raised the profile of apatite as a jewelry stone. The stones are sought after not only for their beautiful color, but for their striking fluorescence as well. Violet fluorapatite also fluoresces.

Blue apatite is normally small in size, approximately 1 to 2 carats; on rare occasions, Myanmar produces blue apatite in 10-carat sizes. Yellow apatite from Mexico can cut to 15 carats. The rarest and smallest apatite is violet and they are under 2 carats. Clean blue-green stones are mainly under 5 carats. Green can be very large and yellow cat's eyes can range up to 15 carats and green up to 20 carats.

Apatite usually comes in a mixed cut or a step cut, both to show off the color and for durability. Cutting apatite requires skill as it is so brittle; it's easy to chip facet edges as you work on them. Apatite beads can be problematic; the stringing process can lead to damage and, as the knotting is tightened, any cracked beads will break.

The main sources for gem-quality apatite are Brazil, Canada, India, the USA (Maine), and Mexico. Other sources are Russia, East Africa, Sweden, Germany, Portugal, and Spain.

GEMMOLOGICAL INFORMATION

CRYSTAL SYSTEM Hexagonal. Usually prismatic or stubby with pyramidal ends. Massive, granular, and compact.

MOHS HARDNESS 4–5

REFRACTIVE INDEX 1.598–1.667

SPECIFIC GRAVITY/DENSITY 3.10–3.35

LUSTER Vitreous in crystals

CHEMICAL COMPOSITION Calcium phosphate. Most gem apatite is the fluorapatite variety.

COMMON TREATMENTS Heating can improve the color for blue and blue-green stones.

OPTICAL PROPERTIES Chatoyance. Pleochroism—blue-green stones have blue/yellow. Luminescence. Fluorescence appears in some stones.

CUTTING AND STONE CUTS Poor cleavage with conchoidal fracture. Very heat sensitive. Avoid rough handling.

IMITATIONS/SYNTHETICS Synthesized, but only for medical research.

NOT TO BE CONFUSED WITH... Tourmaline, chrysoberyl cat's eye.

Cat's eye apatite (top)
Light hitting the internal fibers and hollow growth tubes of this cabochon has created chatoyance.

Raw stone
Translucent material with prismatic crystal habit.

Blue apatite necklace with diamond rondelles
The necklace is made from the most popular color of apatite, blue. The faceted gem rondelles are interspersed with diamond-set gold beads.

CHRYSOCOLLA

Chrysocolla has a unique, opaque, greenish-blue color with interesting patterns. Its distinctive greasy luster and the fact that it's very soft can help with identification.

Chrysocolla is prized for its color and unusual multicolored patterns. It is generally found in bright greenish-blue to cyan-blue to green colors as a microcrystalline crust or a compact botryoidal (grape-like) form. It occurs with copper deposits or is mixed with copper carbonates such as malachite or turquoise. Chrysocolla has inclusions of brown copper ore. It is nearly always opaque and when polished has an attractive greasy to vitreous luster.

Chrysocoalla belongs to a small group of copper-bearing gems, which includes malachite, azurite, larimar, smithsonite, variscite, Oregon sunstone, paraiba tourmaline, and turquoise. These stones can be easily confused with each other because they have similar colors and luster.

Fine blue chrysocolla is very crumbly in its pure form and so needs to be in a mix to be workable. Blue-green Eilat stone (or pseudomalachite) contains a mix of chrysocolla, malachite, turquoise, and other materials, and is hard enough to cut.

Chrysocolla with clear, druzy quartz crystals on the surface is also suitable for jewelry. Often, the chrysocolla crystals intergrow with quartz or opal, or form a gel with silica that hardens to a workable chrysocolla-chalcedony. Stellarite is a trade name for a light blue mixture of chrysocolla and quartz. Parrot wing is a mix of chrysocolla and jasper with a brownish-green appearance.

Chrysocolla is commonly treated with a coating of colorless resin to stabilize the stone and make it easier to cut. It is also a difficult stone to set, so needs soft fine silver or a high-carat gold for the collet or setting. Avoid mechanical cleaning such as ultrasonic cleaners. Instead, use a soft toothbrush with detergent and warm water. Store your chrysocolla separately to other jewelry in order to avoid scratches and damage.

Chrysocolla is usually found in locations where copper is mined, such as in Chile, Russia, and Zaire. The main sources include Israel, the Congo (Zaire), Chile, England, Mexico, Peru, Russia, and the USA. Arizona is known to produce some of the best chrysocolla available. Chrysocolla is often bought by collectors as specimens, so it does have a value.

GEMMOLOGICAL INFORMATION

CRYSTAL SYSTEM Monoclinic—crystals are microscopic in aggregates; cryptocrystalline.

MOHS HARDNESS 2–3

REFRACTIVE INDEX 1.46–1.63

SPECIFIC GRAVITY/DENSITY 2.20

LUSTER Greasy/waxy to vitreous

CHEMICAL COMPOSITION Hydrated copper silicate

COMMON TREATMENTS Not treated

OPTICAL PROPERTIES Nothing specific

CUTTING AND STONE CUTS Very soft

IMITATIONS/SYNTHETICS There are simulants on the market such as chalcedonies dyed to resemble chrysysocollas.

NOT TO BE CONFUSED WITH... Malachite, gem silica, turquoise.

Chrysocolla cabochon (top)

Typical green color with small blue patches; the beads also contain brown copper ore inclusions because chrysocolla is found alongside copper deposits.

Chrysocolla beads (left)

A row of 8mm diameter beads with lovely blue-green colors and a few brownish inclusions.

Chrysocolla raw stone by R. Holt & Co.

This stone is comprised of microscopic crystals in an aggregate.

RHODOCHROSITE

Rhodochrosite can be identified as a pink and white banded material that's carved as a decorative stone. There is also a beautiful, translucent, pink gem that resembles the flesh of a watermelon.

The name rhodochrosite comes from the Greek word for "rose-colored." It became commercially available from about 1940.

The colors range from pale pink to rose-red to deep pink to orange-red to yellowish and brown. Rhodochrosite occurs as massive opaque to silky translucent material. Fine gemmy crystals are occasionally faceted, but the fine-grained, pink and white banded stone is more common. The pink comes from manganese impurities; indeed, rhodochrosite is found in veins associated with manganese—copper, silver, and lead deposits. The calcium in the composition of rhodochrosite reduces the refractive index and specific gravity, while iron and zinc increase them.

Rhodochrosite is birefringent, so the doubling of the back facets is pronounced. The stone is very sensitive to heat, and the perfect cleavage and softness can make it difficult to cut and set. It's a good idea to design a protective setting and talk to your customer about the durability of this stone. It's not really suitable for rings, so pendants and earrings are more practical. Size-wise, 2 to 4 carats is average for faceted stones, while banded opaque material can be as large as 20 carats or more.

The oldest source of rhodochrosite banded material is Argentina; it was called Inca rose. The USA is now the main producer. Large faceted gemstones are rare, but they do come out of South Africa from time to time. Colorado, in the USA, produces very fine pink gem material, which is highly valued. Some Peruvian material is very fine, whereas Argentinian rough is opaque and less expensive. Mexico only produces small sizes. In Argentina's Catamarca Province, it's possible to find amazing carving material that has unusual fine patterns. Often, there are huge stalactites over 4ft (1.2m) long, which are sliced up or cut as carving material. Overall, the finest material is from Colorado, in the USA, or Africa.

Avoid using ultrasonic cleaners and chemicals with rhodochrosite as it is fragile. In addition, try to avoid polishing the metal once the stone has been set.

GEMMOLOGICAL INFORMATION

CRYSTAL SYSTEM Trigonal hexagonal. Habits are stalactites and massive compact.

MOHS HARDNESS 4

REFRACTIVE INDEX 1.578–1.84 (birefringent)

SPECIFIC GRAVITY/DENSITY 3.70 (heavy)

LUSTER Pearly to vitreous

CHEMICAL COMPOSITION Manganese carbonate

COMMON TREATMENTS Wax or plastic impregnation.

OPTICAL PROPERTIES Fluorescence. Birefringence.

CUTTING AND STONE CUTS Perfect cleavage with uneven and conchiodal fracture. The stone can be faceted despite its softness.

IMITATIONS/SYNTHETICS Synthesized for research purposes.

NOT TO BE CONFUSED WITH... Rhodonite.

Two faceted rhodochrosites, marquise and kite (top)

These are beautiful transparent gems with a pretty orange-pink color.

Raw stone

This is the more common pink and white banded stone and is a cross-section of a stalactite. The banding, color, and density identify it.

Rhodochrosite marquise (left) and cabochon (far left)

The marquise is a clear coral. Using a loupe, it's possible to see the interlocking crystal structure. The cabochon is colored by manganese impurities.

FLUORITE

Also known as fluorspar.

Fluorite is recognizable for its great color range, producing multi-colored gemstones with attractive zoning. Its many optical properties also help with identification.

Fluorite has been recorded as a gemstone since 1530. For 1500 years, the English mined a banded fluorite called Blue John in Derbyshire; it was carved into vases and bowls. Fluorite has often been described as the most colorful mineral in the world and is frequently misrepresented.

The colors range from yellow to blue to pink to purple and green. Chemical impurities and natural irradiation contribute to all the colors. There is frequent color banding in both gem-grade and massive material with a patchy distribution of color.

Sometimes fluorite intergrows with other minerals. Canada produces banded violet material in a calcite mix, while in Switzerland very rare octahedral, pink fluorite crystals grow on quartz. Many varieties of fluorite display fluorescence under ultraviolet light; it's not a definitive identification of the gemstone, but it is strongly associated with this gem. Fluorescent material is typically blue, so Switzerland, as well as Illinois and New Hampshire in the USA, are potential locations for fluorescent fluorite. In some rare cases in Switzerland, color-change fluorite occurs—it shows blue in daylight and purple or lavender in incandescent light. Rare chrome fluorite is mined in Colombia.

Also, there's a variety of fluorite that's thermoluminescent. It emits a bright green to blue-green light when heated. This is called chlorophane.

Fluorite has perfect cleavage in two directions; when cleaved, it produces a prefect octahedron with smooth faces. Even though fluorite has a low refractive index, it still takes a high polish, so faceted stones are brilliant.

Crystals are large with good symmetry and clarity. Inclusions tend to be mineral crystals such as hematite, cavities, and healed fractures. Both faceted gems and cabochons are cut; however, care should be taken during cutting as fluorite has a habit of chipping. Because it's so soft, fluorite cabochons are sometimes capped with rock crystal for increased durability.

Store fluorite away from direct sunlight, as it may fade with prolonged exposure. Finally, never submerge fluorite in water because it is slightly soluble. Clean the stone with a damp cloth and toothbrush, and avoid ultrasonic cleaners.

Other sources of fluorite are Canada, the USA, South Africa, Thailand, Peru, Mexico, China, Poland, Hungary, the Czech Republic, Norway, and Germany.

GEMMOLOGICAL INFORMATION

CRYSTAL SYSTEM Cubic or isometric with cubic habit. Orderly crystals of octahedral and cubes. Also massive and granular.

MOHS HARDNESS 4

REFRACTIVE INDEX 1.43

SPECIFIC GRAVITY/DENSITY 3.18

LUSTER Vitreous. Transparent to translucent.

CHEMICAL COMPOSITION Calcium fluoride

COMMON TREATMENTS Irradiation with gamma rays to produce neon colors and change colors. Composite stones. Dyeing. Impregnation with resin for increased durability. Heat treatment to lighten colors. Coating.

OPTICAL PROPERTIES Strong fluorescence to blue/violet. Color change is rare.

CUTTING AND STONE CUTS Soft and difficult to facet because of the perfect cleavage in four directions.

IMITATIONS/SYNTHETICS Synthetics exist.

NOT TO BE CONFUSED WITH... Glass, feldspar, beryl, quartz, calcite, tourmaline, apatite.

Raw stone (top)
Fluorite crystals in matrix showing the cubic crystal habit, visible octahedral cleavage lines, and colour zoning.

Faceted briolettes
The briolettes display fluorite's beautiful colour banding and colour range.

MALACHITE

Malachite is unmistakable due to its color and banded appearance. Many people buy it as a decorative stone as well as a gemstone.

The first malachite deposits to be mined were in Egypt and Israel over 4,000 years ago, as part of the copper production in those regions. It was popular in Ancient Egypt, Greece, and Rome, and used for jewelry and also in powdered pigment form. The Russian Urals were heavily mined to produce huge amounts in the 1800s.

The color of malachite is a result of the copper in its composition, which means that it's an idiochromatic stone. The color is always green, ranging from pastel green to bright green to a very dark green that is almost black. Crystals are rare, but are bright green and translucent with a vitreous to adamantine luster. Unlike some other opaque green stones, this gemstone has a green color that doesn't fade over time or when exposed to light. This property has allowed it to be ground to a powder and used as a popular pigment and coloring agent. Opaque material polishes brightly to a vitreous luster. Malachite's high specific gravity makes it weigh heavy; this is due to it being a copper mineral and makes it easy to identify.

Malachite is soft with perfect cleavage, which limits its use for making jewelry. It is mainly cut as cabochons and slabs, used as an inlay material, or carved as a decorative stone to show off the color and reveal the concentric bands of light and dark green. It is sensitive to heat and reacts with acid, so care needs to be taken during the working process, including polishing. Malachite dust is toxic, so it should not be inhaled during cutting or polishing. It is often treated with paraffin wax to fill small pits or to improve the luster, and it is coated with epoxy resins in order to harden the material and make it more robust.

Malachite intergrows and mixes with other copper minerals such as azurite (to become azurmalachite), chrysocolla, turquoise, and pseudomalachite (Eilat stone). This can make identification difficult. It is found worldwide in copper-mining areas, but Zaire is the most important source, followed by the Congo, Namibia, Australia, France, and Arizona.

Two cabochon malachites

Malachite is usually cut as cabochons or slabs due to the softness of the material.

GEMMOLOGICAL INFORMATION

 CRYSTAL SYSTEM Monoclinic with acicular (needle-like) to tabular habits. Found as aggregates with a botryoidal form. Also stalactitic structure.

MOHS HARDNESS 4

REFRACTIVE INDEX 1.85 (average)

SPECIFIC GRAVITY/DENSITY 3.80 (heavy stone)

LUSTER Vitreous to silky. Fibrous habit is silky, while massive habit is dull to earthy.

CHEMICAL COMPOSITION Copper hydroxycarbonate

COMMON TREATMENTS Stabilized to make the stone less crumbly.

OPTICAL PROPERTIES Nothing specific

CUTTING AND STONE CUTS Perfect cleavage in one direction; fair in the second direction. Conchoidal fracture.

IMITATIONS/SYNTHETICS Synthetic malachite exists for making jewelry. Poor synthetics have an unnatural color and the banding is not the same as natural banding with concentric eyes.

NOT TO BE CONFUSED WITH Azurite, azurmalachite, Eilat stone, chrysocolla mixes.

Antique malachite bracelet by Lang

A rare 19th-century gold bracelet with oval plaques of green banded malachite.

Raw stone

Natural green banded malachite with copper ore matrix.

NATURAL FRESHWATER AND SALTWATER PEARLS

Natural pearls have a particularly beautiful depth of luster and each pearl is unique in color, shape, size, and luster. It's not really possible to identify an undrilled natural pearl without taking an X-ray. As larger pearls can have a considerable value, it's advisable to ask a laboratory to test a pearl.

Pearls are the oldest gems known to man and have been used as adornment since 3500 BC. The oldest surviving pearl necklace is approximately 2,000 years old. Pearls were popular because, unlike mineral gemstones, they didn't require cutting, faceting, or polishing. They were simply pierced. They were a symbol of wealth and power, and sought-after and prized by the Ancient Egyptians and Romans and other kingdoms. Over the centuries, lagoons and coastlines were plundered by the pearl-fishing industry until by the 1880s the lagoons were empty! The development of cultured pearls around 1920 allowed more people to wear them as jewelry, but prior to that most antique jewelry used natural pearls (or a man-made imitation). Sadly, the over-fishing of natural pearl beds, plus pollution, has meant that only a tiny number now remain.

Pearls are one of five organic gemstones that are created by living creatures or plants. In the case of pearls, bi-valve mollusks (oysters and mussels with two shells) create them as an immunity defense to protect themselves. An "intruder" is isolated either between the shell and the fleshy mantle or in the mantle itself. The outer skin, or epithelium, forms a sac around the intruder, encrusting it with nacre (mother of pearl) to produce a pearl. If the irritant is inside the mantle, the pearl will be round; if it's attached to the shell, the pearl shape will be baroque. Shapes, sizes, and occurrence vary, depending on the mollusk. A natural black Tahitian pearl occurs in one of every 10,000 to 15,000 mollusks. In the Persian Gulf, smaller white natural pearls are found in approximately one in every 40 oysters.

GEMMOLOGICAL INFORMATION

CRYSTAL SYSTEM Orthorhombic. An aggregate composed of tiny orthorhombic aragonite crystals and hexagonal calcite crystals.

MOHS HARDNESS 3–4 (pearls are soft, but very compact, so it is difficult to crush them).

REFRACTIVE INDEX 1.53–1.68

SPECIFIC GRAVITY/DENSITY 2.68–2.74

LUSTER Pearly

CHEMICAL COMPOSITION Calcium carbonate, conchiolin, and water.

COMMON TREATMENTS Cultured pearls are dyed, irradiated, bleached, and buffed.

OPTICAL PROPERTIES Light interference causes iridescence/the orient.

CUTTING AND STONE CUTS Sensitive to heat and chemicals.

IMITATIONS/SYNTHETICS See Imitation Pearls on page 178.

NOT TO BE CONFUSED WITH... Cultured freshwater pearls, cultured saltwater pearls.

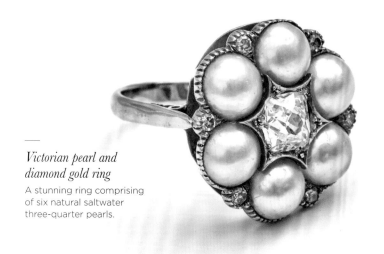

Victorian pearl and diamond gold ring
A stunning ring comprising of six natural saltwater three-quarter pearls.

Certified natural freshwater pearls
The surface quality and luster are excellent. To find a matching pair of natural pearls in this color, quality, and shape is rare.

Natural saltwater pearl varieties
Clockwise from top left: Pair of natural saltwater white-rose pearls; two natural black saltwater pearls; natural gold and white angelwing pearl; beautiful natural black saltwater baroque pearls.

A natural pearl is comprised of nacre (mother of pearl), which is transparent and colorless. The nacre is made of calcium carbonate in the form of aragonite hexagonal platelets. The micro-crystals are held together by a non-crystalline binding agent called conchiolin, which contains the pigment. The crystals form many concentric layers and the pearly luster is produced by the overlapping platelets and a film of conchiolin. When light enters the pearl, the layers cause interference and the light splits into spectral colors, resulting in iridescence, which is called luster or the orient.

THE COLORS ARE:
Saltwater: Cream to white, gray to purplish to black, yellow to golden.
Freshwater: Cream to white, lilac to purple, peach to pink to bronze.

SOURCES OF NATURAL PEARLS TODAY:
Saltwater: The warm waters either side of the equator... the Red Sea, Bahrain (Persian Gulf), the Caribbean, the Gulf of Mexico, Guatemala and Venezuela, the Gulf of Manaar (Indian Ocean between India and Sri Lanka).
Freshwater: Angelwing pearls from the Mississippi River, in the USA, Scottish river pearls, Ireland, France, and Germany. There are laws preventing people from taking pearl oysters from rivers.

1920s Art Deco natural pearl and diamond platinum sautoir
Saltwater pearls are riveted to mounts.

CULTURED SALTWATER PEARLS: AKOYA, SOUTH SEA, TAHITIAN, KESHI, CONCH, AND ABALONE

The traditional saltwater cultured pearl should be perfectly round and have a high luster. If the cultured pearl has a drill hole, then it is possible to see the nucleus and the depth of the nacre layer using a x10 magnification loupe.

In the early 1900s, there were very few natural pearl beds left and there were simply not enough pearls to meet demand. There was intense pressure to develop a reliable method of culturing round pearls, and a Japanese pearl producer, Mikimoto Kokichi, led the way. The first Japanese saltwater farms were founded in 1913 in southern Honshu and the first Mikimoto store was opened. However, it wasn't until 1920 that there were sufficient harvests of cultured pearls for them to become commercially available.

GEMMOLOGICAL INFORMATION

CRYSTAL SYSTEM Orthorhombic. Aggregates of tiny hexagonal aragonite platelets in concentric layers.

MOHS HARDNESS 3–4

REFRACTIVE INDEX 1.53–1.68

SPECIFIC GRAVITY/DENSITY 2.70–2.79

LUSTER Pearly

CHEMICAL COMPOSITION Calcium carbonate in the form of aragonite and an organic, non-crystalline horn substance called conchiolin.

COMMON TREATMENTS Dyeing and irradiating. Silver salts/nitrate treatment, plus bleaching, buffing, coating, and filling.

OPTICAL PROPERTIES Iridescence/the orient and luster.

CUTTING AND STONE CUTS Drilling of pearls for mounting on posts or stringing as necklaces. Damaged pearls are cut into half or three-quarter pearls.

IMITATIONS/SYNTHETICS See Imitation Pearls on page 178.

NOT TO BE CONFUSED WITH... Cultured freshwater pearls, natural pearls.

Saltwater South Sea pearl and diamond earrings by Bentley and Skinner
A pair of large silver-white cultured South Sea pearls of fine grade sit beneath an asymmetrical arrangement of diamonds.

Damaged cultured pearls
The cultured pearls have broken down, showing the mother of pearl bead nucleus and the nacre layer. This can happen if the pearls are badly farmed or cultured.

Freshwater (left) and saltwater
Akoya cultured pearls (far left)
The freshwater pearls are a good-quality
row with good luster, but the Akoya
pearls outshine them.

Saltwater Akoya cultured pearls   **173**
The white pearl has a fine mirror-like
luster, whereas the black has a lower
luster due to the fact that it is dyed. The
only natural black pearls are saltwater
Tahitians.

THE AKOYA oyster was chosen by the Japanese because it reliably produced a round pearl with good nacre, a high luster, and a smooth surface quality. A three-year-old oyster would be implanted with a number of mother-of-pearl beads, 6–7mm in diameter, which would grow to 7–8mm round pearls. The largest pearl that could be produced was 10mm in diameter. Using a large nucleus reduced the growing time in the oyster and minimized the risk of damage to the pearl. The Akoya mollusk produces approximately 0.35mm of nacre each year. The deeper the nacre layer, the better the luster and iridescence.

Mikimoto always kept the pearls in the mollusk for three years, while many of his competitors only allowed two years because of the risk of disease. Japanese Akoya pearls are always harvested in the winter months, as that is when the luster is best. Mikimoto only used the best pearls of the harvest, which equated to just 10 percent of the crop.

The natural Akoya color range is white with a rose or green overtone, cream to yellowish-gold, and natural blue-gray. Akoyas are dyed black and blue, and also sometimes treated with silver salts/nitrate to darken the nucleus. The treated black Akoyas don't have the luster of the natural colors and the blues can be inconsistent.

The pearl sizes are 2.5–10mm in diameter. The very small sizes cost more because they are difficult to farm and process. Large sizes are also expensive as the mollusk dies and there's a greater investment of time. The shapes are full round, off-round, and semi-baroque. The Japanese led the way in producing fine cultured pearls, but the Chinese came into the market relatively recently and are now also farming saltwater cultured pearls.

Akoya colors
From left: Akoya pearls enhanced blue; natural
brownish-gray pearls; and natural gray pearls.
All three rows have a full round shape and the high
luster typical of the Akoya mollusk.

SOUTH SEA and TAHITIAN pearl farms are based in the warm waters of Australia, the Cooke Islands, Indonesia, French Polynesia, and Tahiti. Saltwater Tahitian and South Sea pearls are bigger than Akoyas, as the oyster is larger and they spend three to five years in the shell.

The color range of these pearls is silver-white, light yellow to deep golden, and gray to black. Tahitian pearls are the only natural black pearls you can buy. The color of Tahitian and South Sea pearls has two components: the body color and the overtones (or iridescence). Gray and black Tahitian pearls can have pink, green, and blue overtones. The white South Sea pearl usually has a silver overtone. Golden South Sea pearls can have a light yellowish-gold to intense deep gold body color. The more intense the color, the more expensive the pearls become. Golden pearls are often dyed, so be careful.

Tahitian and South Sea pearls start at approximately 9mm in diameter and go up to 15–16mm diameter in a row. You will pay a premium for pearls with a diameter above 14mm. Some baroque-shaped pearls can be as large as 20mm.

The range of shapes is full round, off-round, oval, button, drop, circled, semi-baroque, and baroque. Full rounds carry a premium as only 5 percent of the South Sea and Tahitian pearl harvest has that shape. Well-proportioned drop shapes are also difficult to find, especially as a pair, so they can cost more. The baroque and semi-baroque shapes grow attached to the shell; they are more plentiful, so are cheaper, and the irregular form emphasizes their high luster.

Surface quality can vary from small pits to large blemishes, holes, circles, and cracks. The odd pit is not serious, but larger flaws can weaken the pearl. You don't want to see the nucleus, while cracks in the nacre will affect durability over time.

The reason rows of Tahitian and South Sea pearls are expensive is that it is difficult to find matching pearls of the same size, shape, body color, and overtone. The investment of time in growing the pearls also adds to the price. Common treatments are dyeing and irradiation to darken the nucleus and make the color more intense.

Golden South Sea pearls (above)

The color intensity of a golden South Sea pearl will affect the price. Of these four, the smallest has the best color.

South Sea pearl shapes (top)

The shape also affects the value. Here, the full-round white pearl has the highest value.

Tahitian pearls: body and overtone colors

The large 15mm full-round Tahitian pearl has a dark gray body with strong blue-green overtones, the 12mm gray pearl has a silvery-green overtone, and the small 10mm full-round pearl has a medium gray body with very strong pink and green overtones.

Two rows of Tahitian pearls

The top row of drop-shaped pearls is the finer grade, with a better surface quality, distinct overtones, and high luster. The lower row of Tahitians has a semi-baroque shape, the pearls are circled, the luster is not so intense, and the overtones are less distinct.

*Row of saltwater
Tahitian Keshi pearls*

The pearls have grown spontaneously without a nucleus. The luster is very good as the nacre layer is thick and the row has a mix of colors and overtones.

*Golden South Sea pearl and
diamond ring in 18kt gold*

The golden pearl is secured by two curved prongs that split from the band, one of which is set with small, brilliant-cut diamonds.

Akoya Keshi pearls

Three white Akoya keshi pearls from Japan displaying an amazing luster and surface quality. They have a baroque shape.

SALTWATER KESHI PEARLS grow spontaneously in the Akoya or Tahitian/South Sea mollusks while a cultured pearl is growing. They are, as such, natural pearls because they have no nucleus. They are the same colors as the cultured pearls, but are a plump baroque shape and have a fabulous luster. They range in size from 2.5mm up to 17mm. They are rare, difficult to source, and valuable.

SALTWATER CONCH and **ABALONE PEARLS** come from large marine snails. They are very rare and always natural; they cannot be implanted with a nucleus, as they bleed to death when the mantle is cut. They appear in Art Nouveau and Art Deco jewelry pieces and are valuable.

Conch (left) and abalone pearls

The pearly layer of the conch is made of concentric layers of fibrous calcium, which produce a flame structure or pattern. Abalones come in all sorts of shapes and sizes, but always have rich coloration.

CULTURED FRESHWATER PEARLS AND MABE PEARLS

The Chinese are now producing the majority of cultured freshwater pearls on the market. These can normally be identified by their size, shape, color, and luster; they don't have the nacre quality and shape of saltwater pearls.

CULTURED FRESHWATER PEARLS are much cheaper than saltwater varieties. They are cultured in rivers, ponds, and lakes, and were introduced by the Japanese who grew them in Lake Biwa, in Japan. Biwa pearls had exceptional luster and unusual non-round shapes but, unfortunately, pollution stopped the farming. The Chinese now dominate the market and are culturing freshwater pearls much more quickly; they can have as little as eight months in the shell.

The natural colors of freshwater pearls are cream to white, pink to peach, lavender to violet, yellowish-green, and golden-orange to copper. They do not occur in gray or black naturally; both of these colors are dyed.

Freshwater pearls are rarely round; they are nucleated with mantle tissue or beads and come in a wide variety of shapes. It took some time to culture round freshwater pearls due to the type of freshwater mollusks. There are ovals, button shapes, sticks, disks, and coins, cornflake and keshi-type shapes, plus potato and rice pearls. Rice pearls have a wrinkled appearance as they are cultured in large quantities for only eight to ten months. There's no space for the

GEMMOLOGICAL INFORMATION

CRYSTAL SYSTEM Orthorhombic. Aggregates of tiny hexagonal aragonite platelets in concentric layers.

MOHS HARDNESS 3–4

REFRACTIVE INDEX 1.53–1.68

SPECIFIC GRAVITY/DENSITY 2.68 (average)

LUSTER Pearly

CHEMICAL COMPOSITION Calcium carbonate in the form of aragonite and an organic, non-crystalline horn substance called conchiolin.

COMMON TREATMENTS Dyeing and irradiation. Pearls are irradiated to darken the nucleus and then dyed. Irradiation can result in a bluish-colored bloom. Dyeing can make pearls all look the same color, while normally there's a variation in body color and overtones.

OPTICAL PROPERTIES Iridescence/the orient and luster.

CUTTING AND STONE CUTS Drilling of pearls to mount on posts or for stringing as necklaces. Pearls with damaged areas are cut into half or three-quarter pearls.

IMITATIONS/SYNTHETICS See Imitation Pearls on page 178.

NOT TO BE CONFUSED WITH... Saltwater cultured pearls and natural saltwater and freshwater pearls.

Dyed freshwater pearls

From top: Light gray pearls with pasty low luster areas; copper-colored potato pearls with dye deposits in pitted area; and long baroque pearls that have been dyed to a teal blue color.

"A" grade freshwater cultured pearl buttons (top)

These pearls have a super mirror-like luster in a natural lavender pink. The excellent surface quality and luster are due to a very good nacre layer.

Freshwater Biwa
pearl necklace

Biwa pearls were put into the mollusk twice for a better shape and luster.

Biwa sticks

Typical Biwa sticks that are chunky with a good nacre layer.

mollusk to turn them, so the nacre layer is poor and the surface quality is heavily marked. Potato pearls are large in size, but irregular in shape, with flat patches due to overcrowding. There's a lack of nutrients because of the overcrowding and, as a result, the quality of nacre is poor. These pearls are often circled and pitted due to the short growing time.

It is possible to source high-grade freshwater pearls where the surface quality, luster, and color are very fine. They are sometimes called Orient pearls.

In general, freshwater pearls are less than 12mm in size. Non-nucleated seed pearls are about 2mm, with nucleated off-rounds measuring 3–12mm. It's possible to find very large 17mm to 20mm baroque shapes, but they can have dull pasty areas with little luster.

Freshwater pearls do not usually have the longevity of saltwater pearls. The growing methods and dyeing process reduce their lifespan, as the nacre layer is thin, and dyed pearls will also discolor over time.

MABE PEARLS are composite freshwater pearls; the nucleus is attached to the inner shell of the mollusk so that a hemispherical pearl is grown. At harvest, they are cut out from the shell, filled with wax, and backed with mother of pearl. They are not very robust because the nacre layers can lift off.

Oval, pear, and round
freshwater mabe pearls

Different shapes can be produced by attaching a different-shaped nucleus to the shell.

Potato and rice pearls

From top: Dyed copper-colored rice pearls; dyed peacock potato pearls; and dyed peacock rice pearls.

IMITATION PEARLS

Imitation pearls have been with us since Ancient Roman times. They can usually be spotted by their surface quality or texture and the lack of nacre. Use a loupe to inspect drill holes if possible.

Faux or imitation pearls go back thousands of years; the Ancient Romans produced Roman pearls made of glass with iridescent foils. In the Middle Ages, such was the popularity of pearls that homemade pearl recipes using egg white, dew, and snail slime were used. In the late 1600s, Jaquin of Paris received a royal warrant from Louis XIV for glass pearls, which were coated with *essence d'Orient* (fish scales and varnish). His basic method was used until the 1950s in the form of Japan pearls by US jewelry designers, Miriam Haskell and Stanley Hagler. A French company, Maison Gripoix, made hand-poured glass pearls for Chanel and Dior's costume jewelry ranges from the 1920s onward. We now have glass faux pearls that are coated with a modern, synthetic *essence d'Orient*!

CHECKLIST: HOW TO SPOT A FAUX PEARL

Surface quality—when looked at with a x10 magnification loupe, a real pearl has a very smooth surface, while faux pearls have a stippled, slightly granular surface quality.

Weight—real pearls are dense and feel heavy. Often, faux pearls are light in weight, especially if made from plastic.

Drill holes—there should be a sharp edge to the drill hole and a tubular hole. Faux glass pearls have a conical hole that flares at the top, and is often surrounded by a couple of ridges.

Nacre layer—real pearls have a visible nacre layer that looks approximately 3mm thick when viewed through a loupe. Glass pearls only have a very thin coating of lacquer that often rubs off, leaving the glassy surface.

Knotting—good pearls are usually knotted to protect them from rubbing against each other; faux pearls are not normally knotted, so they do rub against each other.

The clasp—on faux pearls the clasp is usually silver or a base metal with paste stones. Quality clasps aren't used on costume jewelry.

The tooth test—don't do this, as it will damage the dealer's pearls and can also give you hepatitis!

A pair of 1970s glass emerald and pearl earrings by Henkel and Grosse

The cream glass pearls in these earrings are in mint condition.

Faux pearl and crystal bracelet by Miriam Haskell

These glass "Japan pearls" were coated with 18 layers of *essence d'Orient* and polished between layers so they have the quality of luster and weight of real pearls.

NOBLE/PRECIOUS CORAL, SEA BAMBOO, AND SPONGE CORAL

Noble/precious coral also known as corallium rubrum.

Coral is well known for its red and pink colors. It also has a distinct pattern in the coral branches—like striped wood grain. Don't confuse coral with dyed sea bamboo and sponge coral.

NOBLE/PRECIOUS CORAL has a long history; it's been found in Neolithic graves and has been used and carved by the Chinese for over 2,000 years. It has a long tradition of use for medicinal and talismanic purposes.

Precious coral is an organic gemstone; it is an animal, not a plant. It forms on rocky seabeds in dark environments over 500ft (152m) deep. The coral is built slowly by tiny marine animals called polyps, which are soft-bodied creatures that form hard shells. These accumulate as the colony grows and form branches like a tree. The deeper the reef, the darker red the coloration. Coral often has a white core of calcium carbonate in the form of aragonite or calcite, which is covered in polyps connected by living tissue. This in turn is covered in algae, which gives the coral its color. It is a symbiotic relationship. Coral has a very slow growth rate of approximately 1mm per year.

The colors of coral are deep ox-blood red (Moro), deep red (Sardegna), salmon-pink (Momo), pale pink (Angel-skin), white, and blue, which are colored by the organic material carotenoid. Uniform color is desirable, but coral frequently has whitish streaks and spots.

Fine natural Sardegna (Sardinian) coral

The pendeloques are an intense red that is the most sought-after color. They have a high value and are difficult to source.

GEMMOLOGICAL INFORMATION

CRYSTAL SYSTEM Trigonal. Microcrystalline habit. Organic gemstone.

MOHS HARDNESS 3–4

REFRACTIVE INDEX 1.48–1.66

SPECIFIC GRAVITY/DENSITY 2.6–2.7

LUSTER Dull to vitreous

CHEMICAL COMPOSITION Calcium carbonate or conchiolin (an organic horn-based material)

COMMON TREATMENTS Dyeing and staining.

OPTICAL PROPERTIES No specific properties

CUTTING AND STONE CUTS Coral is sensitive to heat, chemicals, and acids. It can fade, so avoid the sun and temperature fluctuations. To cut and grind, use fine-grained sandstone and emery, then polish the coral with a felt wheel. It is used for carvings, cabochons, and beads. It has a splintery, uneven fracture and can contain liquid and tubular inclusions. It's easy to lose the polish, as it's so soft.

IMITATIONS/SYNTHETICS Imitations are made of porcelain, dyed bone, glass, plastic, and rubber-based material. Gilson of France produced a glass-based pink coral stone. Vegetable ivory is often stained as an imitation and sea bamboo passed off as precious coral. There is also reconstituted coral.

NOT TO BE CONFUSED WITH... Carnelian, rhodonite, rhodochrosite.

Japanese Momo coral

The coral has a few white spots, which is common to Japanese material. The beads are polished sections of coral branches and have a fine wood-grain appearance when viewed through a loupe.

Ladybird brooch by David Webb

The body is natural red Sardegna coral and cabochon emeralds plus brilliant-cut diamonds and enamel make the eyes.

Row necklace of Sardegna coral

The beads are sections of natural coral branches, and the color is an even, natural red with no white patches. The small indentations and holes are where the marine polyps lived.

1930s faux coral beaded bracelet

This "coral" is made from glass but it looks very effective. The weight is different from natural coral and the drill holes are sloping with concentric ridges, both of which identify it as glass. The beads are also a uniform color without any wood-grain pattern, which is distinctly faux.

Black and golden coral are made of a horn-like substance called conchiolin. The gold coral can be semi-chatoyant and is rare, so it's heavily regulated and protected (as are black and blue coral).

Coral has an intricate banded structure with striations, which are between 0.25 and 0.5mm apart. In the rough, it has a soft outer skin that can be rubbed off. It has a dull luster, but can take a high polish.

Coral is found in warm waters. Red and salmon-pink coral is found in the western Mediterranean (Sardinia) and the Bay of Biscay, the Pacific Ocean (Japan), the Red Sea, Malaysia, Taiwan, and off the African coast. Black and golden coral come from the West Indies, Australia, and the Pacific Islands. Blue coral comes from the Great Barrier Reef (Australia), Hawaii, and the Philippines. The finest coral comes from Hawaii, the Mediterranean, and Japan.

The main trading center for coral is Torre del Greco near Naples, in Italy. This has been the top coral trading center for over 200 years and processes nearly 75 percent of the world's supply.

Licensing and fishing methods are controlled: coral can only be taken by scuba divers, the size of the coral that can be harvested is regulated, and there are yearly quotas and permitted areas. The industry self-regulates in this way so that coral can be traded without endangering reefs. Most red noble coral grows in deep water, so they are less affected by pollution, acidity, and global warming. Blue corals come from shallow reefs, such as the Great Barrier Reef, so are more susceptible to these environmental factors and, as a result, the Reef is heavily controlled. In the Mediterranean, measures are in place to ensure that the areas where fishing is permitted are rotated and the amount and size of coral that can be taken are limited.

Natural blue coral

This is a tremendous row of beautiful natural blue coral beads. The natural mottled coloration is lovely. The harvesting of blue coral is heavily restricted now and the reefs are protected.

Natural branch coral

Natural branch coral is an organic gem created by living organisms. It grows at the rate of 1mm per year.

Angelskin coral carved pendeloque

Its large size means it's a valuable piece, but angelskin doesn't quite have the same high value as the red Mediterranean Sardegna coral. The paler color means the coral grows in shallow waters.

Dyed sea bamboo

The color of these coral look-alike beads is a very bright, flat orange-red, which indicates dyeing. Natural coral doesn't have such an intense orangey color and there's usually some variation in color among the beads. In the close-up you can see the the parallel veins running through the material.

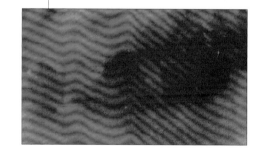

SEA BAMBOO is naturally beige in color, so it is bleached and dyed to red and orange. It looks like a tree as it has heavy striations, but there are organic nodes. Sea bamboo is mainly cut into disks for beads and is found in vintage jewelry. It imitates precious coral and has proved so popular that stocks are now depleted. Dealers should advise on the treatment and make it clear that sea bamboo is not precious coral.

SPONGE CORAL is a naturally red, soft coral with beige veins. Soft coral has a less compact skeleton than precious coral. As a result, it is less stable as a gemstone and is impregnated with resin to stabilize it and enable polishing. This makes it more comfortable to wear. Sponge coral is found in the Indian and Pacific Oceans, as well as the China seas.

Sponge coral cabochon and necklace

The natural patches and veins are an indicator that this is sponge coral rather than noble coral. It is significantly cheaper because it is more plentiful.

Butterfly brooch by Bentley and Skinner

A salmon-pink Momo coral branch has been decorated with a gold foliate design and supports an engraved yellow gold butterfly.

AMBER

Amber is typically light in weight with a resinous luster. It's possible to see inclusions of air bubbles and even occasional plant life or insects.

Amber is one of only a few organic gems; it is the fossilized resin of pine trees, specifically *Pinus succinifera*. The gemstone has undergone a chemical transformation into a polymer—a natural plastic.

The color range is creamy white, golden-yellow to golden-orange, with rarer colors of green, red, blue, violet, and black. The green and blue to violet tints are due to extreme fluorescence.

Amber is found as nodules and weathered lumps with crusts. It is transparent to opaque. Inclusions can include pollen, leaves, moss, lichen, pine needles, and insects (beetles, spiders, mites, and ants). More rarely, frogs, toads, and lizards have been found which were trapped in the sticky resin. It dates from 30 million years ago to the Tertiary Period of over 50 million years ago. It often contains cloudy air bubbles, which can be cleared by heating, and may also have flattened starburst shapes—these are internal fractures caused by stress that radiate from a central point. The highest values are for amber that has good clarity, a light color, and visible insects.

Amber has a long history; it was used as jewelry in Ancient Roman times and carved amber dating from the Neolithic period (10,200 to 4500 BC) has been found in Eastern Europe. The main sources are in the Baltic region—"resinite" amber is found in coal seams and deposits on the Baltic seabed are brought to Polish and Lithuanian

Polish/Baltic amber cabochon

The deep cognac brown color and spangles of air bubbles indicate that this is amber. The low density also helps identify this organic gemstone. Polish amber is protected, so dealers and traders have to be licensed by the Polish authorities.

GEMMOLOGICAL INFORMATION

CRYSTAL SYSTEM Amorphous

MOHS HARDNESS 2.5

REFRACTIVE INDEX 1.54–1.55

SPECIFIC GRAVITY/DENSITY 1.08 (low)

LUSTER Resinous

CHEMICAL COMPOSITION Mix of hydro-carbons, plus resins, succinic acid, and oils.

COMMON TREATMENTS Amber is heated to darken the color and is also dyed. There are clarity enhancements using oil baths. Amber softens at 302°F (150°C) and melts at 482–572°F (250–300°C).

OPTICAL PROPERTIES Fluorescence

CUTTING AND STONE CUTS Heat sensitive, (heat can cause cracking). Tumbled beads, polished cabs, and faceted stones (rare). Avoid chemicals, as amber can be partially dissolved by solvents and alcohol. No ultrasonic cleaners.

IMITATIONS/SYNTHETICS Glass and plastic synthetics. Ambroid is made by warming and heavily compressing small pieces of amber and adding color.

NOT TO BE CONFUSED WITH Carnelian copal, ambroid, cherry bakelite.

Raw stone

This rough amber was washed up by the Baltic Sea in Lithuania and is completely natural with no clarity or color enhancements. The weathered crust on the outside and a typical resinous luster both help identify the stone.

Insect inclusion

Aged between 30 and 50 million years old, this amber contains a fully intact mosquito-like insect that got trapped in the sticky pine-tree resin. It's a good example of the inclusions that can be found in amber. Pieces such as this are highly collectable and can have a reasonable value.

*Art Deco reconstituted
amber earrings*

Reconstituted material has
been on the market for years;
small pieces of natural amber
are ground up, mixed with
resin, then re-cut into beads
and stones.

*Victorian amber
necklace c.1885*

This Victorian reddish-brown
amber is more opaque than
the modern necklace (left)
but it has a lovely color and a
tactile feel.

coastlines during storms. In Poland, amber is part of the national
heritage and is protected—only licensed dealers can trade. The
Dominican Republic has fine yellow-orange amber with good insect
inclusions and also produces around 220 pounds (100kg) of rare blue
fluorescent material each year. It's a younger deposit. Russia is the
largest source; the amber is buried under a layer of clay
approximately 98ft (30m) deep. Other sources are Myanmar
(Burmite), Sicily (Simeite), Mexico, France, Spain, Italy, Germany,
Romania, Canada, the USA, and the Lebanon (very old deposits).

To test amber, rub it vigorously on a piece of wool and the negative
electrical charge becomes strong enough to pick up ash. When
warmed, amber also gives off a pleasant scent of pine and it should
also float in salty water.

Amber can be confused with copal, which is preserved tree resin
from the copal tree. Copal is much younger than amber—only a few
hundred thousand years old! To distinguish amber from copal, leave a
drop of acetone (nail-polish remover) on the stone for three seconds
and then wipe it off. It will leave a mark on copal, while amber will
have virtually no change.

There were large amounts of cherry bakelite in jewelry in the
Art Deco period and it can look very similar to some amber.
Reconstituted amber was also produced from the early 20th century
onward, so just be cautious.

Baltic amber necklace

This necklace contains three colors of amber—
yellow, orange-brown, and a very deep cognac.
The material is lovely, very clean, and the cutting
is excellent.

Birthstones

Birthstones are gemstones associated with each month, which are considered lucky or are thought to have healing properties. They have been used since the first century to bring good fortune to an individual on their birthday. Each month has a designated stone that has certain qualities attached to it; there are often several gems associated with the month, as there's a traditional list of stones that is centuries old and a modern list.

MONTH	JANUARY	FEBRUARY	MARCH	APRIL
Traditional	Garnet	Amethyst	Bloodstone	Diamond
Modern	Garnet	Amethyst	Aquamarine	Diamond
Options	Rose Quartz	Moonstone, Onyx	Rock Crystal	White sapphire

MONTH	MAY	JUNE	JULY	AUGUST
Traditional	Emerald	Pearl	Ruby	Sardonyx
Modern	Emerald	Alexandrite	Ruby	Peridot
Options	Chrysoprase		Carnelian	Jade

MONTH	SEPTEMBER	OCTOBER	NOVEMBER	DECEMBER
Traditional	Sapphire	Tourmaline	Citrine	Turquoise
Modern	Sapphire	Opal	Yellow Topaz	Tanzanite
Options	Lapis Lazuli	Zircon, Aquamarine	Diamond	Topaz

ZODIAC SIGNS

Since ancient times, astrologers have been aware of the positive effects that certain gemstones have when worn by people belonging to particular zodiac signs. The most powerful gem zodiac signs are as follows.

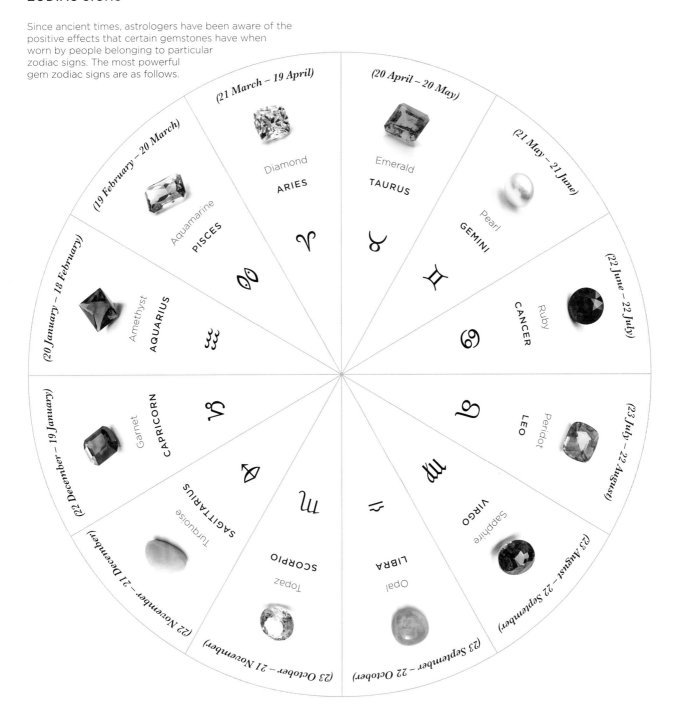

(21 March – 19 April)
Diamond
ARIES
♈

(20 April – 20 May)
Emerald
TAURUS
♉

(21 May – 21 June)
Pearl
GEMINI
♊

(22 June – 22 July)
Ruby
CANCER
♋

(23 July – 22 August)
Peridot
LEO
♌

(23 August – 22 September)
Sapphire
VIRGO
♍

(23 September – 22 October)
Opal
LIBRA
♎

(23 October – 21 November)
Topaz
SCORPIO
♏

(22 November – 21 December)
Turquoise
SAGITTARIUS
♐

(22 December – 19 January)
Garnet
CAPRICORN
♑

(20 January – 18 February)
Amethyst
AQUARIUS
♒

(19 February – 20 March)
Aquamarine
PISCES
♓

Glossary

ACICULAR CRYSTAL HABIT Needle-like crystal shape.

ADULARESCENCE The bluish-white optical effect that is caused by the interference of light within a gem's layered structure.

AGGREGATE Gem material that occurs as a dense, fibrous fine-crystalline mass.

ASTERISM A four- or six-ray star-effect that appears on cabochons and is caused by the reflection of light on fibrous or rutile inclusions.

AVENTURESCENCE The colorful glittering reflections of small plate-like or leaf-like inclusions of minerals such as hematite or fuchsite.

BEZEL A type of stone setting that uses a wall of metal to surround and secure a gemstone. Also, the horizontal wire that runs between the prongs of a claw setting.

BIREFRINGENCE The difference between the highest and lowest refractive indices in gemstones with double refraction.

BOTRYOIDAL A mineral shape or formation that looks similar to a bunch of grapes.

BRILLIANT CUT An ideal cut of mathematically calculated proportions that was designed to maximize a diamond's fire and brilliance.

BRIOLETTE A rounded drop-shaped gemstone that is fully faceted and often drilled for suspension.

CABOCHON A type of gemstone cut that has a flat base and a smooth domed upper surface.

CARAT The measurement of weight used by the international gem trade. 1 carat equals 0.2 grams.

CHANNEL SETTING A type of setting in which rows of square or baguette-cut stones are butted up in a channel and secured on two edges.

CHATOYANCY A cat's-eye effect that occurs in stones cut as a cabochon when light reflects off parallel fibers, channels, or rutile needles.

CLAW SETTING A raised, open setting with wire prongs that grip the outer edge of a faceted gemstone.

CLEAVAGE PLANE The flat plane along which a crystal can be split. Some crystals cleave easily (perfect cleavage) and others cannot be cleaved (no cleavage).

COLLET A rub-over bezel setting for a faceted stone.

COLOR BANDING Parallel stripes of different colors or shades that occur in gemstones such as agate or malachite as a result of rhythmic or layered crystallization.

COLOR ZONING The variations in color and distribution that occur in gemstones as a result of growth layers and the presence of coloring agents.

CROWN The upper portion of a faceted stone, above the girdle.

CRYSTAL A crystal is a gem's uniform body that has an ordered internal atomic structure called a lattice.

CRYSTAL HABIT The arrangement of faces preferred by a mineral. The term also refers to the crystal's type or form, for instance tabular or octahedral.

CULET The lowest part of a faceted stone, which can appear as a point or a ridge.

DIFFUSION TREATMENT The process of heating of gem material for a prolonged period having introduced chemicals into the surface of the stone. It produces a permanent color change in the outer layers of the gem leaving the center unchanged.

DISPERSION The splitting of white light into its spectral colors (known as fire) as it travels through an angled surface on a gemstone.

DOUBLE REFRACTION The splitting of light rays into two when entering a non-cubic mineral. It causes a doubling of the back facets in a gemstone.

DOUBLET A composite stone of two pieces in which an upper section of clear quartz or synthetic material is cemented to a thin lower section of gem.

DRUSY The crystalline surface of the central/inner cavity of an agate nodule that commonly consists of quartz crystals.

FACETS Polished flat faces on a gemstone that are cut at varying angles so that light travels through the stone making it brilliant.

FANCY CUT Describes gemstone cuts and shapes other than round and oval brilliant cuts.

FLUORESCENCE The luminescence (or emission of visible light) by certain gemstones under ultraviolet light. Occurs when a gemstone's electrons, excited by the UV light, release energy as visible light when back to their non-excited state.

FLUX-MELT PROCESS A process in which powdered ingredients are melted and fused in a solvent (flux) at high temperatures over a period of months. Used in the manufacture of high-quality synthetic gemstones such as rubies and sapphires.

FRACTURE The irregular surface produced when a gemstone is broken upon impact.

FUSING The joining of metals by using heat rather than solder; the metals melt at surface level and fuse together.

GIRDLE The outer edge or widest part of a gemstone, where the crown meets the pavilion.

GRAIN OR BEAD SETTING A type of setting in which a faceted stone is held in place by tiny beads of metal that have been raised by a graver and shaped with a beading tool.

GRANULATION The creation and application of tiny balls of silver or gold to decorate the surface of metal.

GYPSY SETTING A type of setting in which a faceted stone is recessed into metal so that the girdle is flush with the metal's surface.

HARDNESS The hardness value of a gemstone is based on its resistance to abrasion.

HEAT TREATMENT A common gemstone treatment that changes or intensifies the color of a gemstone and sometimes improves the clarity.

IDIOCHROMATIC Term used to describe gems whose color is due to their chemical composition rather than due to the presence of external coloring agents.

ILLUSION SETTING A style of setting that is designed to make a diamond look larger than it is by surrounding it with a white gold or platinum disk.

INCLUSIONS The foreign matter or crystal irregularities that occur within a gemstone that can help identify species, origin and authenticity.

IRIDESCENCE Rainbow-like color play that is produced when light reflects off internal structures within a gem, splitting into spectral colors.

IRRADIATION A gemstone treatment that changes or intensifies the color of a stone. It is not always permanent.

KARAT The measurement of fineness of gold or gold alloy. Pure gold is described as 24 karat while 18 karat means that the metal contains 18 parts pure gold and 6 parts alloy (by weight).

LOST-WAX CASTING A process in which a one-part mold is formed around a three-dimensional wax model that is removed by controlled, incremental heating. The subsequent void is then filled with molten metal.

LOUPE A magnifying lens for viewing gemstones. The standard magnification is x10.

LUSTER The shine of a gem caused by external surface reflection. The highest luster is adamantine and the lowest is dull.

MAKE Describes the overall cut of a gemstone, including proportions, shape, symmetry and finish.

MATRIX The host or parent rock that naturally surrounds gem material.

MOHS SCALE The Mohs scale of 1 to 10 indicates a gem's scratch hardness (10 Mohs is the hardest).

MOKUME-GANE A process in which layers of different colored metals are fused together as a laminate so that areas can be filed back to expose a rippled surface pattern.

MOUNT The section of a ring that contains gemstones, for example a group of settings consisting of a central stone and two side stones.

OPALESCENCE A bluish white milky effect caused by selective scattering of shortwave light from small particles in a stone.

OVERTONE The colored highlights that overlie the body color of a pearl.

OXIDIZATION The blackening of metals with chemicals or the chemical reaction that occurs when a metal is exposed to the air.

PATINATION A process for coloring metals by exposure to different chemicals.

PAVE SETTING A type of setting in which small round faceted stones are bead-set close together in a massed arrangement.

PAVILION The lower section of a faceted stone, from the girdle to the culet.

PEGGED SETTING A type of setting in which small round cabochons are grouped tightly together and secured by small metal pegs.

PLAN VIEW The top view of a gemstone.

PLEOCHROISM The collective description of a gemstone that appears to have two or more different colors, or shades of color, when viewed from different directions.

POINT SIZE The diameter size of small faceted gemstones in relation to their calibrated weight, which is measured in points of a carat (1 ct equals 100 points).

PRONGS The vertical or upright posts of a claw setting; the tips of the prongs are shaped into claws to hold the gemstone in place.

REFRACTION The bending of light as it passes from air into a different medium such as a gemstone.

RETICULATION The process of heating metal to a point at which the surface appears to ripple, creating a decorative molten effect.

RING SHANK The part of a ring that encircles the finger.

ROLLING-MILL TEXTURING The embossing of a decorative surface onto silver or gold by means of passing annealed metal through a rolling-mill with textured material.

ROSE CUT A diamond cut dating from the 1600s that has a flat base and a faceted dome. It was often foil backed.

RUB-OVER SETTING Describes a bezel setting in which the top of the wall is either pushed against the side of a stone or is burnished over the edge of a girdle.

SCHILLER A sheen similar to iridescence, produced by the interference of light reflecting off internal layers within a gemstone.

SILK A misty appearance in transparent gemstones that is caused by the reflection of light on fine needle-like inclusions or canals.

STEP CUT A system of cutting straight-sided stones with a series of rectangular parallel facets that follow the shape of the girdle in a stepped arrangement.

TABLE The flat surface on top of a faceted stone; the largest facet, or face.

TABLE CUT An early form of diamond cut that simply cleaved an octahedral crystal to create a flat table and culet.

TENEBRESCENCE The reversible color-change phenomenon in which a gemstone's color fades when exposed to one wavelength of light but is restored by a different wavelength of light, or by being placed in darkness. Heating destroys the effect.

TENSION SETTING A type of setting that uses tension in the metal to support and hold a stone set between two ends of a shank.

TRIPLET A composite stone of three pieces in which one part is genuine gemstone and the other parts either glass, foil, synthetic or low-grade material.

WINDOW If a gemstone's pavilion is cut too shallow and the proportions of the crown and pavilion are incorrect, then the gem will have a glassy "window" when viewed through the table. It will lack brilliance.

Index

190

PICTURE CREDITS

The publisher would like to thank the following sources for their kind permission to reproduce the photographs in this book:

On the cover:
Front: DK Rinos Necklace Oxidised Silver with Lemon Citrines © Daphne Krinos/daphnekrinos.com; Jean Scott Moncrieff Snowflake Diamond Cuff © Jean Scott Moncrieff/Photo FXP; Shutterstock/Bjoern Wylezich. Back: Cartier ring © Cartier; Shutterstock/photo-world; Page 13(cr): Alamy/Patrizio Martorana.

Page 13(tl): Shutterstock/HelloRF Zcool; Page 20(bl): Shutterstock/S_E; Page 21: Shutterstock/Mivr; Page 22: Kent Raible/goldensapherestudios.com; Page 27: Shutterstock/Dennis van de Water; Page 28: Shutterstock/Radu Bercan; Page 38(bl): Jean Scott-Moncrieff/Photo FXP; Page 40(cr): Shutterstock/eFesenko; Page 40(bl): Shutterstock/Daleen Loest; Page 41(tl): Graff; Page 42(tl): David Webb; 42(tr): Graff; Page 43(t): Charlotte De Syllas/Photo: Simon B Armitt; (br): Shutterstock/Reika; Page 44(tr): Graff; Page 44(bl): Shutterstock/Bjoern Wylezich; Page 45(r): Graff; Page 47(br): Charlotte De Syllas/Photo: Simon B Armitt; Page 47(tr): Graff; Page 48(br): Emma Farquharson Jewellery; Page 49(b): Daphne Krinos/daphnekrinos.com; Page 49tl): Jean Scott Moncrieff/Photo FXP; Page 49(tr): Josef Koppmann; Page 51(tr): Graff; Page 51(br): Shutterstock/Manamana; Page 52(bl): Graff; Page 53(c): Graff; Page 55(t): Graff; Page 55(bl): Shutterstock/J.Palys; Page 56(r): Bentley & Skinner (Bond Street Jeweller Ltd); Page 56(bl): Cartier; Page 57(cl): Emma Chapman Jewels; Page 57(tr): Louise O'Neill; Page 57(br): Zaffiro Jewelry/zaffirojewelry.com; Page 58(r): Graff; Page 60(bl): Cartier; Page 61(br): Shutterstock/photo-world; Page 62(tr): Emma Farquharson Jewellery; Page 63(cl): Graff; Page 63(c): Graff; Page 64(bc): Bentley & Skinner (Bond Street Jeweller Ltd); Page 65(c): Daphne Krinos/daphnekrinos.com; Page 65(tr): Josef Koppmann; Page 65(br): Shutterstock/Imfoto; Page 66(bl): Zaffiro Jewelry/zaffirojewelry.com; Page 67(br): Charlotte De Syllas/Photo: Simon B Armitt; Page 67(tr): Josef Koppmann; Page 67(tl): Shutterstock/S_E; Page 67(tc): Shutterstock/S_E; Page 68: Shutterstock/Dan Olsen; Page 69(cl): Lang Antiques, USA; Page 71(bl): Alamy/The Natural History Museum; Page 71(t): Fellows Auctioneers Ltd; Page 73(tr): Jean Scott-Moncrieff/Photo FXP; Page 73(br): Milena Kovanovic/crucibleLondon.com; Page 73(bl): Shutterstock Imfoto; Page 74(bl): Josef Koppmann; Page 74(tr): Zaffiro Jewelry/zaffirojewelry.com; Page 75(c): Catherine Mannheim/catherinemannheim.com; Page 76(bl): Emma Chapman Jewels; Page 77(tr): Emma Chapman Jewels; Page 77(br): Shutterstock/Henri Koskinen; Page 78(l): Bentley & Skinner (Bond Street Jeweller Ltd); Page 78(br): Bentley & Skinner (Bond Street Jeweller Ltd); Page 79(t): Jean Scott-Moncrieff/Photo FXP; Page 79(l): Louise O'Neill; Page 79(br): Zaffiro Jewelry/zaffirojewelry.com; Page 80(br): Shutterstock/William G Forbes; Page 81 (cl): Fellows Auctioneers Ltd; Page 81(tc): Zaffiro Jewelry / zaffirojewelry.com; Page 81(r): Zaffiro Jewelry/zaffirojewelry.com; Page 82(br): Cartier; Page 82(tr): SuShilla/Sushilla Done; Page 83 (bl): Graff; Page 83(br): Shutterstock/Epitavi; Page 84(t): Zaffiro Jewelry/zaffirojewelry.com; Page 84(bc): Zaffiro Jewelry/zaffirojewelry.com; Page 85(bl): Jean Scott-Moncrieff/Photo FXP; Page 85(br): Shutterstock/Dan Olsen; Page 86(tr): Shutterstock/Roy Palmer; Page 89(bl): Shutterstock/J.Palys; Page 90(bl): Shutterstock/J.Palys; Page 91(bl): Josef Koppmann; Page 93(tl): Josef Koppmann; Page 94(br): Shutterstock/J.Palys; Page 95(c): Daphne Krinos/daphnekrinos.com; Page 95(b): Emma Farquharson Jewellery; Page 96(bl): Shutterstock/J.Palys; Page 96(tr): Zaffiro Jewelry/zaffirojewelry.com; Page 97(bl): Shutterstock/Dafinchi; Page 98(bl): Daphne Krinos/daphnekrinos.com; Page 99(br): Fellows Auctioneers Ltd; Page 100(bl): Heritage Auctions, USA; Page 101(br): Shutterstock/J.Palys;

Page 101(bra): Shutterstock/J.Palys; Page 103(br): Shutterstock/J.Palys; Page 103(bra): Shutterstock/J. Palys; Page 103(cb): Shutterstock J.Palys; Page 105(bc): Shutterstock/Vangert; Page 106(bl): Shutterstock/farbled; Page 106(bla): Shutterstock/Moha El-Jaw; Page 107(tl): Daphne Krinos/daphnekrinos.com; Page 107(br): Fellows Auctioneers Ltd; Page 108(br): Shutterstock/Moha El-Jaw; Page 108(bl): Zaffiro Jewelry/zaffirojewelry.com; Page 109(tl): 123rf/tenra; Page 109(cr) Shutterstock/vvoe; Page 110(br): Shutterstock/Imfoto; Page 110(bl): Zaffiro Jewelry/zaffirojewelry.com; Page 111(tr): Lang Antiques, USA; Page 111(bl): Zaffiro Jewelry/zaffirojewelry.com; Page 112(br): Shutterstock/Jiri Vaclavek; Page 113(bc): Shutterstock/S_E; Page 114 (bc): Shutterstock Imfoto; Page 115: Lang Antiques, USA; Page 116(tr): Fellows Auctioneers Ltd; Page 117(cl): Milena Kovanovic/crucibleLondon.com; Page 117(br): Shutterstock/vvoe; Page 118(bl): Shutterstock / Dan Olsen; Page 119(cl): Emma Chapman Jewels; Page 119 (br): Shutterstock/Albert Russ; Page 120(bl): Bentley & Skinner (Bond Street Jeweller Ltd); Page 121(bl): Lang Antiques, USA; Page 121(br): Shutterstock/Albert Russ; Page 122(bc): Bentley & Skinner (Bond Street Jeweller Ltd); Page 125(bl): Shutterstock/vvoe; Page 126(br): David Webb; Page 127(tr): David Webb; Page 127(c): Shutterstock/ Roy Palmer; Page 127(tl): Zaffiro Jewelry/zaffirojewelry.com; Page 129(bl): Shutterstock/William G Forbes; Page 129(tr): SuShilla/Sushilla Done; Page 131 (br): Shutterstock/Imfoto; Page 132 (br): Shutterstock/J.Palys; Page 133(bl): Emma Chapman Jewels; Page 134(bl): Shutterstock/J.Palys; Page 137(br): Catherine Mannheim/catherinemannheim.com; Page 137(bl): Zaffiro Jewelry/zaffirojewelry.com; Page 138(br): Catherine Mannheim/catherinemannheim.com; Page 138(c): David Webb; Page 138(tl): Zaffiro Jewelry/zaffirojewelry.com; Page 139 : Monica Vinader; Page 141(tl): Emma Chapman Jewels; Page 141(tr): Shutterstock/J.Palys; Page 142 (br): Shutterstock/Imfoto; Page 144(bl): Shutterstock/Bjoern Wylezich; Page 145(bl): Fellows Auctioneers Ltd; Page 145(tl): Jean Scott-Moncrieff/Photo FXP; Page 147(br): Bentley & Skinner (Bond Street Jeweller Ltd); Page 147(tc): Fellows Auctioneers Ltd; Page 149(tr): Bentley & Skinner (Bond Street Jeweller Ltd); Page 150(bl): Zaffiro Jewelry/zaffirojewelry.com; Page 151(tr): Heritage Auctions, USA; Page 151(bl): Shutterstock/Bjoern Wylezich; Page 152(br): Daphne Krinos/daphnekrinos.com; Page 152(bl): Shutterstock/vvoe; Page 153(tr): Jean Scott-Moncrieff/Photo FXP; Page 153(bl): Shutterstock/Stellar Gems; Page 153(tl): Zaffiro Jewelry/zaffirojewelry.com; Page 155(br): Shutterstock/bjphotographs; Page 156(bl): Shutterstock/vvoe; Page 157(br): Emma Chapman Jewels; Page 157(tr): Shutterstock/vvoe; Page 158(bl): Shutterstock/Vereschagin; Page 159(b): Bentley & Skinner (Bond Street Jeweller Ltd); Page 159(tl): David Webb; Page 160(bc): Josef Koppmann; Page 160(br): Milena Kovanovic/crucibleLondon.com; Page 160(bl): Shutterstock/J.Palys; Page 161(tr): Bentley & Skinner (Bond Street Jeweller Ltd); Page 161(bl): Bentley & Skinner (Bond Street Jeweller Ltd); Page 162(bl): Shutterstock/Bjoern Wylezich; Page 163(t): Josef Koppmann; Page 165(br): Heritage Auctions, USA; Page 165(bl): Lang Antiques, USA; Page 165(bl): Shutterstock/vvoe; Page 169(br): Shutterstock/Epitavi; Page 172(cl): Bentley & Skinner (Bond Street Jeweller Ltd); Page 179(bl): David Webb; Page 180 (bl): Shutterstock/Seashell World; Page 181(bl): Bentley & Skinner (Bond Street Jeweller Ltd); Page 184: Shutterstock/Africa Studio; Shutterstock/al_1033; Page 184 : Shutterstock/Alexander Hoffmann; Shutterstock/Byjeng; Shutterstock/Fribus Mara; Shutterstock/koroboky; Shutterstock/Manutsawee Buapet; Shutterstock/Mehmet Gokhan Bayhan; Shutterstock/richpav.

I'd like to thank R Holt & Co, who sold my last book, The Jeweller's Directory of Gemstones, *for numerous years and who lent me gemstones for photography for this book. I would also like to thank the owner of R Holt & Co, Mr Robert Holt, who sadly passed away, for his support and help when I started out as a gem trader.*